B.   ontation

Beyond Confrontation

Learning Conflict Resolution
in the Post–Cold War Era

John A. Vasquez
James Turner Johnson
Sanford Jaffe
Linda Stamato
EDITORS

Ann Arbor

THE UNIVERSITY OF MICHIGAN PRESS

1998   1997   1996   1995   4   3   2   1

A CIP catalog record for this book is available from the British Library.

Library of Congress Cataloging-in-Publication Data

Beyond confrontation : learning conflict resolution in the post–Cold
War era / [edited by] John A. Vasquez . . . [et al.].
    p. cm.
  Includes bibliographical references and index.
  ISBN 0-472-09554-4 (acid-free paper)
  1. Pacific settlement of international disputes. 2. Dispute
resolution (Law) 3. Arbitration, International. I. Vasquez, John
A., 1945–   .
JX4475.B49   1995
341.5′2—dc20
                                                    95-3890
                                                       CIP

To peacemakers
wherever they may be found

Contents

Introduction: A Time for Resolution

Disputes arise, angers flare, force is tried, violence breaks out. These are familiar events in life at the interpersonal, domestic, and international level. No matter how acrimonious the times, however, eventually there comes a time for resolution—for settling differences, for trying to make peace. Yet how differences are settled and the ways in which peace is made vary considerably, and these variations have important effects. Whether a child-custody case goes to court or a war is ended punitively has profound effects on future relations.

This book is based on the assumption that how differences are settled and peace is made is something that is learned and therefore can be improved. The volume brings together some of the best scholars in a number of relevant disciplines to see how the learning of peace at the domestic level might inform the learning of peace at the global level in the post–cold war era. The history of domestic politics has been the history of individuals and groups learning to make peace with each other. Conflict resolution techniques have played and continue to play a role in this process. They may be able to play a similar role in certain areas of global politics. The chapters in this book outline how to go beyond confrontation and power politics in international relations and establish a politics of resolution.

Such an analysis is particularly relevant to global politics, which, because of the cold war, has long neglected traditional techniques of conflict resolution, since they were thought to be irrelevant and generally inapplicable to the relations between states. With the cold war rivalry dominating world politics, it was believed that disputes and their underlying issues could be settled and resolved only through a struggle for power. The ending of the cold war has led to a change of sentiment. It is now recognized that for some of the most important issues on the global agenda—for example, intra-allied and intra-European issues—power politics and coercion are not very effective means of contention and resolution. The waning of military "security" issues among major states has also led to the realization that regional disputes and ethnic-nationalist issues now pose the greatest dangers to the peace. Many of these issues are, in fact, domestic disputes spilling over into the international arena. These shifts in the global agenda have spurred new attention to questions of domestic and global conflict management and conflict prevention. A vast literature and practice relevant to these questions have grown up on the domestic level, but they have been largely ignored by international politics specialists.

To review that literature to see what insights it might provide for creating a more peaceful and stable post–cold war world order, the editors brought together scholars and practitioners of domestic and global conflict resolution for a series of multidisciplinary seminars. Funded by the United States Institute of Peace, the project focused on whether the theory, research, insights, and techniques of one area could be of use to the other. The fields represented include political science, social psychology, law, management, sociology, and ethics. Each of the chapters grew out of a paper prepared for discussion in one of the seminars and reflects both the disciplinary orientation of the individual author and the multidisciplinary character of the critical exchange that took place over the original drafts. The present collection of essays reflects the outcome dialogue, and its aim is both to convey the insights and conclusions reached by that dialogue and to stimulate further conversation between theoreticians and practitioners of conflict resolution in the domestic and global spheres.

We believe these sorts of multidisciplinary dialogues have a potential for helping to recast and invigorate conceptions of how to deal with global politics in the post–cold war era. With the end of the cold war and the accompanying changes within the international order, both contemporary international relations theory and diplomatic practice are in an awkward position. So much of the theorizing and practice of the post-1945 period has been devoted to the role of power and the use of force that it is unclear how other techniques might be employed to manage or resolve problems. Despite the new willingness of the United States, Russia, Britain, France, Germany, Japan, and China, as well as other states, to work together to resolve regional disputes and ethnic conflicts, there is little understanding of how the parties directly involved in such disputes might be brought together so that the issues will not continue to fester. Even less is known about how suggestions about crisis prevention or war avoidance that have been offered in recent years might be extended to regional problems. Thus, a pressing need exists for a new and comprehensive conception of the post–cold war order and for new techniques for management and resolution of international tensions to preserve and strengthen that order.

It was with these questions in mind that the editors began their investigation. It was felt that dispute resolution in the domestic sphere had much to offer in the attempts to create and manage a new world order. The Alternative Dispute Movement, for example, encompasses a variety of activities in different social contexts, including extrajudicial legal dispute resolution, arbitration and mediation processes (formal and informal, compulsory and noncompulsory), ombudsmen, neighborhood justice centers, and other approaches emphasizing negotiation between disputants as the way of resolving conflicts. A principal focus is to offset the tendency for disputants to move toward legal action within the courts while positively increasing social cohesion and overall societal good through creative satisfaction of the needs and interests of the parties in dispute.

In the international arena, the concept of conflict resolution encompasses procedures of international law; arbitration or mediation of disputes by third parties (including international organizations); the establishment of "regimes" among interested parties to head off potential conflicts; diplomatic initiative between disputants; "bridge-building" measures between disputants; and so-called Track II diplomacy. It includes conflict management aimed at preventing the use of armed force or at regulating such use so as to minimize destruction. The principal focus of conflict resolution in the international sphere is avoidance of resort to armed force to settle conflicts, while positively seeking to increase international cohesiveness through the creative satisfaction of interests and needs.

The last ten to fifteen years have seen the development of a considerable body of literature in each of the two spheres. Because of the greatly different political contexts provided by the domestic and international arenas and because of the natural preoccupation of each field with its own issues and problems, development has generally proceeded along two substantially separate roads, although a few scholars and practitioners have always maintained a foot in each camp.

Nevertheless, as the chapters of this volume demonstrate, despite differences on the level of practice, there are areas of theoretical convergence between the two spheres. Even within the divergences of practice and political context, there are fundamental similarities in the problems faced and approaches taken to overcome common obstacles. These include an emphasis on analysis of conflict to uncover the actual needs of the parties; rank-ordering interests, goals, and policies in terms of their relation to the underlying needs; and helping the parties to develop options for solving the conflict or dispute.

Part 1 provides an overview of conflict resolution theory, research, and practice. Robert Baruch Bush begins by providing an analysis and short history of the Alternative Dispute Resolution (ADR) movement within the United States. He shows that ADR arose in part because of a dissatisfaction with the dominant court-based legal system. He identifies the structural incentives and constraints that exist within the United States and analyzes the similarities and differences between the domestic and global arenas. In his concluding section, he reviews some of the major questions facing ADR, with an eye to their implications for global conflict resolution. Ronald Fisher follows with an overview of global conflict resolution. He examines third-party intervention in international conflicts and research on it, with emphasis on mediation and third-party consultation. He shows that the various conflict-resolution techniques—for example, mediation, consultation, peacekeeping—are not necessarily competing, but different, techniques appropriate to different stages in a conflict.

Part 2 examines the interconnections between domestic and global conflict resolution from a variety of disciplinary perspectives. Deborah Kolb and Eileen Babbitt describe how mediators of interpersonal and intergroup conflicts actually behave. They try to identify the tactics and techniques of effective practice, and they conclude with an analysis of how mediation at the domestic level might provide insights for mediation of disputes at the global level. Louis Kriesberg discusses how ideas about conflict resolution derived from one set of cases might be applied to other sets of cases, but cautions against the danger of misapplication. He begins by comparing domestic and international conflicts—the similarities and differences between them. He then delineates specific ideas and methods of conflict resolution that are relevant to problems found in both domains. These include preventing conflict, limiting escalation, prenegotiating, problem solving, and reaching high quality agreements. Illustrations are provided for each area. Dean Pruitt analyzes the dynamics of social conflict, especially interpersonal conflict and its resolution. He describes some of the basic cognitive processes and behavior associated with conflict and how these need to be addressed if conflict is to be resolved peacefully. Specific techniques that can be used by third parties are discussed in detail. John Burton makes some important distinctions between dispute settlement and conflict resolution. He argues that there is a need for a paradigm shift and makes a persuasive case for adopting a conflict-"provention" approach over the typical coercive approach of domestic and international politics. He then goes on to argue that conflict "provention" can form the kernel of a new political philosophy and a new kind of political system.

Part 3 looks at the special problems that exist in applying conflict-resolution techniques to global politics. It is often facilely stated that domestic politics is so fundamentally different from world politics, because the latter has no government and the former does, that domestic conflict-resolution techniques cannot be applied to interstate disputes. Such assertions underestimate the amount of order that can be present in a regional or global system. The absence of a global government does not mean that there is no *governance* whatsoever. Objections to global conflict resolution stemming from the view that world politics is anarchic and prone to violence overlook the fact that the bloodiest disputes are more likely to occur within nation-states (in the form of civil wars, revolutions, and political/ethnic purges) than between nation-states. John Vasquez tackles a number of these intellectual objections. He makes it clear that what is important in assessing the possibilities for conflict resolution is not so much the distinction between domestic and global politics, but the nature of the political structure, regardless of the level, in which politics takes place. He argues that domestic and global structures should not be treated a priori as ordered or anarchic systems, but examined in terms of the specific incentives and constraints they provide for the practice of conflict resolution. He offers a common framework for explaining the dynamics of conflict that can be applied to either domestic or global political contention. He concludes with an analysis of how conflict resolution can help prevent and mitigate war in an era of rising nationalism and ethnic conflict.

The remaining two chapters look, respectively, at the political structure of the modern interstate system and the incentives and constraints that structure provides for the practice of conflict resolution. James Turner Johnson examines the specific incentives and constraints the current global *legal* structure provides. He looks at how existing international law provides a structural context within which global conflict resolution can take place. In addition, he delineates how international law has structured relations among states on the basis of certain principles and norms that have sought to regulate conflicts and keep them from endangering the overall relationships among states. Charles Doran examines the foundation of power upon which any given international system is based. He delineates how changes in power can have an important effect on the potential for disputes to arise and escalate to war, while simultaneously pointing out that whether they do so will depend very much on the ability of the political system to assimilate actors who undergo major shifts in capability. He examines the dramatic structural shifts occurring in the world in light of this theoretical analysis, to assess the possibility for the nonviolent transformation of the system. He maintains that conflict resolution is more apt to work under some structures than others. His emphasis on perceptions and role leave many openings for conflict resolution, but his realist emphasis also makes clear the limitations of conflict resolution and the constraints under which it must operate in international relations.

In the closing chapter to the volume, John Vasquez reviews each of the previous chapters to see what lessons can be derived by comparing domestic and global conflict resolution. He argues that peace is something that is learned and that learning to better make peace involves a clearer theoretical understanding of conflict and an identification of useful conflict-resolution techniques. Each of the previous chapters is reviewed with these concerns in mind. The analysis concludes with a discussion of some of the obstacles to improving global conflict resolution and the specific ways in which further multidisciplinary work can aid us in "the learning of peace."

Support for this project has been provided by a United States Institute of Peace grant (#USIP-102–1–89). We are grateful to USIP for allowing us to bring together a group of scholars to explore the interconnections between domestic and global conflict resolution. The views expressed in this volume, however, are those of the authors and should not be attributed to USIP. Nor should the views of one author or editor be attributed to another; we often disagree, but we have found that disagreement fruitful and useful, as we hope our readers will. Our appreciation is also extended to Rutgers University for a supplemental grant and for hosting the seminars. Tom Walker, a doctoral student in political science, provided editorial assistance in preparing the proceedings of the seminars and in selected chapters of the final manuscript. A grant from the Dean of the College of Arts and Sciences at Vanderbilt University facilitated the preparation of the manuscript for publication. Malcolm Litchfield and the editorial staff of the University of Michigan Press were very helpful in bringing the book to fruition. Finally, a special thanks to Henriette Cohen who handled all the arrangements for the seminars professionally and expeditiously.

James Turner Johnson
John A. Vasquez

Part 1
Overview: The Nature of Conflict Resolution

CHAPTER 1

Dispute Resolution—The Domestic Arena: A Survey of Methods, Applications, and Critical Issues

Robert A. Baruch Bush

The aim of this chapter is to provide some background on the current state of the domestic dispute-resolution field, as a basis for examining the possible connections between that field and the field of global conflict resolution. Therefore, the presentation here is an introductory survey, not an in-depth examination. It includes: (1) a description of the range of dispute-resolution processes currently in use in the domestic arena; (2) a short (modern) history of the dispute-resolution field in the United States, incorporating a survey of the current uses of particular processes in different substantive contexts; (3) a summary of the critical issues presently facing the dispute-resolution field; and (4) some reflections, based on the above, on similarities and differences between the domestic and global fields.

At the outset, a few definitions and qualifications are called for. As referred to herein, the "domestic" field means dispute-resolution practice within the United States, at the state and federal levels, including both private and governmental activities. It also means the study of this phenomenon by scholars in different disciplines. Current usage often employs the term *alternative dispute resolution* (ADR) to describe this field, and that terminology is used here. The discussion that follows omits any reference to the field of labor-management dispute resolution. The modern ADR field, although it has derived much from the labor field both in theory and practice, has always regarded the labor area as a distinct, sui generis field. In short, ADR in practice means ADR *outside* the labor area, and that is what will be discussed here.

The term *alternative dispute resolution* suggests that the processes referred to are often seen as alternatives to the formal court system. One implication of this characterization is that much of the work in domestic dispute resolution can be seen as related in one way or another to the legal system, and this explains the involvement of legal academics in the field. Of course, domestic dispute resolution can be and is analyzed from other, entirely nonlegal perspectives. The legal orientation provides a useful framework, though like all others it has limitations. This comment is meant to place what follows in perspective for the reader. A social or political scientist might survey the field quite differently.

Processes in Current Use: A Brief Dictionary of Domestic Dispute Resolution

Discussion of "dispute resolution" in the domestic arena usually focuses on a number of fairly well-defined processes that are more or less widely used to resolve disputes at the present time. While most of these probably need no explanation, some brief definitions derived from current practice and scholarship (American Bar Assoc. 1987; Wilkinson 1990, chap. 1) will provide a common vocabulary.

Adjudication refers to the compulsory judicial (or administrative) process, in which the parties present their cases in a formal, adversarial public proceeding to a judicial official, who makes a decision according to substantive legal rules and embodies that decision in a written opinion. The decision is reviewable by a higher court for errors of law, and after final review, it is binding on all parties and has precedental effect.

Arbitration refers to a voluntary process in which the parties present their cases in a quasi-formal, quasi-adversarial private proceeding to a privately selected neutral third party, who makes a final and binding decision on any basis s/he deems appropriate (or which the parties mutually specify). The decision is reviewable only on very limited grounds and has no precedental effect.

Private judging, a voluntary process, is a combination of the above two processes in which a privately selected retired judge conducts a formal, adversarial private proceeding, and makes a decision according to substantive legal rules. The decision is reviewable by a public higher court for legal errors, but has no precedental effect.

Advisory (or "nonbinding") arbitration refers to arbitration in which the arbitrator's decision is, in effect, only a recommendation, not binding on the parties. The decision may be accompanied by findings of fact, and the process is usually intended as a spur to negotiated settlement.

Court-ordered arbitration refers to a form of advisory arbitration ordered by a court (usually under a statutory scheme) and conducted by a court-appointed lawyer-arbitrator applying substantive legal rules to make an "award." Either party may reject the award and return to court for adjudication, but if neither does, the award becomes final and binding.

Mediation refers to a process, either voluntary or court-ordered, in which a neutral third party (court-appointed or privately selected) conducts an informal and nonadversarial meeting to help the parties identify the issues in dispute and reach a mutually acceptable settlement on their own terms. The mediator has no power to impose a settlement and ordinarily does not even make recommendations.

Med-arb, usually a voluntary process, is a combination of mediation and arbitration in which the neutral third party first attempts to resolve the dispute by mediation; however, if no mediated settlement is possible, the med-arbiter disregards the prior discussions, hears the parties' arguments in a private arbitration hearing, and renders a binding award as an arbitrator.

Negotiation needs no definition here, but several processes should be noted that are essentially add-ons to the negotiation process intended to promote settlement.

Mini-trial is a voluntary process, usually involving corporate parties, in which both parties' lawyers, after an expedited and limited exchange of information, give an adversarial summary presentation of their cases to the managers or corporate officers of both sides. The corporate decision makers then conduct direct negotiations.

Summary jury trial is a court-referred process in which both parties' lawyers, after limited exchange of information, give an adversarial summary presentation of their cases to a sample jury. The jury's verdict is used as the basis for direct negotiations.

Early neutral evaluation is a process, either voluntary or court-referred, in which a mini-trial-like session is conducted by a retired judge or similar "experienced" neutral, who then gives the parties his assessment of the likely outcome if a trial were held. The parties then conduct direct negotiations.

Policy dialogue is a negotiation-based process that involves the convening of sessions where people representing diverse viewpoints on a particular set of issues can both speak and listen to one another, outside of the pressured context of a particular dispute. The dialogue may lead to consensus about how to define issues and problems or how to approach them, or it may simply help the parties to better understand each other's diverse viewpoints and the bases on which they rest.

These processes can be distinguished and characterized on a variety of dimensions, and identifying the most useful framework for comparing processes has interested many scholars. They have suggested distinguishing factors such as whether the process is formal/informal, adversarial/nonadversarial, voluntary/compulsory, binding/nonbinding, public/private, or precedental/nonprecedental; whether the decision is based on legal rules, or other rules, or no rules; the degree of third-party involvement in and control over the proceeding; and so on (Goldberg, Green, and Sander 1985, 7–10). Such distinctions as these all focus on how the processes operate.

Another basis for comparison is impact or outcome. Scholars here have suggested comparing different processes in terms of effects, such as time and

cost (public and private); subjectively defined party satisfaction; preservation/
destruction of relationships; dilution/preservation of rights; exacerbation/ame-
lioration of economic and political inequality; promotion/obstruction of self-
determination and autonomy; furtherance/obstruction of economic efficiency
(aggregate societal welfare); preservation/compromise of public order; and
so on (Bush 1984; Bush 1989a, 347–53).

Comparison of effects, naturally enough, has led to analysis of the relative appropriateness or preferability of different processes, whether in specific
types of cases or generally. The key question here, which is discussed more
fully later, is whether different processes differ in impact in predictable and
significant ways, so that disputants and policymakers can rationally choose
which process to use by matching predicted impact to desired goals. Comparison of operational features has produced different and somewhat contradictory insights. Some scholars have tried to link operational differences and
impact differences, suggesting that different features predictably lead to different impacts, and using that analysis to answer the question of rational
process choice just mentioned (Bush 1984, 951–62; Riskin and Westbrook
1987, chap. 7; Sander 1976). Others, however, have questioned whether the
operational distinctions described in theory are so clearly found in practice,
suggesting that real-world versions of the ADR processes described above are
much more ambiguous than theory implies—and therefore more difficult to
neatly classify, predict, and choose between (Esser 1989). Suffice it to say for
now that on both of these questions—predictability of process impacts and
distinguishability of process features—there is much disagreement in the field
itself.

However, regardless of the continuing lack of consensus on how to
analyze and evaluate ADR processes, their utilization in practice has grown
enormously in the last two decades and continues to do so. This growth itself,
in a context of considerable informational and analytical unclarity, gives rise
to many of the current problem issues. First, however, it is important to
picture that growth by describing in a summary way the development and
current range of utilization of the processes.

Development and Current Uses of ADR Processes: A
Brief History and Overview of the Domestic Arena

Some scholars have traced the development of ADR processes in the United
States to the colonial period (Auerbach 1983). However, most of the current
interest in ADR in the domestic arena focuses on development over the last
20 years or so, beginning in the late sixties. This chapter focuses on developments in this "modern" era of ADR in three areas: mediation, arbitration, and
negotiation variants. This capsule history draws from numerous sources, espe-

cially Singer 1990; as well as Folberg and Milne 1988, chap. 1; Goldberg, Green, and Sander 1985; and Tomasic and Feeley 1982.

Mediation. Over the past 20 years, the use of mediation has developed in many types of disputes. However, the major milestones in the development of mediation, from which it spread more broadly, occurred in three main areas: so-called community mediation, divorce mediation, and environmental mediation. A fourth very recent phenomenon is the development of court-ordered mediation for civil cases generally, which reflects the extent to which the earlier developments have taken root and spread. In each of these areas, the impetus for using mediation came from several directions at once, operating from quite different motivations.

In the domestic field, *community mediation* is understood to encompass resolution of both small-scale interpersonal disputes at the neighborhood level and major multiparty disputes involving different groups within a community (such as racial or ethnic conflicts). Shortly after the major urban disorders of 1968, mediation attracted interest as a possible device for addressing the conflicts behind the violence. This interest came from a few different directions. On the one hand, local and national governmental agencies (like the federal Law Enforcement Assistance Agency) joined with major business/civic-oriented nonprofit agencies (like the American Arbitration Association [AAA] and the Ford Foundation) to sponsor programs that would try to resolve major and minor community disputes by mediation. The U.S. Department of Justice's Community Relations Service and the AAA's National Center for Dispute Settlement were major actors in this area. In both, but especially in the AAA's program, the conception of mediation was based squarely on the precedent and model of labor mediation, and many of the early figures in the field were prominent labor mediators. The first efforts focused on mediation of major disputes involving community groups and government agencies, such as school desegregation and public housing conflicts. Soon the notion developed that major conflicts were often triggered by minor disputes left unresolved, so that mediation at the interpersonal level could avoid escalation into major conflict. The result was the development, again under joint government and private sponsorship, of programs for mediation of minor civil/criminal disputes, in cooperation with local courts and prosecutors (Sander 1976; Stulberg 1975). Often, in such programs, mediation was presented as "an alternative to criminal prosecution," since many of the disputes involved would typically surface as complaints to local law-enforcement agencies.

Parallel to this fostering of community mediation by business, civic, and governmental organizations, a separate "track" of interest in mediation developed during the late sixties and early seventies in the then thriving "grass roots" community-organization sector. Spurred by organizations like the

American Friends Service Committee, and by the activist traditions of the community organizing and neighborhood legal services movements, the community mediation "movement" was modeled on non-Western traditional dispute-resolution institutions such as African "moots" (Danzig 1973; Wahrhaftig 1982). The resulting projects were usually community-based, with minimal involvement of the official justice system and a strong emphasis on education and involvement of the community itself in the program. Here mediation was presented as a means of developing individual and community self-determination without reference to the formal justice system (Shonholtz 1984).

Over the next decade, both court-connected and community-based "neighborhood mediation" programs spread across the country. In the midseventies, the U.S. Justice Department's sponsorship of three model Neighborhood Justice Centers put the official stamp of approval on community mediation, and through the eighties such programs were widely institutionalized at the local and state levels (McGillis 1982). As the field developed, the court-connected and government-sponsored programs—and their approach to mediation—came more and more to predominate over community-based programs. Several hundred government-sponsored programs now exist across the country, and in some states, like New York, Florida, and others, they are organized under statewide programs handling hundreds of thousands of cases annually.[1]

The second major milestone in mediation's history was the development, in the late seventies, of *divorce mediation* (American Bar Assoc. 1982, chap. 1; Folberg and Milne 1988, chap. 1). Several factors led to interest in the use of mediation in divorce cases. First, the broad shift in the substantive law toward nonfault divorce obviated the need for proof or admission of cruelty, desertion, and so on, and signaled a change from a policy favoring preservation of marriages to one favoring facilitation of divorces without undue exacerbation or prolongation of conflict. The shift toward nonadversarial divorce in substantive law led naturally to an interest in the nonadversarial mediation process (Winks 1980). In addition, there was a tradition of mediative processes already extant in the family courts. In the fault era, many family courts used optional or mandatory "conciliation" by in-house staff conciliators (usually social workers), to see whether the marital problem could be overcome and divorce avoided. The end of the fault era closed the conciliation offices, but after the transition to nonfault, the history of conciliation made it easy for family-court judges to see the potential for mediation of the terms of the divorce itself. Starting in the late seventies, family courts began referring contested cases with children to staff mediators (also usually social workers), for mediation of the of the "human" issues of the divorce (i.e., custody and visitation). Further development occurred in the mid-eighties. With studies showing high rates of party satisfaction and compliance with mediated agreements, several states adopted laws *mandating* mediation of all contested custody cases—the first use of mandatory mediation (Folberg and Milne 1988, chaps. 10, 21). More recently, legislation and court rules have expanded the mediation process to deal with financial and property issues as well, so the entire case is sent to mediation.

Parallel to this development within the courts themselves, the nonfault era saw a development in the private marriage counseling profession to extend counseling services not only to help preserve but to help amicably terminate marriages. The result was the development of *private* divorce mediation, with mediation offered on a fee-for-services basis by both therapists and lawyers to couples seeking help in achieving amicable dissolution (American Bar Assoc. 1982, 173). Where court mediation existed, private mediators offered an alternative; where no court mediation existed, they offered a unique service. In both places, tensions arose for obvious reasons between divorce mediators, especially nonlawyer mediators, and the organized bar. However, after a turbulent decade, by the late eighties private mediation was well established in many states, and steadily growing.

The growth of public and private divorce mediation is especially significant because it represents the first instance, outside of the labor field, of an emerging *profession* of mediation, in which significant numbers of practitioners pursue mediation as a full-time paid occupation. Reflecting this unique situation, divorce mediation was the first field of mediation to see significant attention paid to the development of standards of practice and qualification for mediators (Folberg and Milne 1988, chaps. 18–20). In many ways, divorce mediation may have considerable influence as a precedent in the development of general civil mediation, discussed below.

The third milestone in modern mediation history was the development, beginning in the seventies, of *environmental mediation* (Goldberg, Green, and Sander 1985, chap. 10). The increased consciousness of environmental issues in the seventies, and the corresponding increase in regulation and litigation, gave rise to a whole new class of high-stakes, multiparty conflicts with major public policy dimensions, such as disputes over the siting of hazardous facilities or the undertaking of major development projects. The use of mediation here was probably inspired by its early use in intergroup community conflicts as described above. In any event, the development of environmental mediation has been important not only in itself, but because it highlights the possibilities for using mediation to resolve public policy disputes of other kinds. As such, this use of mediation probably foreshadowed the development of publicly funded dispute-resolution offices at the state level in several states.

A fourth major development in mediation that grew out of the other three is the recent growth in the use of mediation for resolving civil litigation generally, including complex commercial, corporate, insurance, liability, and other types of civil claims (Singer 1990, chap. 4). Developments include both court-sponsored (voluntary or mandatory) and private mediation. As to the latter, it is closely connected to the growth of private arbitration services described in the next section, and is still in its nascent stages. This new industry, as it were, it still shaking itself out, and the field is far from stable, as several new entrants have found. Court-sponsored mediation is also still in its early stages, but it is developing quite rapidly. In several states, legislation provides for court-referred or court-ordered mediation of specific kinds of civil disputes including, for example, farmer-creditor disputes, medical malpractice cases, personal injury claims, workmen's compensation claims, and so on. A few states, notably Florida and Texas, have authorized courts to order mediation (or other ADR processes) in *any* civil case, and at least in Florida the process is being used extensively for all types of civil claims. Under such legislation, the utilization of mediation is undergoing rapid and major expansion. Like the development of divorce mediation, the rise of civil mediation means a new—and much larger—body of professional mediators, and this development itself will have major economic and political consequences wherever it occurs, as is already the case in Florida.

One final point is that, in a quite controversial development, the use of mediation is increasingly being urged upon judges themselves, especially in the federal courts, to settle cases pending before them (Menkel-Meadow 1985). Judicial mediation, to be distinguished from judicial *referral* to mediation, is encouraged under the Federal Rules of Civil Procedure as part of the judge's greater role in case conferencing and management of the litigation process. The extent to which federal judges actually do engage in mediation themselves is not yet clear, but it is certainly an important field to note.

Arbitration. As with mediation, the last two decades have seen enormous growth in the use of arbitration in different fields. Three general areas of growth are most notable: private commercial or business arbitration; consumer arbitration in a number of different areas; and statutory or court-ordered arbitration.

Private business arbitration has a long history in the United States, beginning with the arbitration tribunal of the New York Chamber of Commerce, established by the colonial Dutch merchant community in the mid-eighteenth century. The modern era of arbitration began in 1926, with the founding of the American Arbitration Association (AAA), a joint creation of the business community and the bar (Auerbach 1983, chap. 4). Essentially an administrative organization, the AAA (and other newer companies in its image) offers business disputants access to a pool of experienced private arbitrators, as well as administrative services including hearing sites, scheduling, stipulated rules of procedure, and so on, to facilitate the arbitration process. As reflected in the AAA's activities and other developments, the visibility and utilization of private business arbitration greatly increased beginning in the late sixties and early seventies. This development has been tied to a growing perception among business disputants of the ineffectiveness of litigation—both because of its rising costs and, perhaps more so, because of the fear that neither juries nor judges could appreciate the increasingly complex issues (financial, technological, etc.) presented in business disputes and thus render sound decisions (Wilkinson 1990, chap. 1).

From the seventies on, the AAA itself has steadily expanded, as indicated by its establishment of a series of new, specialized arbitration tribunals (each with its own pool of arbitrators and rules) for commercial, construction, insurance, and complex civil cases, among others. Further, a number of competing private arbitration organizations emerged beginning in the early eighties, including firms such as Endispute, Judicial Arbitration and Mediation Services, the Center for Public Resources, and others. While not all have had great success, the growth of the market for arbitration is undeniable. Many of these companies offer mediation and other ADR processes as well as arbitration, and they vary in their rules and the character of the arbitrators in their pools. In certain states, such as California, there has in recent years been a great demand among the business and legal community not only for arbitration but for "private judging," which is conducted by retired judges and is seen as combining the advantages of arbitration and adjudication.

Finally, another major area of business arbitration that has also grown steadily is intraindustry arbitration, in which industry or trade associations use arbitration to resolve disputes between member businesses. The most notable examples of this are the securities and commodities exchanges, whose members agree as a condition of admission to resolve all intermember disputes via arbitration. The same model has been adopted by other industries as well, and it is frequently found in the international business sphere as part of international trade agreements (Wilkinson 1990).

Related to this last phenomenon—intraindustry business arbitration—is the second major area of arbitration's growth. *Consumer arbitration*, despite its label, was really a creation of business in response to increased consumer awareness and the consumer protection movement of the sixties. Like business arbitration, consumer arbitration is found in both generalized and specific industry (or manufacturer) programs (American Bar Assoc. 1983). For example, the Better Business Bureau (BBB), a national retail trade association, has an arbitration program for all kinds of consumer-merchant disputes involving its member merchants (although in recent years they have focused heavily on disputes over newly purchased automobiles). On the other hand, in "AUTOCAP" and "MACAP" (the "CAP" stands for "consumer arbitration program"), associations of auto and appliance manufacturers offer arbitration to purchasers of those specific products. Such industry programs were given encouragement by federal legislation in the late seventies. In a different area, all the major securities and commodities exchanges now extend their arbitration programs to disputes between exchange members and customers, so securities arbitration now includes a consumer sector. In all of these different areas, the common framework is that the business party agrees in advance (usually as a condition of membership in the association) to submit disputes with consumers to arbitration, while the consumer simply has the *option* of doing so when a dispute actually arises. So consumers are generally free to go to court when disputes arise. If the consumer does agree to arbitration at that time, both parties are bound by the decision.[2]

The third major area of arbitration's growth is the field of *court-ordered arbitration,* as defined earlier. The first court-ordered arbitration program was established in Philadelphia in 1952, and such programs spread across Pennsylvania in the sixties. Beginning in the seventies, many states and federal judicial districts have instituted court-ordered arbitration, and it may be the fastest growing form of ADR (Hensler 1986). It is typically adopted under enabling legislation and judicial rules—to avoid legal and constitutional challenges—and typically provides for mandatory arbitration of all civil claims for monetary damages under a certain dollar amount (today, usually $25–50,000). Most programs make no attempt to screen cases for "suitability" for arbitration, and refer as many cases as the available pool of arbitrators can handle. The result is that a very large number of civil cases, of different kinds, are shifted from the courts into the arbitration process. The process itself is run by lawyer-arbitrators applying legal rules, and the "decisions" can be rejected by either party, in effect making this a form of *advisory arbitration.* Nevertheless, in most cases both parties accept the decision, with rejection rates varying between 15 and 50 percent, depending on how long the program has operated. Beyond its use in general civil cases, court-ordered arbitration is also widely used in small-claims cases, and, under special legislation in some states, in certain kinds of consumer disputes such as no-fault insurance claims and medical malpractice cases.

Negotiation variants. As noted earlier, ADR processes in current use include a number of variants of the negotiation process, such as mini-trial, summary jury trial, and several others (Wilkinson 1990). All of these processes are essentially used to spur negotiations by giving the parties a clear idea of what the outcome of a litigation is likely to be, in the absence of a negotiated settlement. The mini-trial is used primarily in complex intercorporate civil litigation, especially as an antidote to problems of massive and extended pretrial discovery and motions in court. "Early neutral evaluation" (ENE) is used in both corporate and noncorporate civil litigation, including personal injury cases. Both of these are services offered by the various private dispute-resolution companies mentioned earlier. ENE is also used in certain state and federal courts as a court-referred ADR technique. Summary jury trial is also used as a court-referred process, primarily in personal injury cases but also in some commercial litigation.

There are a few other important areas where negotiation-based ADR processes have been suggested and used, which are somewhat controversial. One is called "regulatory negotiation," or reg-neg. It is a process in which regulatory agencies like the Environmental Protection Agency, instead of simply promulgating regulations and then conducting hearings to elicit comments and objections, *begin* the promulgation process by convening a meeting of interested and potentially affected parties to collaborate in "negotiating" a set of proposed regulations acceptable to all. Public hearings still follow, but with fewer objections anticipated because of the initial negotiations. A second area is land-use or zoning cases, in which local boards, instead of flatly applying zoning and land-use restrictions, increasingly engage in "negotiated zoning." That is, they negotiate with developers and others seeking variances, extracting various promises and commitments for public amenities in exchange for permission to build at variance from local codes. Both of these examples illustrate ADR processes as alternatives, not to the judicial process, but to the administrative and political processes. They have raised difficult questions, as has public-sector labor arbitration, regarding whether ADR involves an inappropriate (or even unlawful) abdication of responsibility by elected or appointed public officials.

A final development that deserves mention is the proactive use of negotiation-based, consensus processes to help parties address potentially contentious issues *before* specific disputes arise. These processes have been called by different names, including "collaborative problem-solving," "policy facilitation," and, most recently, "policy dialogue." Whichever name is used, these processes generally involve the convening of group sessions, at which people representing diverse viewpoints on a particular set of issues can both speak and listen to one another, outside of the pressured context of a particular dispute. The exchange of views is usually moderated by one or more professional group facilitators, so the process falls somewhere between mediation and negotiation on the ADR continuum. The dialogue may lead to common understandings or consensus about how to define issues and problems or how to approach them, or it may simply help the parties to better understand each other's diverse viewpoints and the bases on which they rest. If specific disputes arise at later points, the foundation laid by the dialogue process may make other ADR processes more productive.

In recent years, certain organizations and projects, such as Common Ground, the Listening Project, and the Public Conversations Project, among others, have concentrated on facilitating broad-ranging dialogues on controversial public issues including abortion, gun control, and race relations. (Public Conversations Project 1992) The dialogue process has also been used in situations involving particular policies, such as policies on urban and regional planning, or environmental protection and economic development (Susskind and Cruikshank 1987, chap. 6; Bingham 1985; Moore and Carlson 1984). Indeed, reg-neg, mentioned just above, can be seen as a form of policy dialogue. The growth of policy dialogue has been closely connected with the growth of public policy and environmental mediation. However, policy dialogue generally deals proactively with issues before specific disputes arise, while policy mediation is normally employed to deal with concrete disputes that have arisen over specific issues or actions. Some have suggested that, like processes such as reg-neg, policy dialogue can be seen not simply as an element of the ADR field, but as a means of enhancing the democratic process. This suggestion has some interesting implications for the global conflict-resolution field.

Structural Incentives and Constraints: Some Comparisons between the Domestic and Global Arenas

The foregoing history and overview suggest, at least implicitly, several important structural or contextual factors in the domestic arena that have worked either to encourage or to constrain the development of ADR processes. It is useful to identify these factors explicitly in order to offer some comparisons with structural factors in the global context.[3]

One strong force behind the development of ADR processes in the domestic arena has been disappointment and dissatisfaction with the formal adversary process offered by courts of law. This force works both negatively and positively. ADR offers a way to avoid the negatives of litigation—delay, expense, constrained win/lose outcomes, and unpleasantness. At the same time, ADR offers a way to secure goods that disputants consider important per se—the power to retain control over outcome, the opportunity to treat others and be treated with respect and concern, and the chance to have one's needs met as fully as possible in a given situation. Offering parties the option both to avoid more of what they dislike and to get more of what they prefer, by comparison to the dominant or primary system, constitutes a powerful incentive for the use of ADR. In the global arena, disappointment with the "system" or regime of power politics, including the use of war or violence, is seen by some as providing a similar incentive to explore conflict-resolution processes, at least as a way of avoiding the negative (Vasquez, in this volume).

In other respects, the domestic and global arenas seem to present contrasting structures—but it is important not to overstate the contrasts. Thus, it is suggested that the difference of "scale" between domestic and global conflict makes the two incomparable. This view portrays domestic conflict as involving relatively small-stakes, two-party disputes between individuals, and global conflict as involving very high-stakes, multiparty conflicts between institutions. In reality, the contrast is less sharp. Many disputes in which domestic ADR is used, such as environmental and public policy cases, involve high-stakes, multiparty institutional conflict; at the same time, many believe that global conflicts can be segmented in conflict resolution so that they can be seen and handled in a two-party, interpersonal framework (e.g., Pruitt, in this volume). Another suggested contrast is that the domestic arena represents a highly ordered environment, especially because of the pervasiveness of law and legal institutions, while the global arena is an essentially anarchic context lacking any strong ordering principles or agencies. Here too, in reality the contrast is not so sharp. Law and legal institutions have far less penetration in the domestic arena than generally assumed (Galanter 1983). At the same time, as Johnson (in this volume) suggests, the structure of international law and organizations has brought considerable order to the global arena (see also Vasquez, chap. 7, herein).

Nevertheless, if framed a bit differently, the order/anarchy distinction does help to identify significant differences in how domestic and global structures create incentives for and constraints on dispute/conflict resolution. Specifically, a distinction can be drawn between "directive" institutions that operate on a formal, authoritative, coercive basis and "connective" institutions that operate on an informal, relative, persuasive basis. While both arenas certainly contain both kinds, directive institutions play a larger role in the domestic than global arena, and vice versa. The impact of this on dispute and conflict resolution is significant.

In the domestic arena, the greater presence of directive agencies provides a greater capacity to pressure or compel the use of ADR; and this has in fact served as a great spur to ADR's expansion, as shown in the historical survey above. However, the same factor can operate to block access to ADR, or to routinize or formalize it and limit its flexibility and creativity, and this has been and continues to be a serious constraint on the development of ADR as a real alternative to existing processes, as will be discussed shortly (see also Kolb, in this volume; Kolb 1989). On the other hand, in the global arena, the greater presence of connective institutions allows for continued and relatively unconstrained experimentation with conflict resolution, both within and without recognized international agencies (Vasquez, chap. 7, herein). However, the same factor can and often does result in real problems in finding an authoritative and effective convenor to get conflict resolution going in the first place. The contrasting pattern is: in the domestic arena, there is more direction toward ADR, but there are also more constraints on its creative development; in the global arena, there are fewer constraints on the creativity of conflict resolution, but also less direction toward using it.

The challenge to both fields suggested by the comparison is how to develop structures that can effectively encourage dispute and conflict resolution without unduly constraining and limiting the flexibility and creativity of these processes. As yet, neither arena seems to possess such structures. Perhaps comparative exploration will help both to move in this direction.

In this connection, one insight suggested by the historical discussion is that, despite the constraints of directive institutions, the domestic field has been enriched and expanded by the regular emergence of new forms and processes from *outside* existing institutional structures. In the development of processes such as community mediation, divorce mediation, mini-trial, public policy mediation, and policy dialogue, a major part of the original impetus was "from the bottom up," or "demand-driven." Parties sought new ways to address disputes and issues, and individual practitioners and organizations tried new forms of dispute resolution in response. Although directive institutions, like the courts, have tended to move in and routinize these processes once they are introduced, the emergent nature of the field has kept pushing practice one step beyond the institutional bounds, so that new approaches and processes continue to develop. In the global field, one can see a similar phenomenon at work—or at least the potential for it—in the new environment created in Eastern Europe and the former Soviet Republics by the political changes of the last few years. The weakening or collapse of old institutions has created an environment in which new methods of addressing issues, solving problems, and resolving conflict are demanded. Indeed, one response to this has been a growing flow of information and consultants from the domestic ADR field into Eastern Europe and the former Soviet Republics, where consensus and ADR processes are seen as ways of enhancing and building more democratic institutions.

The point is that, in both the domestic and global arenas, crises in existing or failed institutions have driven a demand for new ways of addressing and resolving conflict, and the ADR field has continued to be creative in responding to this demand. In a sense, the pressures of crises have accomplished what we have not been able to achieve through intentionally designed structures—to encourage dispute-resolution efforts without constraining their flexibility by rigid routinization. Nevertheless, how to do this *intentionally* remains a real challenge, in both the domestic and global fields.

To return the focus now to the domestic arena itself, the challenge just described is one of the most important issues facing the field—the issue of how to institutionalize the use of ADR. However, there are actually several critical issues confronting the domestic ADR field. The next section summarizes these issues, in order to provide a foundation for further comparative discussion.

Current Issues and Questions in Domestic Dispute Resolution: A Selective Sampling

A number of important theoretical and policy questions have been raised by the use of ADR processes in the domestic arena in recent years. Some of these questions have been suggested already. The aim of this section is to highlight several of the most important of these issues—issues that are still being vigorously debated in the field. What follows is by no means a complete survey of current issues; it is a selective sampling. However, it is not a random sampling. The issues selected go to the heart of the domestic ADR enterprise as it now stands. Pointing to them here can help pose a larger question relevant to the theme of this volume: Can these central issues in domestic dispute resolution be related to important issues in the global conflict-resolution field? Are the pressing issues at all similar in the two fields, so that each might learn from the other? Consider these larger questions in connection with the following issues, each of which is summarized as a series of open questions that are currently the subject of study and debate in the domestic arena.

The critique of ADR. The expansion in the use of ADR processes, and scholarly support for ADR, has provoked a body of very trenchant criticism of ADR theory and practice (Abel 1982; Tomasic and Feeley 1982; Auerbach 1983; Harrington 1985). Although the arguments of the critics are manifold, they cluster into two major and powerful objections to ADR. The objections are that all ADR processes work (in varying degrees) either to *privatize* justice or to *deny* justice, or both. The argument behind the first objection is that, by removing cases from a public forum where public officials decide cases according to public norms, ADR processes allow and encourage outcomes that satisfy the private interests of the parties but injure or compromise the public interest (Fiss 1984; Nader 1979). Thus ADR, the institutional child of the age, exalts private interests over the public good and risks the despoilation of important societal resources. The argument behind the second objection is that, by abandoning (in varying degrees) the framework of rights and protections that has gradually been built into formal legal procedures and substantive law, in favor of ad hoc bargaining, compromise, and discretion, ADR processes allow and encourage outcomes that satisfy the powerful at the expense of the weak (Abel 1982, chaps. 6, 8, 10; Tomasic and Feeley 1982, chap. 12; Harrington 1985). Thus ADR takes from the poor to give to the rich, turning the justice system into injustice and contributing to an oppressive society. It is no answer, say the critics, to speak of peacemaking and conflict resolution as values in themselves. For peace may hide injustice, and conflict may be a positive force for justice. ADR, they say, offers peace without justice (Fiss 1984, 1085).

These critical arguments are probably somewhat overstated here, as they sometimes are in the critique itself. Even the critics allow that ADR does not *always* facilitate greed and oppression. However, they argue that it almost always carries substantial *risks* of these twin evils, and that in view of these risks it is a bad bargain indeed.

ADR scholars and practitioners have offered responses to the arguments of the critique (Goldberg, Green, and Sander 1986; Menkel-Meadow 1985; Bush 1989c). However, the point here is not to review and judge this debate, but to signal the issues and questions it presents. The questions raised by the critique are important, and they are far from being definitively answered. The important open questions include the following: Is it true that ADR processes tend to produce the twin evils of compromising the public good and oppressing the weak, and if so, to what degree? Is this equally true of all ADR processes, in all situations? Is it true, as the critique implies, that using formal legal procedures and substantive legal rules poses much lower risk, if any, of these evils? Is there some enormous good that ADR processes serve that simply outweighs the stated evils, even assuming their existence and severity? Is there any way to modify ADR processes to preserve some of their value but lessen the risks of the stated evils? All of these questions are implicit in the argument over the ADR critique. None have yet been answered satisfactorily. Indeed, much of the current theoretical and empirical work is directed to these very questions (see, e.g., Bush 1989c; Silbey and Merry 1986).

ADR "science" and ADR ideology. The earlier discussion referred to scholars' attempts to devise a framework for rationally choosing which dispute resolution process to use in a given case. This interest in constructing what could be called a "scientific" approach to comparing and choosing between dispute-resolution processes has its origins in early ADR scholarship, especially the work of Lon Fuller and Frank Sander in the seventies (Fuller 1971, 1978; Sander 1976). While some supported this approach in the early eighties (Bush 1984), there was little serious interest in it at that time. Today, however, the notion of a rational and principled system for assigning cases to different dispute-resolution processes, and thus scientifically "designing" dispute-resolution "systems," is extremely popular in the ADR field (Goldberg, Green, and Sander 1985, 545; Ury, Brett, and Goldberg 1989).

This growing popularity of ADR "science" is in part a result of the pressure of the ADR critique as described above. That is, it grows out of the desire to find a sensible middle ground that acknowledges that ADR is indeed inappropriate in some cases (because of the kinds of risks the critics suggest) but maintains that ADR is entirely appropriate in other cases (where these risks are minimal or other values much more important). Such a middle ground would not dismiss the critique, but neither would it abandon ADR. It would allow that both have their place, in different cases. However, the crucial condition for attaining this middle ground is the ability to tell which cases (and processes) are which.

This is the current issue: the practical feasibility of such a "scientific" approach to ADR utilization. The key questions here are: Can cases be identified in which no significant public interest is at stake and no potential for oppression is present, so that ADR is unobjectionable? Or, can certain ADR processes be distinguished from others by their greater capacity for preserving the public interest and preventing oppression, so that at least these processes are unobjectionable? Or, can cases be identified in which other values, furthered by ADR, clearly outweigh any concerns for the public interest or protection of the weak, so that ADR is clearly preferable despite its "twin evils"? If these kinds of distinctions can be made in practice, then a "pluralistic" approach to ADR utilization can be taken, employing different processes in different cases to serve different values--sometimes court, sometimes ADR; sometimes one ADR process, sometimes another (Sander 1976; Menkel-Meadow 1985). However, if such lines cannot be rationally drawn in concrete terms, then the scientific approach to ADR, however appealing in theory, is no more than a dream (Esser 1989; Bush 1989a, 370–79).

Furthermore, the possibility that a scientific approach to ADR use is *not* feasible gives rise to another major issue: the *philosophical or ideological* basis of ADR. That is, if scientific sorting of cases to processes is impossible, then ADR must be justified (or the critique accepted and ADR rejected) across the board. Such a justification would have to rest on ideological—i.e., philosophical or moral—grounds. For example, one might argue that self-determination—often stressed by proponents of ADR—is a supreme value that ADR processes further and that adjudication undermines, and therefore ADR processes are always preferable to the courts in the first instance (Bush 1989c). The argument might also rest on some other comparably important value (Bush 1989c; Riskin 1984; McThenia and Shaffer 1985; Menkel-Meadow 1984). The key question here is: Can one articulate a general ideological justification for ADR processes as preferable to adjudication in all cases, and could any such justification be powerful enough to defeat the critique?

In short, questions regarding the feasibility of ADR "science" remain unanswered, and new questions regarding possible ideological justifications for ADR processes have emerged as another central issue of ADR theory.

The ambiguous character of ADR. Related to the previous issue is another major point of concern. As ADR scholars have begun to explore possible ideological justifications for the use of ADR, it has become clear that

ADR is, and long has been, a phenomenon of highly ambiguous character. ADR processes have been advocated on very different grounds by different interests (Tomasic and Feeley 1982, chap. 9). Government, civic, and business leaders sponsoring community mediation were clearly interested in mediation as an instrument for preserving public order (i.e., the status quo). Community groups and organizers, on the other hand, saw mediation as a means of individual and group empowerment, leading to personal growth and social change or transformation. Businessmen today see both mediation and arbitration as ways to maximize gain at minimum cost, and courts see both as ways to cut costs and reduce backlogs—both essentially utilitarian perspectives. In short, ADR has been supported on all three of these very different grounds—social control, private satisfaction/court efficiency, and citizen/community empowerment and transformation—and on others as well. ADR processes can in theory serve all of these values, though probably not all at the same time. However, all three are not equally powerful as *justifications* for ADR in the face of the ADR critique. Private satisfaction and court efficiency, for example, are unlikely to stand up as justifications against concerns for protecting public interests and preventing oppression. Thus, ADR in theory has different faces, and not all of them are equally attractive (Bush 1989a, 370–79).

If, despite this ambiguity in the sources or motivations for ADR, it was evident that ADR *in practice* was fairly uniform in approach—if practice was generally directed to just one of the goals cited by theory—then we could focus on the justification underlying that single approach. If, however, the different views of the purpose and goals of ADR have translated into differences in the way ADR operates in practice, the matter is far more complex. That is, if there are different *versions* of mediation, arbitration, and so on, being practiced—for example, an empowering or transformative version, a controlling version, and a utilitarian version—then *no* general justification of ADR can be found that would apply equally to all of them. Indeed, it is unlikely that all are equally justifiable or defensible vis-à-vis the ADR critique. Thus, if the ambiguity of ADR exists at the operational level, the question of which process to use applies not only to different processes but to the different versions of each process that probably exist in practice. This is also true for both the scientific and the ideological modes of analysis.

The questions raised by the issue of ambiguity are just beginning to be articulated in ADR scholarship (Bush and Folger 1994; Folger and Bush 1994; Bush 1989b; Silbey and Merry 1986; Kolb, in this volume). Some of the important ones are: Do processes like mediation and arbitration operate in practice according to different "versions," emphasizing different goals and producing different impacts? If so, what determines which version is used by a given mediator or arbitrator—for example, does one version usually predominate in a given context (i.e., is environmental mediation usually empowering, community mediation usually controlling, business arbitration usually utilitarian, etc.)? Are all the different versions equally justifiable vis-à-vis the ADR critique? If not, is there any effective way to ensure that the "best version" is the one employed in practice? These questions reflect the increased depth that ADR study has begun to reach.

Institutionalization and professionalization. A final major issue is presented by the increasing pressures in the field to "institutionalize and professionalize" ADR processes and practice. This development was mentioned in the historical discussion of ADR. For example, the development of court-annexed ADR, both mediation and arbitration, fixes ADR in a particular and powerful context, one effect of which may be to constrain and even distort the development of the processes. The emergence of a significant population of full-time paid mediators is another sort of solidification of ADR. The significance of these and other developments is that they give some permanence and status to the use of ADR generally, and perhaps also to the use of particular *versions* of processes. The issue presented is whether such permanence and status is really deserved, given the many unanswered questions detailed above.

This issue is made sharper if it is true that institutionalization tends to establish certain versions or forms of ADR, and to place certain groups in control of them, to the comparative exclusion of others. For example, institutionalization in community mediation may mean starvation of community-based programs and extension of court-based programs (Wahrhaftig 1982; Silbey and Merry 1986). It may also mean exclusion of volunteers in favor of paraprofessionals. In other areas, like divorce and civil mediation, it may mean exclusion of all but lawyers and therapists from the ranks of mediators, and the subsequent domination of professional education and discipline by these groups alone. Therefore, the push for institutionalization raises important questions, such as: Does institutionalization tend to favor particular versions of mediation, arbitration, and other ADR processes, and if so, which ones? Are the favored versions the ones that have the soundest underlying justifications? Does institutionalization tend to vest control of ADR processes and practice in certain groups to the exclusion of others, and if so, which ones? Does institutionalization weaken the "disfavored" versions and the excluded practitioners, or does it simply create parallel "tracks" of ADR?

Some Tentative Propositions on the Critical Issues in Domestic Dispute Resolution

Regarding the questions identified in the previous section, no definite conclusions are offered here, because none of these questions have easy answers.

However, based on current theory and practice, some tentative propositions can be suggested regarding each of the critical issues in the domestic arena. A full justification of these propositions is beyond the scope of the present chapter, though the author has offered such justifications elsewhere, as indicated in the references given below. Instead, the propositions are offered here without extended argument, as a preamble to the final section's discussion of the overall theme of this volume: the possible connections between the central issues of domestic dispute resolution and those of global conflict resolution. The propositions suggested reflect the general view that the domestic dispute-resolution field faces serious questions at present, despite its steady expansion, and that the prospects for the future depend on realistically facing and answering the kinds of questions described above, debating the issues honestly and hard, and making choices with clear heads—and high ideals. The same may be true in the global arena. Consider the following propositions about each of the critical issues in the domestic dispute-resolution arena, as a preface to some final thoughts on the connections between the two fields studied in this volume.

Propositions regarding the critique of ADR. ADR processes probably do pose risks of compromising the public interest and/or oppressing the weak—not in all cases, but in a significant number. Of course, it should not be forgotten that such risks are very real in court as well (Goldberg, Green, and Sander 1986; Menkel-Meadow 1985). Nevertheless, these kinds of risks may often be larger in ADR than in the courts; and modification of ADR processes to reduce the risks, if it were possible, would probably undermine ADR's capacity to serve other valued goals (Bush 1989b). In short, the critique has some real validity, as far as it goes, that cannot and should not be ignored. However, the possibility remains open that the risks can be minimized by "scientific" use of ADR, that other values justify ADR despite its risks, or that certain versions of ADR processes are relatively risk-free.

Propositions regarding ADR science and ADR ideology. The distinctions that have to be drawn to make the scientific approach feasible probably cannot be drawn with any confidence in practice—either at the process or the version level. Scientific ADR, despite its great appeal, is most likely a pipe dream, attractive primarily because of its capacity for avoiding the underlying and difficult ideological issues (Esser 1989; Bush 1989a, 370–79). That leaves philosophy or ideology—political and moral. My view is that, on ideological grounds, a basis *can* be articulated to justify ADR generally, by reference to the "relational"[4] values of self-determination and consideration for others (or compassion), which many hold superior to the largely individualist values underlying the ADR critique (Bush and Folger 1994; Bush 1989c). Indeed, the likelihood is that many long-time advocates of ADR support it precisely because of their commitment to these relational values, and their belief that

ADR processes further them while the formal adversary system subverts them. That is, many if not most ADR supporters probably do have a (largely unstated) value orientation that underlies and explains their interest in ADR. This orientation can—and should—be made explicit and justified (Bush 1989c). However, this possibility of an ideological justification for ADR in *general* opens the question of whether different *versions* of ADR may exist, and if so whether the general justification covers them all equally.

ADR ambiguity. ADR appears to be as ambiguous in practice as it is in theory, and different versions of mediation and arbitration probably do exist in practice (Kolb, in this volume; Bush and Folger 1994; Silbey and Merry 1986). The most important of these are the three suggested above: the controlling, the empowering/transformative, and the utilitarian versions of ADR. Of the three versions, only the empowering/transformative version can overcome the ADR critique, because only this version of ADR rests on the relational value bases mentioned above (Bush 1989b), and it is largely free of the risks cited in the critique. However, ensuring that this approach to ADR processes is used may prove difficult, because of the institutional interests, structures, and incentives surrounding the use of ADR. It is therefore important to clarify the unique value of the empowering/transformative version of ADR and to support it wherever possible (Bush and Folger 1994).

Institutionalization. Institutionalization as currently operating probably favors certain versions of ADR processes and certain groups of practitioners and gives more permanence and status to these than they deserve. The versions favored are probably the utilitarian and controlling versions. However, both are ideologically indefensible. In short, institutionalization is probably no great help to the productive development of the field at this point. Continued diversity and openness are necessary to preserve the possibility of continued survival of the ideologically defensible versions of ADR. In this respect, the continuing expansion of the field into areas such as policy mediation and policy dialogue, which may be less susceptible to "capture" by institutional interests and values, is a positive and welcome phenomenon.

Concluding Thoughts: Are the Issues Similar in the Domestic and Global Fields?

There are some striking similarities, but also some important differences, between the key issues in domestic dispute resolution and global conflict resolution. This chapter concludes by pointing to some of these comparisons, with an emphasis on the issues identified above as key issues.

The critical view. Proponents of conflict resolution in the global arena are vulnerable to a critique very similar to that leveled against domestic dispute resolution. First, they present an implicit view of war and violence as undesirable per se that, it could be argued, tends to exalt peace over justice and to delegitimate altogether a tool that may sometimes be the best means available for the have-nots to challenge the haves. Wars of national liberation and political terrorism, for example, are justified by some as the only effective means for oppressed peoples to gain recognition and justice. Second, they seem to ignore or at lest deemphasize international law, instead of insisting on making it a more effective and powerful tool for protecting the weak and oppressed, for example in the human rights area.

What is interesting, by comparison to the domestic arena, is that despite a similar potential for critique, one does not seem to have arisen so forcefully in the global field. There is some acknowledgment in this volume of both the peace/justice element (Kriesberg, in this volume) and the loss-of-law element (Johnson, in this volume) of the critique. However, by comparison to the intensity and centrality of the critique in the domestic field, it seems to occupy a much less important place at present in the global conflict resolution discourse. There seems to be more of a consensus that global conflict is so dangerous that peaceful conflict resolution is a clear, if not totally unmitigated, good. Of course, there may be a well-known body of critical thought that this author, as an outsider to the international field, simply has not seen. If not, however, then the difference is striking indeed.

"Science" and ideology. As great as the difference between the fields on the previous issue is the similarity between them on this issue. First, "the matching, coordinating, and sequencing of different but complementary third-party interventions" (Fisher, in this volume), to meet the contingencies of the situation, is an important theme for a number of global conflict-resolution scholars. Some see the question as how to match the "stage" of the conflict with the appropriate kind of intervention (Fisher, in this volume). Others suggest allocating different types of situations to different processes—disputes over interests should go to negotiation or mediation, conflicts over needs to facilitation and resolution (Burton, in this volume). The common thread is the notion of rationally sorting and matching situations to methods of intervention, the very same "scientific" notion that domestic ADR scholars are pursuing in their field.

Second, despite this pursuit of a rational conflict-resolution "science," the strong impression given by the chapters of this volume is that in the global field, as in the domestic arena, there is an ideological dimension underlying the interest in peaceful processes of resolution. Thus, when discussing models for choosing among methods of intervention, global scholars tend to place these methods in a defined ordering that implicitly or explicitly views some methods, and the results they achieve, as preferred or superior to others. For example, Burton (in this volume) presents resolution of underlying human needs as superior to settlement of interests. While, according to Fisher (in this volume), even in contingent or stage models, the goal is always to move from more impositional to more empowering interventions, and from more immediate and superficial to longer range and profounder outcomes (e.g., interests to needs or relationships). This is not to criticize these views; on the contrary, they are highly defensible. The point here is that this whole framework of choice or sequencing implies a hierarchy of interventions, and that the hierarchy rests on a set of values or ideology that defines what is higher and lower. As in the domestic arena, ideology underlies the preference for certain methods of resolution over others.

Moreover—and this point is even more striking—the values underlying interest in global conflict resolution seem very similar to those underlying support for informal and nonadversarial resolution of domestic disputes. Some advocates of domestic ADR support it because of their commitment to the values of self-determination, compassion, and community (Bush 1989c; Riskin 1984; McThenia and Shaffer 1985), values served better by ADR than by formal adversary justice. In addition, some seem to prefer ADR because they place a high value on meeting "human needs," and believe that ADR processes do this much better than the adversary system (Menkel-Meadow 1984; Ury, Brett, and Goldberg 1989). Turning to the global field, we find implicit and explicit reflections of strikingly similar values.

Fisher's strong emphasis (in this volume) on fostering mutual understanding and strengthening relationships through "third-party consultation" suggests an underlying commitment not just to world peace, but to the value of understanding and relationship per se. Doran's (in this volume) theory of the "power cycle," and the need for "great understanding" by declining powers to make adjustments for rising powers, also reflects something beyond realpolitik—the moral dimension of a state's decision to abnegate its own interest and yield to another for the sake of the whole. In some cases, the value basis is more explicit. Burton (in this volume) ties the importance of conflict resolution, as an alternative to power politics, to the value of meeting "inherent and universal human needs," and others use similar language. In all of these contributions from the conflict-resolution field, there are remarkably strong similarities to the value orientations of domestic ADR supporters—toward either relational or human-needs values or both.

If it is true that values—and certain values in particular—underlie both the domestic and global conflict-resolution fields, then it is all the more important that those values be articulated with honesty and clarity. If "conflict resolutionaries," as James Laue calls those of us in both the domestic and global fields, are really following a certain ideology, then that ideology should be clearly identified. Doing so is important in order to build support for the use of dispute and conflict resolution and justify them against possible critiques. Doing so is also important in order to understand, for ourselves, precisely why we are involved in the enterprise altogether, and how to pursue it more effectively. A final similarity between both fields on this issue is that neither has seen sufficient exploration of the significance or character of the underlying ideological dimension, and both could benefit from more work in this direction.

Ambiguity of processes. This is another issue on which similarity is evident. For example, Fisher (in this volume) discusses mediation, "mediation with muscle," and third-party consultation. However, while he presents the three as distinct processes, others suggest that the difference may really derive from the choice of third party—that is, who is conducting the process (Kolb and Babbitt, in this volume). This raises the same kinds of concerns presented by the ambiguity or malleability of processes in the domestic arena. The pervasiveness of this issue suggests the importance, in both fields, of developing greater sophistication in describing—and monitoring—what individual "neutrals" do; because (for example) "mediation" may often simply be arbitration by another name, and this may lead to misunderstanding and even abuse of resolution processes. In this area, there is considerable progress and continuing work in the domestic arena (see Kolb and Babbitt, in this volume), from which scholars in the global field might gain good ideas of how to pursue the inquiry in their domain.

Institutionalization. On this final issue, there is significant contrast, as discussed earlier, between the two fields in terms of the structural context in which they operate. One important practical consequence of that structural contrast is that the domestic field is, at present, much farther along in the direction of institutionalization than the global arena. However, there is a real concern on the part of many that progress in institutionalization has brought with it a change in the character of the "alternative" processes themselves. That is, as their use is routinized, they display less of the informal, nonadversarial, creative character that engendered interest in them to begin with, and begin, as Kolb (1989) has put it, to look more and more like the processes they were supposed to replace. Whether, and how, this tendency can be avoided—or reversed—is an important and troubling question for many in the domestic arena today. Here, the contrasting structure of the global arena may be a distinct advantage, since it may contain fewer structures with enough gravitational pull to "capture" or co-opt the initiatives of conflict-resolution practitioners, and ongoing freedom to experiment and develop independently is more likely.

In this connection, it is possible to see parallels in some of the recent developments in both the domestic and global fields that suggest ways of avoiding the constraining effects of institutionalization. In both fields, there have been efforts recently to focus on dealing with conflict proactively rather than reactively, both by earlier timing of interventions, and by expansion of activities from resolution per se to education. As to the first, processes like policy dialogue in the domestic arena and consultation in the global arena (Fisher, in this volume), both involve moving intervention to an earlier point in the time line of a conflict cycle, to the predispute stage. Doing so removes certain kinds of barriers to communication between parties; it also avoids institutional pressures that are much stronger when an actual crisis exists. In effect, when interventions occur earlier, conflict-resolution efforts have more latitude and flexibility, and institutional constraints are less powerful. Regarding the second kind of proactive effort, student mediation programs and policy dialogue in the domestic arena, and processes like consultation in the global arena, often involve education as much as or more than conflict resolution. That is, they allow and help parties to learn about both substantive issues and problem-solving skills, even where there is no immediate need to resolve a particular conflict. Again, the effect is to allow more latitude and flexibility, and to avoid institutional pressures and constraints. It is also worth noting that these kinds of educational, preconflict interventions strongly express values of empowerment and transformation that, as noted earlier, underlie efforts in both the domestic and global fields. Seen in the broadest context, these kinds of proactive efforts help strengthen civic participation and enhance democratic processes, and it seems clear that these are considered important goals at both the domestic and global levels today.

There is one final pattern to note that is somewhat disturbing from the perspective of the domestic arena: that is what might be called the "emigration" of practitioners and scholars from the domestic to the global arena. A number of the early and very influential leaders of the domestic field have, in recent years, begun to spend more of their time and effort in the global arena. This may be simply a matter of natural growth and expansion, but it may also be that these "charismatic" early figures are beginning to be disenchanted with the effects of institutionalization on the domestic field. For those deeply interested in the continued vitality of the domestic field, it must be hoped that this is not the case. James Laue has suggested that the only thing that counteracts routinization is a continuing focus on the values of the enterprise. This is one area where the two fields appear to have much in common; indeed, the global field is somewhat more explicit about values than the domestic. Joint work such as that undertaken for this volume may, by connecting our efforts and redirecting attention to such basic questions as the values of the enterprise, help to maintain the clarity, vitality—and idealism—of both domestic and global conflict resolution.

NOTES

1. Several other major areas of mediation developed out of the community field, directly or indirectly. In effect, as mediation caught on in the community field, funders and project innovators sought new applications. Often, the same individuals have spearheaded developments in a succession of areas. Mediation of *prison disputes*—including major conflicts and individual grievances—and the development of inmate grievance systems featuring mediation as a central element, was one such development (Cole, Hanson, and Silbert 1985). This field grew rapidly in the seventies, but has been less visible recently. *Landlord-tenant* mediation, for both private and public residential housing, is a second area that grew out of community mediation and continues to spread. A third is the mediation of *disputes involving juveniles*—specifically, mediation of disputes between students in elementary and secondary schools (American Bar Assoc. 1988), and mediation of intrafamily disputes between parents and children in family court cases (American Bar Assoc. 1982, chap. 3). Mediation continues to grow in both these areas.

2. The reason for this consumer-option framework lies: (*a*) in the legal rule that contracts (including agreements to arbitrate) may be unenforceable if the parties have vastly unequal bargaining power; and (*b*) in the constitutional right to trial by jury absent a clear and knowing waiver. In short, consumer agreements to arbitrate made as a condition of purchase are highly vulnerable to legal challenge. A final area of consumer arbitration—medical malpractice arbitration—illustrates this problem sharply (American Bar Assoc. 1983). In that area, hospitals, health-care providers, and medical associations introduced arbitration agreements into patient services contracts, but found it almost impossible to persuade courts to compel patients to arbitrate, no matter how clearly and evenly the agreements were drafted. As a result—and sometimes following legislatively imposed guidelines—such agreements now generally give patients a period after signing within which they can unilaterally rescind the agreement to arbitrate. However, despite this generally accepted legal framework, recent developments have seen the introduction of consumer contract arbitration clauses by banks and brokerages that would require consumers to use arbitration only. These developments have yet to be tested in court.

3. Comparisons here and in the following sections are based on the other chapters in this volume.

4. The term is taken from moral and political philosophy, but has begun to gain currency in law and dispute-resolution literature (Bush and Folger 1994; Bush 1989a, 1989c).

REFERENCES

Abel, Richard L., ed. 1982. *The Politics of Informal Justice.* Vol. 1, *The American Experience.* New York: Academic Press.
American Bar Assoc. 1982. *Alternative Means of Family Dispute Resolution.* Washington, D.C.: ABA.

————. 1983. *Consumer Dispute Resolution: Exploring the Alternatives.* Washington, D.C.: ABA.

————. 1987. *Alternative Dispute Resolution: An ADR Primer.* Washington, D.C.: ABA.

————. 1988. *Education and Mediation: Exploring the Alternatives.* Washington, D.C.: ABA.

Auerbach, Jerold S. 1983. *Justice Without Law?* New York: Oxford University Press.

Bingham, Gail. 1985. *Resolving Environmental Disputes: A Decade of Experience.* Washington, D.C.: Conservation Foundation.

Bush, Robert A. Baruch. 1984. "Dispute Resolution Alternatives and the Goals of Civil Justice: Jurisdictional Principles for Process Choice." *Wisconsin Law Review,* 893–1034.

————. 1989a. "Defining Quality in Dispute Resolution: Taxonomies and Anti-Taxonomies of Quality Arguments." *Denver Law Review* 66:335–80.

————. 1989b. "Efficiency and Protection, or Empowerment and Recognition?: The Mediator's Role and Ethical Standards in Mediation." *Florida Law Review* 41:253–86.

————. 1989c. "Mediation and Adjudication, Dispute Resolution and Ideology: An Imaginary Conversation." *Journal of Contemporary Legal Issues* 3:1–33.

Bush, Robert A. Baruch, and Joseph P. Folger. 1994. *The Promise of Mediation: Responding to Conflict Through Empowerment and Recognition.* San Francisco: Jossey-Bass.

Cole, George; Roger A. Hanson; and Jonathan E. Silbert. 1985. *Alternative Dispute Resolution Mechanisms for Prisoner Grievances.* Washington, D.C.: National Institute of Corrections.

Danzig, Richard. 1973. "Toward the Creation of a Complementary, Decentralized System of Criminal Justice." *Stanford Law Review* 26:1–54.

Esser, John P. 1989. "Evaluations of Dispute Processing: We Do Not Know What We Think and We Do Not Think What We Know." *Denver Law Review* 66:499–562.

Fiss, Owen M. 1984. "Against Settlement." *Yale Law Journal* 93:1073–90.

Folberg, Jay, and Ann Milne. 1988. *Divorce Mediation: Theory and Practice.* New York: Guilford Press.

Folger, Joseph P., and Robert A. Baruch Bush. 1994. "Ideology, Orientations to Conflict, and Mediation Discourse." In Joseph P. Folger and Tricia S. Jones, eds., *New Directions in Mediation: Communication Research and Perspectives,* 3–25. Thousand Oaks, Calif.: Sage Publications.

Fuller, Lon F. 1971. "Mediation—Its Forms and Functions." *Southern California Law Review* 44:305–39.

————. 1978. "The Forms and Limits of Adjudication." *Harvard Law Review* 92:353–409.

Galanter, Marc. 1983. "Reading the Landscape of Disputes: What We Know and Don't Know (and Think We Know) about Our Allegedly Contentious and Litigious Society." *UCLA Law Review* 31:4–71.

Goldberg, Stephen B.; Eric D. Green; and Frank E. A. Sander. 1985. *Dispute Resolution.* Boston: Little, Brown.

———. 1986. "ADR Problems and Prospects: Looking to the Future." *Judicature* 69:291–99.

Harrington, Christine B. 1985. *Shadow Justice: The Ideology and Institutionalization of Alternatives to Court.* Westport, Conn.: Greenwood Press.

Hensler, Deborah R. 1986. "What We Know and Don't Know about Court-Administered Arbitration." *Judicature* 69:270–78.

Kolb, Deborah M. 1989. "How Existing Procedures Shape Alternatives: The Case of Grievance Mediation." *Journal of Dispute Resolution,* 59–87.

McGillis, Daniel. 1982. "Minor Dispute Processing: A Review of Recent Developments. In Roman Tomasic and Malcolm M. Feeley, eds., *Neighborhood Justice: Assessment of an Emerging Idea,* 60–76. New York: Longman.

McThenia, Andrew W., and Thomas L. Shaffer. 1985. "For Reconciliation." *Yale Law Journal* 94:1660–68.

Menkel-Meadow, Carrie. 1984. "Toward Another View of Legal Negotiation: The Structure of Problem Solving." *UCLA Law Review* 31:754–842.

———. 1985. "For and Against Settlement: Uses and Abuses of the Mandatory Settlement Conference." *UCLA Law Review* 33:485–514.

Moore, Carl, and Chris Carlson. 1984. *Public Investment: Using the Negotiated Investment Strategy.* Dayton, Ohio: Kettering Foundation.

Nader, Laura. 1979. "Disputing without the Force of Law." *Yale Law Journal* 88:998–1021.

Public Conversations Project. 1992. "American Psychological Association Presentation." Cambridge, Mass.: Family Institute of Cambridge.

Riskin, Leonard L. 1984. "Toward New Standards for the Neutral Lawyer in Mediation." *Arizona Law Review* 26:329–62.

Riskin, Leonard L., and James E. Westbrook. 1987. *Dispute Resolution and Lawyers.* St. Paul, Minn.: West Publishing.

Sander, Frank E. A. 1976. "The Varieties of Dispute Processing." *Federal Rules Decisions* 70:111–33.

Shonholtz, Raymond. 1984. "Neighborhood Justice Systems: Work, Structure and Guiding Principles." *Mediation Quarterly* 5:3–16.

Silbey, Susan S., and Sally E. Merry. 1986. "Mediator Settlement Strategies." *Law & Policy* 8:7–32.

Singer, Linda R. 1990. *Settling Disputes: Conflict Resolution in Business, Families and the Legal System.* San Francisco: Westview Press.

Stulberg, Joseph B. 1975. "A Civil Alternative to Criminal Prosecution." *Albany Law Review* 39:359–76.

Susskind, Lawrence, and Jeffrey Cruikshank. 1987. *Breaking the Impasse: Consensual Approaches to Resolving Public Disputes.* New York: Basic Books.

Tomasic, Roman, and Malcom M. Feeley, eds. 1982. *Neighborhood Justice: Assessment of an Emerging Idea.* New York: Longman.

Ury, William L.; Jeanne Brett; and Stephen B. Goldberg. 1989. *Getting Disputes*

Resolved: Designing Systems to Cut the Costs of Conflict. San Francisco: Jossey-Bass.

Wahrhaftig, Paul. 1982. "An Overview of Community-Oriented Citizen Dispute Resolution Programs in the United States." In Richard L. Abel, ed., *The Politics of Informal Justice.* Vol. 1, *The American Experience,* 75–98. New York: Academic Press.

Wilkinson, John H., ed. 1990. *Donovan Leisure Newton & Irvine ADR Practice Book.* New York: John Wiley & Sons.

Winks, Patricia L. 1980. "Divorce Mediation: A Nonadversary Procedure for the No-Fault Divorce." *Journal of Family Law* 19:615–53.

CHAPTER 2

Pacific, Impartial Third-Party Intervention in International Conflict: A Review and an Analysis

Ronald J. Fisher

The history of humankind is to a regrettable degree the history of war, of conquest and defeat, of destructive social conflict. This most violent form of confronting differences among people continues relatively unabated in the modern era, but with increased effectiveness and impact, and thereby greater human costs. While most domestic societies have been moderately successful in developing mechanisms for the nonviolent management of conflict among individuals and other actors, the international system is marked by its recourse to unilateral and destructive means for confronting disputes among states, as well as among competing identity groups within states.

Much of this contrast in the use of violence relates to the successful evolution of the rule of law within societies backed by the authority and power of the state, while among societies the principles of national sovereignty and military security hold sway over conflict-management mechanisms at the system level. It is therefore reasonable to continue regarding the international political system as a relative anarchy in which states act largely in their own self-interest, without significant regard for the welfare of others, and in which there is no accepted higher authority for adjudicating or resolving differences.

On the positive side, the practice of bilateral and multilateral negotiation has become a common form of dispute settlement, especially in interstate interaction, but less so in intergroup conflict within states. All manner of issues are successfully handled through the processes and outcomes of international negotiation in the form of treaties and similar accords. Thus, many areas of international interaction are regulated by explicit agreements, tacit regimes, and institutional arrangements that prevent, manage, and at times resolve potentially destructive conflict between states.

The pacific intervention of impartial third parties has a long and honorable history in the management of human social conflict, in both the domestic and international arenas (Mitchell and Webb 1988; Rubin 1981). The role of third parties in international relations is now receiving an increasing amount

of scholarly attention, congruent with the apparent attractiveness and frequency of their interventions (Bercovitch 1984; Bercovitch and Rubin 1992;
Carnevale 1985; Touval and Zartman 1985; Young 1967). The most common
form of third-party intervention would appear to be that of mediation, although good offices, fact-finding, and arbitration are also in evidence.

In addition to traditional third-party roles, a number of scholar/practi-
tioners have recently developed an innovative method of interaction involving
problem-solving workshops directed toward intergroup and international
conflict resolution (Burton 1969, 1987; Doob 1970; Kelman and Cohen 1976,
1986). These initiatives can be subsumed under the generic rubric of third-
party consultation, and a model that captures the unique elements of this
approach has been developed (Fisher 1972, 1976).

It is in this area of problem-solving approaches that there may be the
greatest amount of transfer from developments in alternate dispute resolution
at the domestic level to conflict management in international relations. This
is partly because the practice of mediation and related third-party methods at
the international level has a long and relatively successful development, and
there is less need for the infusion of ideas from other arenas.

Finally, at the international level, consideration must also be given to the
relatively pacific third-party intervention of peacekeeping, which is uniquely
applied in this arena to limit hostilities typically following cease-fire agreements in the hope that other nonviolent methods of conflict.management will
subsequently prove successful. At the domestic level, police forces are used
to "keep the peace" through invoking the force of law. The only parallel
globally is the enforcement power of the United Nations charter, which has
only been invoked twice, once in Korea and more recently against Iraq.

These considerations lead to an initial typology of third-party intervention that includes six general categories, each of course having some internal
variation, given the wide diversity of intermediary activities (Fisher and
Keashly 1991; Keashly and Fisher 1990). The first is that of *conciliation,*
which involves a trusted intermediary who provides an informal communication link between or among the antagonists with the purposes of identifying
major issues, lowering tension, and encouraging movement to direct interaction, most often negotiation. Related forms of intervention included here are
good offices, wherein the intermediary acts as an unofficial go-between or
provides a forum for the parties to meet in, and fact-finding, wherein the third
party assesses the conflict and provides a statement or report back to the
parties. The essential distinctions are that the third party does not develop and
propose alternatives for settling the dispute and that the parties seldom meet
face-to-face, the exception being some forms of good offices.

Mediation involves the intervention of a skilled and experienced intermediary who attempts to facilitate a negotiated settlement of the substantive

issues that comprise the dispute. The mediator often combines individual meetings involving each party with joint sessions, and uses reasoning, persuasion, the control of information, and the suggestion of alternatives to assist the parties in finding a mutually acceptable settlement.

The traditional form of *pure mediation* in which the third party has no power over the outcome can be distinguished from *power mediation,* or "mediation with muscle" (Stein 1985), in which a powerful third party uses coercion or "leverage" (Touval 1982; Touval and Zartman 1985) in the form of promised rewards or threatened punishments to motivate the parties toward a settlement. Power mediation, which is really triadic bargaining in the sense that the third party pursues specific interests for its own sake, often leads to agreements that have future implications for the third party as a provider of continuing benefits and/or the guarantor of agreements. Pure mediation is typically assumed in the domestic arena, such as in industrial relations, whereas both approaches are common in international relations, with powerful states being drawn to power mediation by their very identity, while small states and international organizations primarily practice pure mediation. This difference may be one of several that limits the transfer of learning from the domestic to international arenas.

Arbitration involves a legitimate and authoritative third party who renders a binding judgment to the parties that is arrived at by considering the merits of the opposing positions and imposing a settlement deemed to be fair. In the domestic system, where arbitration is institutionalized and often nonvoluntary, rulings usually carry penalties for noncompliance. In the relative anarchy of the international system, submission to forms of arbitration and compliance with outcomes are largely voluntary and comparatively rare, except where specified by international treaty. In the extreme, agreements entailed in judgments flowing from arbitration procedures can be ignored or violated in the interests of national sovereignty.

Consultation, also referred to as problem solving, involves a trusted and knowledgeable third party who facilitates analysis of the conflict and the development of creative alternatives through communication and diagnosis based on social-scientific understanding. The underlying issues in the conflict are confronted directly so that the relationship between the parties can be shifted in the cooperative direction, thus facilitating the settlement of substantive issues. This form of intervention was first developed in the domestic arena by social scientist-practitioners working in organizational settings (Blake, Shepard, and Mouton 1964), but was soon followed by similar developments in international conflict resolution (Burton 1969).

The final form of third-party intervention, *peacekeeping,* involves the provision of military personnel by an outside party to supervise and monitor a cease-fire between antagonists. The intervening force may also engage in a range of humanitarian activities, and may provide day-to-day mediation services around particular incidents or situations. More recently, peacekeeping has provided a civilian component, particularly the organization and monitoring of election processes to democratically resolve conflicts, such as in Namibia. In contrast to the other forms of intervention, however, peacekeeping is not designed to move the parties toward a negotiated settlement, but to provide the breathing space in which that might occur.

The purpose of this chapter is to provide an overview of third-party intervention at the international level in the categories of mediation and third-party consultation. The potential complementarity of these two methods will then be explored in the context of a contingency model of third-party intervention. The conclusion will comment on the potential for the transfer of methodology from the domestic to the international spheres with particular reference to mediation and consultation. The challenge for the future is seen as developing the method of third-party consultation to the point where it can play a useful role alongside mediation in the resolution of international conflict.

International Mediation

The long history of intermediaries in intergroup and international conflict has continued to grow along with the advent of nation-states and the interstate system (Mitchell and Webb 1988). Moreover, recent times have witnessed the development of institutions whose function in part is that of third-party intervention. Particularly since World War II, there has been a shift in the identity of intermediaries from the major powers or coalitions of states to regional and international organizations, especially the United Nations (Levine 1972). This has been particularly the case in the post-cold war era. Arbitration has also been institutionalized, initially through the creation of the Permanent Court of Justice at The Hague and currently through the International Court of Justice within the United Nations system. Parenthetically, the approach of third-party consultation finds some institutionalized expression through the functioning of the Commonwealth of Nations, in which exploratory, problem-solving discussions often serve a useful prenegotiation function (Fisher 1989; Smith 1985).

International mediation, simply defined, is "a form of conflict intervention that attempts to facilitate voluntary agreements through negotiation" (Carnevale 1985) or "a form of third-party intervention in conflict for the purpose of abating or resolving the conflict through negotiation" (Touval and Zartman 1985). Mediation appears to occur most often in international conflict when the dispute is complex and protracted, when the parties are at a stalemate but do not want to risk or invest in further escalation, and are willing to consider cooperative behaviors (Bercovitch 1986).

The functions of mediation are to provide a communication channel between the parties and to assist in the development of proposals for settlement of the dispute. Added to these mediator roles of communicator and formulator, Touval and Zartman (1985) propose that of manipulator, in which the third party enters into triadic negotiation out of self-interest and uses coercion in the form of sticks and carrots to move the parties toward settlement. As noted in the typology above, this form of intervention, power mediation, is distinguished from traditional or pure mediation, which relies solely on the communication and formulation functions, and draws its influence from impartiality and persuasion rather than self-interest and coercion. It is an untested but plausible hypothesis that pure mediation is practiced more by small and middle powers and regional and international organizations, whereas power mediation is more frequently operationalized by the major powers, particularly the United States.

International mediation has received considerable attention through descriptive, anecdotal, and case-study accounts, but it is only in the last two decades that empirical research of varying rigor has been carried out. A number of the more noteworthy studies are reviewed and integrated by Bercovitch (1984, 1986). The apparent attractiveness of pacific third-party involvement in international conflict in the present century is demonstrated by frequencies of intervention approximating 60 percent in crises and wars variously defined. In the post-World War II period, mediation appears to be the most common form of intervention, accounting for approximately 20 percent of all third-party efforts, and the United Nations is the most active third party, intervening in over 40 percent of the cases (Butterworth 1978). Regional organizations, including the Organization of American States (OAS), the Organization of African Unity (OAU), and the Arab League are also frequent mediators.

In terms of timing, mediation efforts are usually initiated after a conflict has manifested itself in hostilities, thus supporting the above comment regarding the existence of a stalemate, but also indicating the frequent motivation of international organizations to expedite cease-fires rather than intervening prior to the outbreak of violence. In relation to the outcomes of mediation, success has been variously defined all the way from simple acceptance of mediation efforts (e.g., Frei 1976) to an instrumental contribution to the achievement of a settlement (e.g., Northedge and Donelan 1971). When settlement is the criterion, rates of success are understandably lower than when the requirement is simply the cessation of hostilities, for example, 26 versus 45 percent for the United Nations in one study of institutional third parties (Haas,

Butterworth, and Nye 1972). Bercovitch (1984) interprets Butterworth and Scranton's (1976) data as indicating that in only 21 of 310 cases (7 percent) did the intervention effort have a strong impact on settling the conflict.

The varying findings on the outcomes of mediation as well as theoretical and practical curiosity raise the important question as to the conditions that foster success versus failure. Frei (1976) and Bercovitch (1986) have specifically and systematically addressed this question. Frei's analysis covers a collection of 65 international mediation cases within the period 1960 to 1974, which, according to Frei, is characterized by the simultaneous presence of both East-West and North-South conflict. Bercovitch's larger universe of 210 mediation cases is drawn from 72 international disputes occurring in the 1945 to 1984 period (each dispute evidencing between 1 and 16 mediation efforts). Both investigators provide an empirical assessment of many of the impressionistic propositions regarding effective mediation that are found in the contemporary literature.

Frei's categories of variables affecting mediation outcomes include the identity and characteristics of the parties, the interrelations among the parties, the characteristics of the conflict, the identity and characteristics of the mediator, and the relationship between the mediator and the parties. Bercovitch's independent variables are more simply grouped into the identity and characteristics of the parties, the nature of the dispute, and the identity and characteristics of the mediator. Bercovitch's definition of success is more complex and demanding than Frei's simple acceptance of mediation and includes complete settlement, partial settlement, the arrangement of a cease-fire, and no success.

Integrating these two sets of results, but with more weight given to Bercovitch's more sophisticated analysis, yields the following list of conditions conducive to successful international mediation:

> the parties are small- to medium-sized states (rather than insurgent groups) who are relatively equal in power and dependent on outside assistance
> the dispute is over tangible interests as opposed to ideological differences and is at a relatively low level of intensity
> the mediation effort follows rather than precedes efforts to deal with the conflict by the parties, who are at the point of exhaustion and stalemate
> the mediator possesses relatively high prestige and access to resources and enacts all three roles of communicator, formulator, and manipulator

These studies thus provide some initial indications of the factors that are related to successful mediation in international conflict. Much more work remains to be done and needs to involve large and diverse data sets and more sophisticated statistical analyses. Quantitative analyses thus provide a complementary picture to the historical and descriptive accounts of intermediary activities that already exist. Eventually, a body of theory based on various forms of evidence will help provide guidelines for third-party practice and training in the field of international conflict resolution.

Third-Party Consultation

One outcome of the varying rates of success for mediation and other forms of conflict management in international disputes has been the search for alternative means of intervention. A variety of such means have recently been grouped under the label of "Track Two Diplomacy," a term coined by Joseph Montville and his colleagues to denote "unofficial, informal interaction between members of adversary groups or nations that aims to develop strategies, influence public opinion, and organize human and material resources in ways that might help resolve the conflict" (Montville 1987). Track Two Diplomacy includes informal initiatives in peacemaking, conferences involving citizens of countries engaged in conflict, and other forums that provide opportunities for unofficial dialogue that may ultimately affect the formal policy and decision-making processes, that is, Track One Diplomacy (McDonald and Bendahmane 1987). Montville and others identify the problem-solving workshop, captured here by third-party consultation, as a specific form of Track Two Diplomacy.

The problem-solving workshop at the international level has its origins in the innovative work of John Burton and his colleagues, both in international relations theory and conflict-resolution methodology (Burton 1965, 1969). Partly drawing on developments in conflict resolution in other fields, including social casework and organization development, Burton and his associates organized and facilitated two problem-solving initiatives in the mid-1960s. The first involved a series of sessions with informal but high-level representatives from Malaysia, Indonesia, and Singapore, which at that time were engaged in armed hostilities. With the assistance of a third-party panel of social scientists following Burton's approach of "controlled communication" the participants analyzed the conflict and looked for mechanisms for de-escalating and resolving it. Three weeks after the end of the sessions, hostilities ceased and an accord was ultimately reached. Informal feedback indicated that the problem-solving sessions had a significant and positive effect on the resolution of the conflict.

The second Burton initiative was focused on the Cyprus conflict at a point in time when United Nations mediation had broken down (Mitchell 1966). Informal representatives of the Greek and Turkish Cypriot communities met for a five-day problem-solving workshop in which a panel of social scientists introduced various concepts and models for analyzing the conflict and the relationship between the two groups. During the session, the parties also actively explored the possibilities of returning to mediation, which they subsequently did. Unfortunately, the possibility of further problem-solving workshops was precluded by the resumption of the U.N. mediation effort, which apparently saw the two approaches as mutually exclusive.

A second innovative development in problem solving was the application of group training methods to the conflict in the Horn of Africa by Leonard Doob and his associates (Doob 1970). Influential individuals from the countries of Somalia, Kenya, and Ethiopia met over a two-week period under the guidance of American organizers and human-relations trainers. In the initial phase, the participants met in two mixed-sensitivity training groups, each of which went on to develop mutually acceptable solutions to the conflict. However, the total workshop could not reach consensus and ended on a note of some frustration. Following the workshop, any possible transfer of positive effects to the actual conflict may have been precluded by a coup in Somalia.

The development of the problem-solving methodology at the international level has also been pioneered by Herbert Kelman, who was a member of the third-party panel at the 1966 Cyprus workshop organized by John Burton. Kelman initially compared and contrasted the Burton and Doob approaches (Kelman 1972) and went on to develop his own unique methodology in collaboration with Stephen Cohen (Kelman and Cohen 1976, 1986). Since 1971, Kelman and his associates have organized and facilitated a continuing series of workshops focusing on the Israeli-Palestinian conflict, which is at the heart of the Middle East question. Kelman's workshops have involved a variety of influentials from each side who are not official decision makers but have access in various ways to the political and policy-making processes. It is highly likely that these efforts over an almost 20-year period have had a beneficial effect on the political climate, fostering peaceful resolution. Kelman has come to conceptualize his work as part of a prenegotiation process designed to help create the conditions for initiating Israeli-Palestinian negotiations toward a mutually satisfactory settlement and stable peace (Fisher 1989; Kelman 1982) that eventually bore fruit.

My own approach has been to conceptualize these various problem-solving initiatives as a new form of intervention termed *third-party consultation* (after Walton 1969) in order to emphasize the unique role of the impartial and skilled intermediary who enters directly into the field of the conflict. Based on an identity as a social scientist/practitioner, the third-party consultant undertakes strategies and behaviors that facilitate the interaction of the antagonists in analyzing and dealing with the underlying attitudes and issues in their relationship and conflict. A review of related interventions at the interpersonal, intergroup, and international levels led to the development of an initial model of third-party consultation (Fisher 1972) that was revised and extended to deal with intergroup conflicts in community settings (Fisher 1976). An extensive review and evaluation of applications at the organizational, community, and international levels (Fisher 1983) was followed by a focus on the potential utility of consultation at the international level, both in general (Fisher 1986) and in specific relation to the prenegotiation process (Fisher 1989).

Up to the present time, there have been about a dozen published initiatives in the international sphere, focusing on a variety of conflicts and employing a range of different approaches and designs. Thus, the actual amount of practice experience is very limited in comparison to other forms of third-party intervention, most notably mediation. In the conceptual work, the intention has been to cast third-party consultation as a new form of conflict-resolution methodology that may have a unique and useful role to play in concert with more developed and accepted methods. At the same time, the range of applications, especially at the international level, is small, the underlying theory is rudimentary, and the supporting research suffers from significant limitations (Fisher 1983). Nonetheless, there is a clear need for the continuing development of the methodology, for the training of social scientist/practitioners who can serve as third-party consultants, for the enactment of action-research programs to assess effectiveness, and for the eventual institutionalization of the method alongside more traditional approaches.

Rather than simply describing the method and model of third-party consultation, it is perhaps more useful to compare and contrast it with the more widely understood intervention of mediation, with which it is at times confused. Fisher (1983) provides an initial contrast between consultation and mediation, while Fisher and Keashly (1988) use the model of third-party consultation to develop a detailed comparison on a number of components and dimensions.

Briefly, consultation places more emphasis on the subjective elements of conflict and focuses more on the basic relationship between the parties in terms of perceptions, attitudes, feelings, qualities such as trust and commitment, communication processes, and orientations toward each other, especially in terms of competitiveness versus cooperativeness. It is assumed that improvement in these areas will facilitate a more collaborative and integrative approach to dealing with the objective side of the conflict. Mediation is not unaware of subjective aspects, but places more emphasis on the objective elements of the conflict (incompatible goals and positions) and attempts to work around subjective factors, usually assuming that a settlement on substantive issues will improve the relationship.

With regard to identity, all types of third-party intervenors need to be impartial, knowledgeable, and skilled; however, the nature of their expertise differs considerably. Mediators require extensive knowledge of the substantive issues in the dispute and the ability to facilitate negotiation toward an acceptable compromise or integrative solution. The expertise of the third-party consultant lies in knowledge about the sources and processes of social conflict and methods of resolution, as well as the human relations skills of enabling participants to share perceptions and feelings, to diagnose or analyze their relationship and their conflict, and to move the problem-solving process to the development of possible alternatives through consensual decision making. This requires the development of greater trust and openness in the consulting relationship than is the case in mediation.

In terms of actual interaction, the mediator is more concerned with "content," that is, ideas and evaluations regarding specific issues and possible alternatives, whereas the consultant focuses on "process," how the parties treat and respond to each other, and how they can shift their orientations in a cooperative direction. At base, consultation attempts to facilitate creative problem solving on the basic relationship, whereas mediation attempts to facilitate a negotiated settlement on a set of substantive issues. Thus, while both types of third parties work to enact core functions of inducing positive motivation, improving communication, diagnosing the conflict, and regulating the interaction, they do so using different tactics and procedures. In general, the mediator attempts to use perceived costs and benefits and the building of momentum to move the parties toward settlement, whereas the consultant offers a low-risk opportunity to improve a difficult relationship through the unique process of face-to-face confrontation of underlying issues. The mediator controls the flow of information and sometimes withholds items in order to facilitate a settlement; the consultant encourages and models open and direct information exchange and discussion, along the lines of an academic seminar. The mediator works to understand the dispute in terms of interests and positions relevant to negotiation and in relation to similar disputes; the consultant facilitates self-diagnosis and understanding of the conflict by the parties. The mediator controls the interaction and the process of successive concession making toward the goal of settlement; the consultant paces the discussions through the phases of differentiation and integration and sees the interaction as a source of information on the nature of the conflict.

In terms of objectives, mediation is directed toward a settlement on substantive issues that balances gains and losses in a manner that is acceptable to all parties; consultation seeks resolution of the conflict through positive attitude change, an improved relationship, and innovative solutions that are jointly determined and self-perpetuating. The contrast between mediation and consultation is therefore highly cognizant of the distinction between settlement and resolution enunciated by Burton (in this volume; see also Burton 1990). In addition, consultation is uniquely designed for the study of conflict, that is, for the parties and the third party in the scientist/practitioner role to learn more about social conflict and its resolution.

Parenthetically, it must be noted that the ideal objectives of consultation are seldom realized, at least in the international sphere, since much work is of a pilot nature and there has been little extensive follow-up to ascertain if and how outcomes are transferred from workshops to the wider relationship between the parties (Fisher 1983; Hill 1982). Thus, there is a continuing need in the development of the method to logically counter arguments, as Mitchell (1981) does, that it is impractical and ineffective until considerably more experience and evaluation have accumulated.

A Contingency Model of Third-Party Intervention

The suppositions that social conflict is a mix of objective and subjective elements and that interventions are differentially suited to deal with these different aspects underlie the rationale of a contingency approach. More specifically, conflict is seen as a dynamic process in which objective and subjective factors interact in varying degrees as escalation and deescalation proceed over time. Thus, different interventions may be most applicable and effective at different stages of conflict, and the challenge is to match the type of intervention to the level of escalation and to coordinate and sequence interventions toward the settlement of specific issues and the ultimate resolution of the conflict. Based partly on the work of Glasl (1982) and Prein (1984) at the organizational level, a contingency model has been developed with a view toward intergroup and international conflict resolution (Fisher and Keashly 1991; Keashly and Fisher 1990).

A stage model of conflict escalation is a prerequisite to developing a contingency approach for third-party intervention. Based on the work of Glasl (1982) with input from Wright (1965) and Kriesberg (1989) at the international level, a four-stage model of conflict escalation has been developed. The four stages are identified conceptually as: (1) Discussion, (2) Polarization, (3) Segregation, and (4) Destruction. These stages are differentiated by changes in the nature of communication and interaction between the parties, their perceptions and images of each other and their relationship, the issues at the fore of the dispute, the perceived possible outcomes, and the preferred strategy for handling the conflict.

Thus, as conflict escalates, communication and interaction move from discussion and debate, to reduced contact and a reliance on the interpretation of actions, to the use of threats, and finally to an absence of direct communication combined with hostilities directed toward the adversary. Perceptions and images change from being more or less accurate, to rigid and simplified negative stereotypes, to images of good and evil, to an ultimate view of the other party as nonhuman. The relationship moves from one of trust, respect, and commitment, to one that still acknowledges the importance of the other party in its own right, to one of mistrust and disrespect, and ultimately to a situation of complete hopelessness and intransigence. The salient issues move from substantive ones and related positions, to concerns regarding the relationship itself, to fundamental needs or core values, to the question of ultimate survival. The perceived possible outcomes begin with joint gain options, move to mutual compromise, to destructive win-lose possibilities, and finally to lose-lose alternatives with the intention of minimizing one's own losses while inflicting maximum damage to the other party. Concurrently, the chosen methods of conflict management shift from joint decision making, to negotiation, to defensive competition, and finally to outright attempts at destruction.

The basic rationale of the contingency approach is to intervene with the most appropriate methods at the relevant stages in order to de-escalate the conflict down through the stages. This is accomplished by matching the initial intervention to the current stage of the conflict and by combining further interventions in an appropriate sequence to further deescalate the conflict. This strategy has considerable similarity to the "scientific approach" in Alternative Dispute Resolution in which different types of cases would be assigned to different dispute-resolution processes (Bush, in this volume). However, it is also acknowledged that the present contingency model is restricted to an almost universal and invariant sequencing of methods regardless of the substance of the conflict. This is partly because the model of conflict escalation is seen as invariant in terms of stages. It is possible that both models of conflict escalation and third-party intervention will need to develop greater conceptual complexity and practical flexibility as our understanding and experience develops.

A diagram of the contingency model is provided in figure 1. In stage one, the focus is on the quality of communication between the parties, since the relationship still involves adequate trust and commitment and perceptions are relatively accurate and positive. However, as the parties confront difficult substantive issues, communication difficulties move the interaction from a discussion to a debate involving adversarial behavior. The appropriate third-party intervention is that of conciliation in order to facilitate clear and open communication on interests and related positions. This would hopefully clear the path to direct negotiations between the parties so that the dispute could be settled before there was damage to the relationship.

In stage two, relationship issues come to the fore as trust and respect are threatened and distorted perceptions and simplified and negative images begin to emerge. The relevant intervention is deemed to be consultation in order to deal with relationship problems before they further escalate the conflict. Once

Intervention Sequence

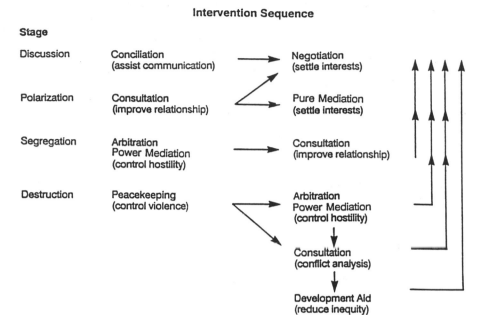

Fig. 1. A contingency model of third-party intervention. (Adapted with revisions from Ronald J. Fisher, *The Social Psychology of Intergroup and International Conflict Resolution* [New York: Springer-Verlag Publishers, 1990].)

a cooperative relationship is reestablished, the parties are in a better position to deal with substantive issues through negotiation. However, given that these issues were contentious enough to foster escalation in the first place, it is possible that mediation in its pure form is an appropriate follow-up. This possibility provides a point of complementarity between consultation and mediation. The initial consultation intervention in improving the relationship would place the mediator in the advantageous position of dealing with difficult enough substantive issues without the added burden of having to work around, and in some cases be hostage to, negative attitudes, hostile feelings, mistrust, and so on. Consultation would also provide a useful premediation function by providing a low-risk forum in which the parties could consider the merits of and the framework for mediation. This conceptualization is of course at odds with existing reality in international conflict management where consultation is not readily available and not seriously considered by parties to disputes, particularly at the relatively low level of stage two escalation. Mediation is typically the intervention of choice when negotiations have reached an impasse, but unfortunately is often unsuccessful, partly because relationship difficulties get in the way. In addition, interests may be interfused with basic needs and thus appear nonnegotiable, and positions may have become immovable through a series of past commitments. Given these circumstances, it is possible that the more frequent adoption of consultation in moderately escalated conflict might improve the success rate of mediation. There are examples of this form of effective sequencing of consultation and mediation in industrial relations (e.g., Birnbaum 1984; Brett, Goldberg, and Ury 1980), but not in international relations, at least in the literature.

In stage three, hostility and defensive competition are predominant and basic needs such as security and identity are threatened. The rationale for intervention is that immediate control is necessary to halt escalation and to demonstrate to the parties that some degree of agreement on substantive issues is still possible. Where available and appropriate, arbitration would be one intervention of choice, but its lack of legitimacy and acceptability in international relations has already been noted. The second alternative is power mediation, wherein the third party can use leverage to gain at least a partial settlement and halt the escalatory spiral. This creates another point of potential complementarity between mediation and consultation, in that the latter could be used to improve the relationship, thus de-escalating conflict down to stage two. Rather than assuming that settlement will improve the relationship between the parties, consultation would be used as a follow-up intervention to increase the probability of de-escalation.

In stage four, the conflict has escalated to the point of mutual attempted destruction, that is, war at the international level. The level of hostilities requires a direct intervention to separate the parties and control the violence. Thus, peacekeeping is prescribed in the wake of a cease-fire agreement to provide for monitoring the cease-fire and possibly restoring normal living conditions. Parenthetically, it is clear that some form of intervention, often including mediation, is required to attain the cease-fire, but the focus is different from mediation designed to deal with the substantive issues in the dispute, which is the concern of the contingency model.

Once the destructive interaction between the parties is constrained, the way is clear for other follow-up interventions. One possibility is arbitration or mediation with muscle to further control hostility and demonstrate that some agreement is possible. A second option is consultation, either following arbitration or power mediation, or directly after peacekeeping. The latter form of consultation would be more directed to providing a full analysis of the conflict, pointing the way toward further resolution efforts. Following an initial intervention, substantive issues that were identified could be channeled to pure mediation, while more complex difficulties could be the focus of continued consultation. In addition, the model suggests that the provision of development aid as a form of peacebuilding could be one outcome of consultation that could assist in dealing with structural inequalities that are often part of protracted intergroup and international conflict. The point is that a combination of efforts would be necessary to de-escalate a stage-four conflict back down to a manageable relationship.

The contingency model provides an initial conceptualization of how the matching, coordinating, and sequencing of different but complementary third-party interventions might proceed. The large gap between such a conceptualization and current practice in international conflict management is immediately acknowledged. However, the potential of such an approach can be illustrated through case-study analyses of third-party efforts in escalated conflicts, such as that provided on the Cyprus conflict by Keashly and Fisher (1990).

The contingency model provides one view of how third-party interventions in international conflict might be selectively applied and coordinated toward greater effectiveness. Given the continuing popularity of third-party efforts, it is important that both conceptual understanding and practical expertise be constantly improved. In particular, the overreliance on a limited array of methods should be critically examined and a healthy eclecticism should be encouraged. One appeal of a contingency approach is that it not only opens the door to a wider variety of possible interventions, but it also stresses the potential complementarity of third-party methods, as opposed to seeing them as competing or contradictory. The rationale and logic of the model appear sound, but what is required is a great deal more practical experience and empirical assessment before the utility of the contingency approach can be properly evaluated. In this regard, the future agenda for work in international conflict resolution is abundantly clear.

Conclusion

The growing interest in international conflict resolution and third-party intervention comes at a time of increasing need for the development and application of effective methods. There appears to be a small but hopefully increasing receptivity on the part of policymakers and diplomatic practitioners to the ideas and approaches of social scientists and other scholars. The establishment of both academic and government institutions to foster interchange between scholars and practitioners is a hopeful sign. Examples include the Institute for Conflict Analysis and Resolution at George Mason University, the Center for International Development and Conflict Management at the University of Maryland, and the United States Institute of Peace. Through the activities of such institutions new ideas and practices can be created and evaluated and eventually be taken forward for assessment and adoption in the real world.

One important task is to assess the degree to which developments at the domestic level can be transferred to the international level, the topic of this volume. Over the past decade or so, the domestic arena in North America and some European countries has seen a virtual revolution in conflict resolution, largely captured by the term "Alternative Dispute Resolution" (ADR) (see Bush, in this volume). While it may be possible to draw many parallels between work in the two different systems, that is, domestic and global, it is not clear which elements of ADR have direct applicability at the international level. This is partly because recent developments in the two systems began from relatively different starting places. In the domestic arena, the burgeoning variety of conflict-management methods have been developed largely as *alternatives* complementary to the existing justice system and are often mandated by legislation or regulated practice. In the relative anarchy of the global system, the rule of law has been less evident, and methods of negotiation and mediation among independent actors have moved to the fore in diplomatic practice. In both the domestic and global systems, there has been a comparative neglect of problem-solving approaches along the lines of third-party consultation, and it is here that the greatest potential for reciprocal transfer may lie. Work at the international level has drawn on domestic developments and has in turn advanced the general field of conflict resolution to the benefit of scholar/practitioners in both systems. Consultation or problem solving is complementary, that is, alternative, to most existing methods in both domestic and global systems since it involves a participative, consensual style of resolution, as opposed to a judgmental, adversarial approach to management or settlement. Substantive areas of conflict that may be more amenable to consultation at both the domestic and international levels are those that involve multiparty, multi-issue disputes and protracted social conflicts among identity groups, both of which often cross borders.

Another possibility for transfer is the "problem-solving theme" of ADR that might be brought to international conflict resolution. This theme is apparent, for example, in the many calls for an integrative approach to negotiation that is deemed to lead to more effective, that is, mutually satisfactory agreements (e.g., Fisher and Ury 1981; Pruitt 1986). It also appears to be infused in newer forms of mediation in the community, criminal justice, and marital arenas that focus on relationship issues as well as substantive interests. In this way, third-party intervention becomes a combination of pure mediation and consultation in which sequencing and coordination of activities may follow some form of internalized contingency approach. In contrast, it appears that mediation in industrial relations continues to follow predominantly a traditional approach, perhaps because such services are relatively institutionalized (e.g., Davis 1987), while consultation continues its primary growth as a separate entity within the field of organization development (e.g., Blake and Mouton 1984). Also in contrast, power mediation appears to be less evident in domestic systems, partly because various forms of arbitration are available when necessary to impose agreements on conflicting parties, and partly because domestic mediators seldom have access to significant benefits or punishments that they can use to leverage parties in the direction of settlement.

The final point on the question of transfer from domestic to international conflict resolution focuses on the complexity and political reality of the global system. Skeptics of third-party consultation typically emphasize these considerations in rejecting the potential of the method in the international arena. It is contended that with such a limited number of participants, small group interventions cannot possibly do justice to the myriad of determinants that influence national policies and interstate interaction. Furthermore, policymaking is impervious to calls for collaborative approaches, since it must deal with the harsh political realities of an anarchic system in which each actor is out for maximum self-gain. These same arguments can be applied to most developments in ADR that seem to have some potential for transfer to the international level. Counterarguments can be made that a good deal of foreign policy-making is already carried out in the confines of small groups, and that the world is now seeing the increasing emergence of common goals (environmental protection, sustainable development) that can only be attained through cooperation.

In short, there are no inherent reasons why collaborative approaches cannot be implemented at the international level. As Mitchell (1981, 141) points out with regard to consultation: *"Difficulties* of implementation are not the same as *impossibilities* and many arguments about 'impracticality' appear to arise more from innate caution and conservatism than from searching analysis of really fundamental differences between the setting of international disputes and other forms of human conflict."

For general theorists of conflict and strategists of conflict resolution, there are ample similarities among various levels to create optimism about transfer from the domestic to the international spheres. However, difficulties will arise if the greater complexity and the unique characteristics of the international system are not taken into account. What is required is a detailed analysis of the determinants of international conflict and its resolution that can then be incorporated in further developing methodologies of intervention. Also required is an acknowledgment that the global system continues to operate with a larger component of power politics limited by fewer institutional constraints than does the domestic arena, at least with regard to conflict management and resolution. However, for those interested in fostering collaborative and coordinated approaches, this simply means that greater conceptual sophistication and practical persistence will be required in order to increase the range of options available for effectively and humanely managing international conflict.

A first step in addressing the question of transfer is to initiate a finer-grained analysis of both domestic and international conflict by developing a set of common dimensions that apply to both (see Kriesberg, in this volume; Pruitt, in this volume). It will then be possible to see which types of domestic conflict are more similar to which types of international conflict and to ask whether similar methods of management and resolution might be appropriate in comparable circumstances. Concurrently, we must ask both philosophical and practical questions that transcend the existing state of knowledge and challenge humankind to move beyond the adversarial, power-based methods of the present. Burton (in this volume) and Vasquez (chap. 7, herein) provide useful and exciting food for thought in these directions.

NOTE

The author wishes to thank Baruch Bush, Sandy Jaffe, James Johnson, and John Vasquez for helpful comments on an earlier version of this chapter. Some portions of this chapter are initially developed in R. J. Fisher, *The Social Psychology of Intergroup and International Conflict Resolution,* Springer-Verlag Publishers, 1990. At the time of the initial drafting of this chapter, the author was a senior research fellow at the Canadian Institute of International Peace and Security, which was abolished in 1992 by an act of Parliament.

REFERENCES

Bercovitch, J. 1984. *Social Conflicts and Third Parties: Strategies of Conflict Resolution.* Boulder, CO: Westview.

————. 1986. "International mediation: A study of the incidence, strategies and conditions of successful outcomes." *Cooperation and Conflict* 21:155–68.

Bercovitch, J., and J. Z. Rubin, eds. 1992. *Mediation in International Relations.* New York: St. Martin's Press.

Birnbaum, R. 1984. "The effects of a neutral third party on academic bargaining relationships and campus climate." *Journal of Higher Education* 55(6): 719–34.

Blake, R. R., and J. S. Mouton. 1984. *Solving Costly Organizational Conflicts.* San Francisco, CA: Jossey-Bass.

Blake, R. R.; H. A. Shepard; and J. S. Mouton. 1964. *Managing Intergroup Conflict in Industry.* Houston, TX: Gulf.

Brett, J. M.; S. B. Goldberg; and W. Ury. 1980. "Mediation and organization development." In *Proceedings of the Thirty Third Annual Meeting of the Industrial Relations Association,* 195–202. Madison, WI: Industrial Relations Research Associates.

Burton, J. W. 1965. *International Relations: A General Theory.* London: Cambridge University Press.

————. 1969. *Conflict and Communication.* London: Macmillan.

————. 1987. *Resolving Deep-rooted Conflict: A Handbook.* Lanham, MD: University Press of America.

————. 1990. *Conflict: Resolution and Prevention.* New York: St. Martin's.

Butterworth, R. L. 1978. *Moderation from Management: International Organizations and Peace.* Pittsburgh, PA: University Center for International Studies.

Butterworth, R. L., and M. E. Scranton. 1976. *Managing Interstate Conflicts, 1945– 1974: Data with Synopses.* Pittsburgh, PA: University Center for International Studies.

Carnevale, P. J. 1985. "Mediation of international conflict." In S. Oskamp, ed., *International Conflict and Public Policy Issues: Applied Social Psychology Annual 6,* 87–105. Beverly Hills, CA: Sage.

Davis, H. 1987. "Managing labor-management relations: A more complete approach." In J. D. Sandole and I. Sandole-Staroste, eds., *Conflict Management and Problem Solving: Interpersonal to International Applications,* 169–77. London: Frances Pinter.

Doob, L. W., ed. 1970. *Resolving Conflict in Africa: The Fermeda Workshop.* New Haven, CT: Yale University Press.

Fisher, R., and W. Ury. 1981. *Getting to "Yes": Negotiating Agreement without Giving in.* Boston, MA: Houghton Mifflin.

Fisher, R. J. 1972. "Third party consultation: A method for the study and resolution of conflict." *Journal of Conflict Resolution* 16:67–94.

————. 1976. "Third party consultation: A skill for professional psychologists in community practice." *Professional Psychology* 7:344–51.

————. 1983. "Third party consultation as a method of intergroup conflict resolution: A review of studies." *Journal of Conflict Resolution* 27:301–44.

————. 1986. "Third party consultation: A problem-solving approach for de-escalating international conflict." In J. P. Maas and R. A. C. Stewart, eds., *Toward a World of Peace: People Create Alternatives,* 18–32. Suva, Fiji: University of the South Pacific.

————. 1989. "Prenegotiation problem-solving discussions: Enhancing the potential for successful negotiation." *International Journal* 44(Spring): 442–74.

Fisher, R. J., and L. Keashly. 1988. "Distinguishing third party interventions in intergroup conflict: Consultation is *not* mediation." *Negotiation Journal* 4:381–93.

————. 1991. "The potential complementarity of mediation and consultation within a contingency model of third party intervention." *Journal of Peace Research* 28(no. 1): 29–42.

Frei, D. 1976. "Conditions affecting the effectiveness of international mediation." *Papers of the Peace Science Society (International)* 26:67–84.

Glasl, F. 1982. "The process of conflict escalation and roles of third parties." In G. B. J. Bomers and R. B. Peterson, eds., *Conflict Management and Industrial Relations,* 119–40. Boston, MA: Kluwer-Nijhoff.

Haas, E. B.; R. L. Butterworth; and J. S. Nye. 1972. *Conflict Management by International Organizations.* Morristown, NJ: General Learning Press.

Hill, B. J. 1982. "An analysis of conflict resolution techniques: From problem-solving workshops to theory." *Journal of Conflict Resolution* 26:109–38.

Keashly, L., and R. J. Fisher. 1990. "Toward a contingency approach to third party intervention in regional conflict: A Cyprus illustration." *International Journal* 45(Spring): 424–53.

Kelman, H. C. 1972. "The problem-solving workshop in conflict resolution." In R. Merritt, ed., *Communication in International Politics,* 168–204. Urbana, IL: University of Illinois Press.

———. 1982. "Creating conditions for Israeli-Palestinian negotiations." *Journal of Conflict Resolution* 26:39–75.

Kelman, H. C., and S. P. Cohen. 1976. "The problem-solving workshop: A social-psychological contribution to the resolution of international conflicts." *Journal of Peace Research* 13(2): 79–90.

———. 1986. "Resolution of international conflict: An interactional approach." In S. Worchel and W. G. Austin, eds., *The Psychology of Intergroup Relations,* 2d ed., 323–42. Chicago, IL: Nelson-Hall.

Kriesberg, L. 1989. "Varieties of mediation activities." Paper presented at the annual meeting of the International Society of Political Psychology, Tel Aviv, Israel, June.

Levine, E. P. 1972. "Mediation in international politics: A universe and some observations." *Papers of the Peace Research Society (International)* 18:23–43.

McDonald, J. W., and D. B. Bendahmane, eds. 1987. *Conflict Resolution: Track Two Diplomacy.* Washington, DC: Foreign Service Institute.

Mitchell, C. R. 1966. *Cyprus Report.* London: Centre for the Analysis of Conflict.

———. 1981. *Peacemaking and the Consultant's Role.* New York: Nichols.

Mitchell, C. R., and K. Webb, eds. 1988. *New Approaches to International Mediation.* Westport, CT: Greenwood.

Montville, J. V. 1987. "The arrow and the olive branch: A case for track two diplomacy." In J. W. McDonald and D. B. Bendahmane, eds., *Conflict Resolution: Track Two Diplomacy,* 5–20. Washington, DC: Foreign Service Institute.

Northedge, F. S., and M. D. Donelan. 1971. *International Disputes: The Political Aspects.* London: Europa.

Prein, H. 1984. "A contingency approach for conflict intervention." *Group and Organization Studies* 9(1): 81–102.

Pruitt, D. G. 1986. "Achieving integrative agreements in negotiation." In R. K. White, ed., *Psychology and the Prevention of Nuclear War,* 463–78. New York: New York University Press.

Rubin, J. Z., ed. 1981. *Dynamics of Third Party Intervention: Kissinger in the Middle East.* New York: Praeger.

Smith, A. 1985. "Commonwealth cross sections: Prenegotiation to minimize conflict and to develop cooperation." In A. Lall, ed., *Multilateral Negotiation and Mediation: Instruments and Methods,* 53–73. New York: Pergamon and the International Peace Academy.

Stein, J. G. 1985. "Structures, strategies, and tactics of mediation: Kissinger and Carter in the Middle East." *Negotiation Journal* 1:331–47.

Touval, S. 1982. *The Peace Brokers: Mediators in the Arab-Israeli Conflict, 1948–1979.* Princeton, NJ: Princeton University Press.

Touval, S., and I. W. Zartman, eds. 1985. *International Mediation: Theory and Practice.* Boulder, CO: Westview.

Walton, R. E. 1969. *Interpersonal Peacemaking: Confrontations and Third Party Consultation.* Reading, MA: Addison-Wesley.

Wright, Q. 1965. "The escalation of international conflicts." *Journal of Conflict Resolution* 9:434–49.

Young, O. R. 1967. *The Intermediaries: Third Parties in International Crisis.* Princeton, NJ: Princeton University Press.

Part 2
Interconnections between Domestic and Global Conflict Resolution

CHAPTER 3

Mediation Practice on the Home Front: Implications for Global Conflict Resolution

Deborah M. Kolb and Eileen F. Babbitt

Mediation is one of the oldest and most ubiquitous forms of conflict resolution in American society and throughout the world. Traditionally a prominent adjunct to labor negotiation, mediation is now used in divorce, family, civil, consumer, commercial, and employee relations; environmental planning and siting; and the development of governmental procedures and regulations. More recently as we have seen the world move beyond the cold war, the possibilities for using mediation to solve international problems have multiplied. Now it is not just political disputes that practitioners mean when they talk of international mediation, but disputes involving environment and resources, business, and other problems analogous to those for which mediation is used in the United States.

As mediation has penetrated into these new areas of social life, curiosity about the practice of mediation, that is, what mediators actually do to bring about settlement, has also increased. Mediation has always been something of a mysterious art, with as many theories of practice as there are mediators. Within the field of practitioners and the scholars who follow their work, there is little consensus about the ways mediation is practiced and whether it is possible to describe adequately what mediators do to bring about settlement. The process is usually described as a specific form of dispute resolution that is distinguished by a general set of activities and stance of the mediator (see, for example, Maggiolo 1971; Folberg and Taylor 1984; Moore 1986; Simkin and Fidandis 1986; Susskind and Cruikshank 1987).

The purpose of this chapter is to review the current state of research on how mediators practice. Currently, there are three generic approaches to describing what mediators do. One, based on formal descriptions of mediation, seeks to distinguish this process from other modes of dispute resolution. Integral to these depictions is the neutral stance of the mediator relative to the parties and the lack of authority mediators have to compel settlements. The first section of this chapter will review research about this stance.

Mediation is also described according to the kinds of tactics and techniques practitioners use in the service of agreements. Based primarily on laboratory field studies, this extensive literature develops a model of practice that is problem oriented. This body of work will be reviewed in the second section of the chapter. A third approach to the description of mediation is based generally on a theory of practice that seeks to link action with interpretation. The aim is to describe how mediators define their roles, strategies, and approaches and how these are influenced by experience and the institutional or professional bases and other facets of context. Findings from this literature will be considered in the third section. Implications from research on the domestic front for practice in international domains will be drawn where possible, and explored more fully in the final section.

The Mediator's Stance

Students of the mediation process disagree among themselves about the best ways to describe what it is that mediators do. Formal descriptions of mediation typically emphasize the stance of the mediator relative to the parties and the process. Moore's (1986, 14) description is typical. "Mediation is the intervention into a dispute or negotiation by an acceptable, impartial, and neutral third party who has no authoritative decision-making power to assist disputing parties in voluntarily reaching their own mutually acceptable settlement of issues in dispute. The concepts of neutrality and authority in mediation have been the subject of some study."

Neutrality

Neutrality is defined in different ways in the context of mediation. Some use it to mean that the mediator has an equidistant relationship to the parties, that one party is not favored over the other (Kressel 1972; Kolb 1985; Dingwall 1987). Others define it more as a stance during the process such that the mediator allows each party to tell his/her story in such a way that they are credited (Douglas 1962; Cobb and Rifkin 1989). Finally, the standard of neutrality is applied to the agreement, and the degree to which the mediator is responsible for ensuring that certain types of agreements are realized (Forester 1989). Within the literature, each of these facets of neutrality has been the subject of empirical study.

Conventional wisdom claims that a mediator's acceptability and the trust the parties have in her is based on the perception that the mediator is neutral with regard to their interests (Kressel 1972). In domains such as labor relations and legal settings, relationship neutrality stems from the fact that the mediator is an outsider. Mediators are not always outsiders and frequently have previous relationships and an ongoing interest in the dispute and its outcome. In nonindustrial societies, for example, mediators are well known to the parties; indeed they are sought out, in part, because of these relationships (Merry 1982). They are often closer to one party, and may even have a kinship relationship with one and not the other. Further, as leaders in their communities they represent the norms and values and typically advocate settlements that accord with these cultural dictates. While they often know disputants and may have crosscutting ties with them, they are usually not directly involved in the particular dispute they mediate.

In emergent mediation settings, where mediators are not formally designated, neutrality is an alien concept. In Kolb's work on mediation in organizations, where she studied ombudsmen and managers as mediators in disputes between subordinates and colleagues she found that, as in international fields, the boundaries between the uninvolved third party and the primary parties blurs (Kolb 1989a). Within organizations, emergent mediators are insiders and seem to derive their influence from that fact. They seem to be trusted because their interests are known.

Likewise, ombudsmen in organizations find a neutral position difficult to maintain. The interests of ombudsmen and parties are not easily separated. Ombudsmen are employed by their organizations and are often caught between protecting the organization and helping a claimant. The balance between these sometimes conflicting requirements is not independent of the ombudsmen's own managerial and career interests. In deciding how to help, whom to involve in a process, and settlement, these concerns figure prominently. To be seen as neutral in a context that is often highly political is to jeopardize the ombudsman's ability to perform her job (Kolb 1987).

These "biased" relationships may also influence the ways the process is conducted and the kinds of agreements achieved. In labor mediation, for example, mediators employ a range of tactics that assist "pros," chief spokespersons with their committees (Kolb 1983; Hiltrop 1985). These tactics include arranging meetings, emphasizing the "pros'" expertise, supporting their position, and helping them maintain and build trust with their committees. It is a symbiotic relationship. Pros are valued allies to labor mediators in making agreements and in the service of that agreement, and the mediator also assists pros to realize their own institutional objectives.

Within the process, mediators wittingly and unwittingly collude with one party in such a way that one side's story or version of events becomes legitimated over others. In studies of divorce mediation, Dingwall (1987) finds that mediators routinely ignore and often demean parties who discuss what the mediator deems to be extraneous topics and who suggest settlement options that run counter to the direction the mediators are pursuing. Dingwall concludes that "the mediator has her own view of what will constitute an acceptable outcome and is able to make use of her control of the encounter frame to push for this" (18).

Ongoing work by Sara Cobb and Janet Rifkin suggest that certain speakers "fix" the story such that others' abilities to participate are constrained. In the ways that stories are told, blame and bad intentions are attributed to the other (Cobb and Rifkin 1989). When this occurs, participation of the other is reduced. This type of "silencing" can also occur in more subtle ways. Pearce, Barnett, and Rifkin (1987) investigated communication patterns in community mediation. They found that mediators frame their task in certain ways, and that this control of the process closes out other ways of addressing problems. In particular, mediators use concepts of instrumental rationality, economic concepts of bargaining utility, and standards of distributive justice in the conduct of their cases. The researchers show how parties who argue on the basis of morality rather than rationality, and emotion rather than reason, can become disempowered in mediation.

Mediators often intentionally violate the dictates of neutrality because they believe that they bear the responsibility for the kinds of outcomes achieved. Some believe that they can fashion better agreements (in the sense of mutual gains) than the parties left on their own (Susskind and Cruikshank 1987). Others argue that in the face of power imbalance, the mediator should intervene to insure that a settlement does not egregiously favor the stronger party (Forester 1989).

The implication for neutrality of these intentional violations is an ironic one. In the former situation, it is clear that interested mediators in their roles as shuttle diplomats and analysts use their expertise and positions to exert leverage over the outcomes of the process in order to balance power between weaker and stronger parties. However, the argument can also be made in the context of public policy disputes (and perhaps the international realm as well) that a neutral stance with regard to process and outcomes is not neutral at all. Rather, it reinforces the social and political status quo. It is ironic that in acting neutral in the face of unequal power and status mediators are decidedly not neutral in that they preserve the existing order rather than contribute to its change (Cobb and Rifkin 1991).

Authority

Conceptions of mediator stance reflect the evolution of the process in the United States. As mediation has evolved from primarily an adjunct to collective bargaining into public policy and other arenas, our definitions of what mediation is relative to other procedures has become blurred. The neutrality of the mediator is one dimension along which this blurring has occurred; the use of power and authority is another. A distinguishing characteristic of mediation, at least as compared to other dispute-resolution procedures, is the presumed lack of power that mediators have to compel agreement. Empirical research has challenged this definition of the process. Within mediation itself and in the ways disputants come to be mediated, power shifts away from the disputants to the mediator.

Mediators are typically seen to lack formal authority to settle disputes. This claim underlies many of the superior benefits of the process; parties control the process and will accept only those terms of settlement that are in their interests. While mediators lack formal authority, they are hardly without considerable resources to influence what occurs in mediation. Certain mediators, Henry Kissinger for example, come to the table with resources of their own (Rubin 1980; Babbitt 1993). However, in more mundane settings and in less visible ways, mediators claim authority for themselves and assert their influence over the parties and process (see Goffman 1959).

Mediators claim authority for themselves on the basis of program association and experience. In the ways they organize the setting, the knowledge they display about the issues and other settlements, as well as the pictures they paint about what happens when agreement is not reached, practitioners strongly influence parties' perceptions of their own choices (Kolb 1985; Pruitt et al. 1989; Silbey and Merry 1986).

Mediators have considerable control over the structure of the process, that is, whether to conduct sessions with the parties face-to-face or in private caucuses. Caucuses serve obvious instrumental purposes; they are a place to ventilate hostility, and are associated with enhanced problem-solving activity (Pruitt et al. 1989). However, this exclusive focus on how caucusing can help also ignores the importance of caucuses to the mediator as a means of control. Silbey and Merry (1987, 14–15) suggest that control over communication— over who talks to whom and for how long—constitutes a major form of mediator manipulation: " ... control over the flow of information creates extended control over the substance of communication as well since the mediators decide what information to pass between the parties." This observation is supported by the finding that when mediators want to leave their imprint on the settlement, they are more likely to spend more time in private caucuses (Kolb 1983; Silbey and Merry 1986). The separate caucus also permits the mediator to claim credit for settlement and to balance perceptions of neutrality (Kolb 1985).

Even if mediators can exert control over the process, one can argue that at least control over the outcomes is left to the parties. In this regard, mediation is defined as a noncoercive form of third-party intervention (Goldberg, Green, and Sander 1985). However, critics argue that it is impossible to separate the referral process, by which disputants come to mediation, from what occurs within the procedure itself. When disputants, who are intent on going to court, are instead channeled into mediation with a mediator assigned to them, and when the structure of the procedure is beyond their control, the parties feel coerced into (and in) mediation (Sarat 1988).

There is some concern that certain types of people and cases are the ones channeled into mediation. It is the poor, minorities, women, and small businessmen who must face a mediation hurdle before they can use the courts. Many of the cases that are channeled into mediation are ones that are labeled "interpersonal" disputes (Harrington 1985; Silbey and Merry 1987) and these are handled in similar ways in court and in mediation. What this work suggests is that the way we define the stance of mediators relative to the parties is more variable than formal definitions suggest.

The Tactics and Techniques of Effective Practice

There are many ways to categorize the vast battery of potential mediator tactics (Wall 1981). One of the most popular, proposed by Kressel (1972), distinguishes among reflexive, nondirective, and directive tactics. Reflexive tactics are used by mediators to orient themselves to the dispute, and to establish rapport with the parties. Thus, "trust-building" activities may help to create rapport and influence the success of mediation (Carnevale et al. 1989; Pruitt et al. 1989). Labor mediators build rapport by creating a sense of shared community with significant others not present; thus, name dropping and reference to other cases are commonly observed (Kolb 1985).

One of the mediator's most important nondirective functions is to enhance communication between the parties, and to structure the agenda so that issues can be dealt with efficiently. It is important for the mediator to act as a communications link (Hiltrop 1989). Open communication, however, does little to enhance parties' ability to reach agreement. Only if mediators help parties to communicate "reasonable and fair" offers, and if they assist each party to put itself in the adversary's shoes, are better outcomes obtained (Deutsch 1973; Druckman 1975; Hiltrop 1985). There seems to be a consensus that aiding the parties to clarify issues and develop an agenda will enhance the chances of agreement (Carnevale et al. 1989; Frohman and Cohen 1970; Pruitt et al. 1989). Along these lines, mediators would be well advised to arrange preliminary meetings to explore issues with the parties (Hiltrop 1989), and to suggest dealing with easier issues first (Pruitt et al. 1989). Assisting the parties to find a common "currency" for their issues, thereby making it easier to assess trade-offs, is another tactic that seems to help (Evans and Crumbaugh 1969; Stevens 1963).

In the context of divorce mediation, Donahue (1989) has defined the concept of "communicative competence." Those mediators who are most successful in securing agreements between the parties are the ones who use their communicative competence to control the interactions between disputants. When emotions run high, for example, parties will interrupt each other more, switch topics, talk past each other, and require the mediator to manage these interactions assertively—so that the conflict does not escalate.

Directive tactics are those the mediator uses to encourage the parties to settle. These include applying pressure for concessions and making suggestions and particular recommendations that would lead to agreements. There is a popular fiction that assertive and directive mediation is a contradiction in terms—that in being directive, mediators risk compromising their neutrality (Douglas 1962). Professional opinion and observation of mediators at work suggests that active and aggressive mediation is more the norm than the exception (see Susskind and Ozawa 1983; Wall and Rude 1985; Zartman and Touval 1985). Further, in situations where hostility is high, directiveness may be the only way to move the parties toward settlement (Carnevale and Pegnetter 1985). It is interesting to note, however, that while commenting and responding to proposals seems to help, actually developing and recommending proposals works only some of the time (Carnevale et al. 1989; Hiltrop 1989). Likewise, pressure tactics and threats seem to be highly risky propositions that can have an impact beyond the immediate dispute (Carnevale et al. 1989; Kolb 1983; Lovell 1952).

In an effort to connect some of these disparate tactics, Carnevale (1986) proposes a strategic model that specifies four strategies; the use of each is contingent on the mediator's assessment of potential common ground and the value of agreement to the parties. These strategies are: integration—helping the parties find joint gain options; pressing—trying to reduce the set of non-agreement alternatives; compensation—making agreement seem more attractive relative to alternatives; and inaction. Strategic choice depends on availability, feasibility, costs and benefits, and mediator incentives.

Others propose a stage model of tactical use. The timing of mediators' tactical response to characteristics of the dispute, their use of different techniques to address specific issues and to work toward specific outcomes (Hiltrop 1985; Shapiro, Drieghe, and Brett 1985), have all been found to vary. International relations analysts have had a particular interest in the role of "timing" and "ripeness" (Kriesberg 1987). It is thought that there is a right moment for intervention in disputes, a point when the conflict is "ripe" for settlement. To intervene before this optimal moment is to risk being ignored by the disputants, who are not yet sufficiently motivated to take their conflict seriously; to intervene too late is to risk being ignored, because the disputants are already so locked into extreme positions that they are no longer able or willing to budge.

Some analysts have suggested a type of stage model within the process itself—that is, that mediators use less directive, facilitative tactics early in the case, and shift to more directive ones later on (Douglas 1962; Kressel 1972). Others have suggested that the stage of negotiation is critical; for example, in labor-management negotiations the closer the parties get to a strike, the more directive the mediator's approaches become (Hiltrop 1985). Finally, some have argued that timing reflects mediators' particular institutional ideology about role and strategy; stages in tactical usage will differ based on these distinctive conceptions of what mediators are supposed to do, and when they are supposed to do it (Kolb 1983).

Carrying it one step further, Jones (1988) argues that mediation resulting in agreements progresses through distinct stages: communication about process issues and exchanges of information in the early segments (e.g., agenda setting and behavioral norms), discussions of alternatives and possible solutions in the middle phases, and talk about agreements in the final phases. Communication in no-agreement mediation does not shift from process and exchanges of information to talk about solutions and agreements.

Mediation is often described as contingent activity. Successful mediators are the ones who can diagnose problems and react accordingly. For example, when parties disagree over issues of principle, and/or when their relationship is especially hostile and conflict-ridden, it is more difficult for them to reach agreement (Carnevale and Pegnetter 1985; Hiltrop 1985; Kochan and Jick 1978). Further, in situations where conflict intensity is high, mediators make use of more varied and directive tactics. Similarly, certain kinds of issues pose more difficulties for mediators; pay disputes are easier to resolve than cases where more basic issues of prerogatives and rights are at stake (Hiltrop 1985; Kochan and Jick 1978; Kressel 1972).

These studies of mediator tactics and strategies have produced a wealth of insights that contribute to our understanding of the interactive dynamics of mediation. Indeed, many of the findings from these studies translate directly into prescriptions for practice. However, the conception of mediation as a discrete set of tactics used in response to certain objective requirements of the dispute setting has not yet been evaluated in the field (Kressel and Pruitt 1985). It has proven difficult to specify what impact any given technique has on outcomes. New directions explore the ways they are bundled together into coherent strategies, and the relationship between occurrences in the case and the tactics used in response (see Kressel and Pruitt 1989).

Framing and the Social Construction of Mediation Practice

A third approach to describing mediation shifts the focus from the mediator's techniques to the situated and meaningful interaction between practitioner and the dispute s/he is mediating. In this view disputes are social events that are embedded within a structure of social relationships and cultural norms for handling conflict (Nader and Todd 1978). Mediation is seen as a highly adaptive process that is practiced in different ways depending upon the mediator's professional background and institutional setting, the character of the disputes in which they are engaged, their interpretation about what is required and the tactics and techniques available to them. Mediators are distinguished by the kinds of frames they use to interpret disputes and the roles they play in the process. The culture and social structure in which mediation occurs and the dispute processing channel of which it is a part influence the forms that practice takes (Kolb and Associates 1994).

Framing is relevant to mediation practice as both a mode of interpretation used to order situations and as a means to control definitions of that situation available to others. Interpretive frames enable mediators, and the parties, to make a situation ordered and sensible. They focus attention on certain matters, give meaning to those issues, and so set direction for how they will be considered. Often practitioners are unaware of the frames they bring to situations and so do not see how they construct the reality within which they function (Schon 1983).

How conflicts between parties are framed also influences the way third parties intervene. A limited number of frames—for examples, rights, interests, and underlying needs or problems—are most relevant to mediation (Sheppard et al. 1989; Silbey and Sarat 1988). When matters in dispute are treated as issues of rights, they are taken to mean that one party or group of parties has a claim against another that is vindicated by a legal or other decisional remedy (Silbey and Sarat 1988). When disputes are framed as conflicts of interest, the situation is seen as one where parties desire or value the same scarce resource. Such situations can be resolved through compromise and trade-offs of demands (Aubert 1965). In more recent prescriptive formulations, interests are defined as the underlying motivation for claims that stand behind positions in negotiation (Fisher and Ury 1981; Ury, Brett, and Goldberg 1988). This formulation is akin to what Sheppard et al. (1989) label an underlying problem frame. Here the focus is not on what the parties demand as a matter of right, or on what they want to satisfy their interests, but on the underlying reason that the dispute has arisen in the first place. These reasons may be understood in terms of basic human wants and needs (Burton 1990, in this volume) or as rooted in social and economic structures. If disputes are framed tracing problems back to their underlying cause, some suggest that it is possible to develop mutually satisfactory options for settlement (Fisher and Ury 1981; Susskind and Cruikshank 1987). However, observers of mediation often find that mediators explicitly narrow the frame from underlying problems to one of interests or rights in order to make the dispute more tractable (Kolb 1983; Silbey and Merry 1986).

Frames are important not only in understanding how problems are interpreted, but also in understanding the ways that they are mobilized to control available definitions of the situation (Goffman 1974). The ways in which problems or issues in dispute are defined, the forms of argument and modes of discourse used during discussion of the issues, and the delineation of alternatives and range of possible settlements are all options mediators can use to create and sustain a particular interpretation of events and possibilities (see Pearce, Barnett, and Rifkin 1987; Kolb 1983; Silbey and Merry 1987). In grievance mediation, for example, union and management representatives come to define a grievance according to a violation of contractual right. This definition prevails during the prior steps of a grievance procedure and will become the basis upon which it will be argued in arbitration if mediation fails. The mediator's agenda is to help the parties focus on underlying interests in order to create a solution that better meets everybody's needs. The problem is that in mediation, parties discuss the grievance in rights-based language and have difficulty shifting the frame to one of interests. In order to assist them in making the shift, the mediator frequently challenges the basis of their case, predicting its success or failure in arbitration. Only then is it possible to redirect the discussion to interests and immediate solutions (Kolb 1989b).

The concept of dispute frames has been important to the study of mediation in diverse contexts (and from other disciplines). Labor mediators shift discussion from local work issues to monetary issues and other broad concerns with widespread institutional impact (Kolb 1983). Community mediators narrow deep-seated family problems into contracts specifying rights and responsibilities (Merry and Rochleau 1985). In grievance mediation, disputes are expanded from a rights focus to one of interests and underlying problems (Kolb 1989b; Ury, Brett, and Goldberg 1988). In policy dialogues, the stakeholder groups in a given policy context are brought together to construct a joint problem and reach consensus about how to solve it, rather than to confront each other in litigation or enforcement procedures (Susskind and Cruikshank 1987).

Managers use a set of simple diagnostic frames to decide what form of intervention they will employ (Sheppard, Blumenfeld-Jones, and Roth 1989). The kinds of outcomes they want to achieve, and the resources available to achieve them, also affect the strategy of grievance mediators and ombudsmen (Kolb 1987; Shapiro, Drieghe, and Brett 1985). In her study of ombudsmen, Kolb (1987) described how the limited authority of ombudsmen, coupled with their position in rich social networks, influenced how these third parties dealt with complaints. Given the complexity of the complaints, and the possibility that they could be dealt with in many different ways, ombudsmen tended to define the problem in terms of what they could do about it (see Emerson and Messinger 1977). For example, when ombudsmen were well connected in the organization's social network, they used that network to help a number of complainants find new opportunities. The way interventions were framed seemed to depend on the ombudsmen's power to resolve problems. Generally, professional interests of the mediator, the intractability of certain problems, mediator ability and authority, and special relationships with certain parties all slant the interpretation of issues and their phrasing in particular ways (Black and Baumgartner 1983; Galanter 1974; Kolb 1987; Zartman and Touval 1985).

Study of mediator roles begins from a "social constructionist" perspective (see Berger and Luckman 1966). This perspective highlights the creative and interpretive work that goes into mediating a dispute, the way issues, parties, and process are named and given legitimacy, and the interactive struggle for control over process and meaning that marks the interaction (Kolb 1983; Silbey and Merry 1986). What emerges from these empirical field studies of mediator practice is a typology of mediator roles and strategies, and the connection of these to institutional structure and procedural form.

In her study of labor mediators, Kolb (1983) identifies two different approaches to mediation: orchestration and deal making. She describes how these two approaches are manifested in the organization of meetings, and in the use, purpose, and timing of particular strategies and tactics. Kolb shows that these roles develop as complements to those played by others in the process, reflecting institutional ideology about the appropriate function of mediation in collective bargaining. Orchestrating mediators, who work primarily in the private sector, concentrate on the process dimensions of agreement making and look to chief negotiators for both labor and management to identity the substantive elements in the agreement. In contrast, deal makers take it upon themselves to fashion the specific elements of the deal. By taking the form it does, orchestrating and deal-making mediation serve in their own ways to maintain the existing institutional order in labor relations.

Silbey and Merry (1986) describe two polar strategies of mediation—bargaining and therapy—that they observed in court-based and community mediation programs. A bargaining approach to mediation is one in which compromise and concession making over specific issues dominate, while a therapeutic focus emphasizes the needs and feelings of those in conflict. While bargaining and therapy are not identified with specific groups of mediators, they do represent distinctive claims to authority, techniques for controlling process and substance, and means to activate commitments in order to obtain settlements. Silbey and Merry show how these strategies transform the everyday problems parties bring to mediation into a new language of relationships that transcends the specific problem and forms the basis for settlement.

The ways practitioners mediate are influenced, not only by the facts of a given dispute, but also by contextual factors, among them the culture and social structure in which mediation is embedded. These contextual issues gain in importance across the international divide. Culture permeates the mediation process. Cultural categories that may have an impact on mediation obviously include explicit and tacit values, beliefs, conceptions of self, and rules for interaction.

Merry (1987) explores the metaphors that dominate mediation in court-based U.S. programs and in *ho'oponopono,* an analogous form of third-party intervention in Hawaii. The metaphor in the U.S. programs is the "contract." As she describes it, "parties come to the mediation table because they have particular interests. The purpose of the process is to uncover each person's bottom line, what it is they really want and will settle for, and reach an agreement that both can live with" (Merry 1987, 3–4). In contrast, *ho'oponopono* suggests a metaphor of untangling or unsnarling relationships. In the process, the techniques are supposed to open discussion so that participation can "loosen" (*kala*) and "cut (*'oki*) the entanglements (*hihia*) of negative affect between the parties. The way is thus open for apology and forgiveness, acts that restore good will, and positive affective exchanges between individuals (Ito 1985). This process is a reciprocal apology-forgiveness exchange.

It is possible to consider culture not only at the societal level, but also in communities, organizations, and occupations. The study of cultural differences suggests that disputants often enter mediation with rather different cultural "frameworks" that, in turn, shape their experience. Across the table from each other, these different frameworks may lead to misunderstanding, confusion, escalation, and exclusion (Friedman 1987; Pearce, Barnett, and Rifkin 1987), as when people from one culture view mediation as a highly intrusive form of seizing control, while others regard the identical form of intervention as nothing more than "gentle advising."

One can argue that with broad definitions of culture in mind, most mediators work cross-culturally even if they remain in one society. Increasing diversity in communities and organizations, and the desire to bring previously disenfranchised groups to the table, means that parties are likely to operate on the basis of different cultural understandings. Mediators who can translate across these cultural boundaries may be most effective. Culture has proven a difficult topic to study in negotiation. It is clear that individuals do not uniformly manifest cultural identities; socialization, education, and other experiences shape understandings as well (Janosik 1987).

Relationships influence mediation practice. The fact that negotiations with people who have longer-term relationships with each other changes the number of the interaction is an accepted fact in studies of negotiation and mediation (Greenhalgh 1987; Nader and Todd 1978). Given the structure of labor mediation—where professional spokespersons service many local unions and management groups and thus have continued exposure to mediation and mediators—there is evidence that helping these "pros" is a prominent feature of mediator strategy (Hiltrop 1985; Kolb 1983). Sometimes these tactics help because they further agreement; at other times they can be seen as furthering the institutional position of the spokesperson, even at the expense of the local parties (Galanter 1974).

Within corporations, Sheppard and his colleagues have inquired of managers (and others) how they handle common disputes they encounter. From these data emerge a number of interesting observations about the structural conditions under which mediation is likely to occur and some of the forms it will take. First, it is clear that managers are not natural mediators. They are more likely to adopt adjudicative or inquisitorial approaches (Lewicki and Sheppard 1985; Sheppard 1983). However, there are occasions when managers *will* mediate, particularly when it is important to maintain a working relationship between the parties. To the degree that managers are held accountable for particular decisions, are concerned about precedent, and personalize the bases of disagreement, however, they are less likely to mediate (Kolb and Sheppard 1985; Lewicki and Sheppard 1985). Further, whether a manager decides to mediate depends on how he or she diagnoses the situation, and the resources available for settling it (Kolb and Sheppard 1985).

These findings suggest that there are likely to be significant differences when bosses mediate with subordinates, or peers do so with each other. Indeed, in a study of cross-functional mediation, Kolb (1989a) found that among colleagues, managers seem to become involved as mediators. What is so interesting about this intervention by managers, however, is not what they do to actually resolve differences, but rather the roles they play in premediation stages. From the positions they hold, managers are able to learn about conflict, legitimize its public expression, involve relevant people, and help shape the dispute in such a way that it can be resolved. Murnighan (1986) has proposed that when mediators are "insiders," they are "intravenors." Intravenors differ from mediators because of their vested interest and the power on which they can draw.

Gender may also be important. In peacemaking efforts behind organizational scenes, there is evidence that women are often sought out for these quiet roles. In a study of conflict management in organizations, Kolb (1992) found that certain people, often women, are sought out in organizations for the maternal and nurturing skills they are seen to possess. Their peacemaking activities are conducted behind the scenes in such a way that they channel conflict into arenas where it can be dealt with in a more public manner.

Study of mediation in different contexts suggests some of the variety in the ways it is practiced. Indeed, some argue that mediation has more in common with the alternatives it replaces than it does with practice across settings. Empirical analysis of the assumed differences between mediation and the procedures for which it is an alternative indicates that considerable overlap exists between what occurs in mediation and the dispute-resolution procedures that follow and/or precede it (Amy 1987; Buckle and Thomas-Buckle 1986; McEwen and Maiman 1984; Vidmar 1985).

In their study of cases in district court and local mediation programs, Silbey and Merry (1987) find that social problems are treated similarly, that negotiation is the method of settlement, and that the kinds of agreements reached in both settings typically involve postponing the resolution of conflict and monitoring the situation instead. In grievance mediation, the structure of the process and the interpretive frames mediators and parties use to understand the process are shaped by the preceding grievance steps and the possibility that arbitration will follow (Kolb 1989b). This line of research suggests that mediation may not be a distinctive dispute-resolution procedure, but one that takes on many of the characteristics of the procedures for which it is an alternative.

Implications for Global Mediation

The domestic practice of mediation has been a subject of significant scholarship. As we think about applying what we know about domestic mediation practice to the international arena, there are a number of issues that we should consider. International mediation, like its U.S. domestic counterpart, takes place in a variety of contexts. The most visible mediators are those who operate in response to a security crisis, like Carter at Camp David, Cyrus Vance and Lord Owen in the former Yugoslavia, or the Algerian mediation between the United States and Iran over the release of hostages. There are others who, although they are not formally designated as mediators, nevertheless play similar roles. These include members of international secretariats and conference chairpersons who facilitate policy decision making in large international forums such as the Law of the Sea.

Like their domestic counterparts, mediators in the international arena can function in formally designated roles or behind the scenes, in less formal capacities. For example, when the Secretary-General of the United Nations (U.N.) intervenes in a dispute, he follows well-defined procedures and works in full view of the world community. However, when the Quakers act as a third party, they stipulate at the outset that participation will cease if the role becomes public.

The primary difference between domestic and international mediation regards the alternatives available to the disputing parties. Since mediation is an alternative to other forms of dispute resolution, it is important to bear in mind the nature of the alternatives. In the United States, mediation occurs in the shadow of the law or bureaucratic alternatives. Regardless of the context, disputants in U.S. domestic conflict have either legal or administrative rules that will provide them with an enforceable outcome, should they choose to use these alternatives. In international conflicts, legal and administrative structures also exist, but they do not have the capacity to enforce a decision without the consent of the parties. The World Court, for example, found the United States guilty of mining the harbors of Nicaragua, but the United States then chose not to accept the Court's jurisdiction on the issue and not to abide by its findings. Further, the potential for violence in the international arena is often present (Kriesberg, in this volume). Thus, mediation in international contexts is likely to have more in common with other forms of diplomacy than it has with mediation in the context of individual or interpersonal disputes. However, in the sense that international mediation involves complex parties of potentially different authority and resources, empirical findings from certain domestic domains may be relevant. We can speculate about these similarities and differences according to the major themes of the chapter.

The research on the stance of the mediator suggests that whether a mediator is neutral varies across settings and has an impact on both the process and its outcomes. So too, potentially, in the international domain. However, there is a real question as to whether neutrality is a useful concept in the international context. In international conflicts where the primary actors are nation-states, neutrality cannot be defined as "equidistant from" the parties. Sometimes the constellation of alliances in the international system and the interdependence among nations make it hard to imagine a mediator country or international organization that would be seen as truly unbiased toward all protagonists in a dispute. (This may also be the case in disputes involving subgroups within a country, although mediation of such disputes is quite recent and has not yet been adequately studied.)

Indeed, work by Touval and Zartman (1989) suggests that the biased mediator is more the norm than the exception in international political conflict. The bias is introduced by virtue of the mediator's preexisting relationship with one party, or by the mediator's own interest in the outcome of the dispute. Their analysis concludes that the parties to the dispute often consider the mediator's bias to be an asset. The disputant who has fewer ties to the mediator may believe that the mediator can use its relationship with the other side to gain concessions. The disputant who is closer to the mediator may believe that its interests will be well represented by a mediator who is its ally. Whether or not these beliefs are actually true, they are powerful inducements that a mediator can use to bring disputing parties to the table.

Bias can also work against involvement. Most international mediators, in contrast to those who work domestically, represent countries or organizations and therefore have their own constituencies. Different international mediators thus speak with different voices and represent different interests. For example, the U.S. secretary-general was not trusted as a mediator in certain disputes such as those involving South Africa or Israel, because the U.N. was seen as being captive of developing country interests and unworkably biased in their favor. More recently, the ending of the cold war and the collapse of the Soviet Union has increased the willingness of the United States and others to use the U.N. as a vehicle for international diplomacy; this has changed the standing of the U.N. in the world and made it more viable as a mediator.

There is another dimension of neutrality that research from the domestic domain illuminates. This concerns the impact of ongoing relationships that develop through negotiations. To the degree that special relationships are formed between a mediator and a spokesperson for a party, they have an impact on the kinds of outcomes achieved. In the domestic context, these relationships develop from continued exposure and interaction. These relationships in the international context may also be affected by cultural affinity between mediators and parties. Thus, mediators from the West may subtly align themselves with those more like themselves. These relationships can have an impact on the process and potential outcomes such that certain positions and possibilities receive more of a hearing than others.

More relevant to international mediation than neutrality is the concept of "standing." Standing is an important element in whether international mediators will be accepted or not. Standing is more than just reputation. It also connotes the relative influence and respect that a country, organization, or person commands in the international community (Babbitt 1993). The greater the standing of a potential mediator, the less likely the disputing parties will be to spurn an offer of assistance.

For example, Jimmy Carter, as a former U.S. president, has standing both politically and personally because of his reputation for honesty and moral integrity. He is seen as someone acting not out of narrow self-interest, but reflecting the humanitarian norms of the larger international community (Babbitt 1994). This puts him in a unique position to offer his services as a mediator in disputes between groups within countries, for example, where the parties may otherwise be reluctant to allow intervention. In these cases, Carter can credibly become the spokesperson for international concern about human rights, famine, war casualties, and regional stability.

If standing, more than neutrality, is what gets a mediator accepted in an international dispute, leverage is what makes it possible for some mediators to settle the dispute. Leverage comes from the ability to change the consequences of actions taken by the disputing parties, for better or for worse (Touval and Zartman 1989; Babbitt 1993). In international disputes, more than in domestic disputes, the mediating party is often a highly visible person or a representative of a highly visible country or organization, with resources that can be brought to bear on the disputing parties. Their involvement in the dispute makes the stakes of settling or not settling much greater for the disputants, because it focuses world attention on the dispute and may change the parties' calculation of the costs versus benefits of settlement. The mediator can use that pressure, especially if there is a power imbalance between the disputing parties and the more powerful party is holding out on a settlement.

The microstrategies and tactics of mediators that are associated with effective mediation are likely to translate across the international divide. Successful mediators are ones who understand why parties need mediation; they know what factors have prevented them from reaching an accord without a third party. Further, once into the process, they are attentive to possible weaknesses and strengths the parties have in solving problems. From this perspective, international disputes are quite similar to disputes in any arena. Mediators must be conscious of building trust, enhancing communication, assessing potential common ground and alternatives to settlement, assisting parties to find joint-gains options, applying pressure when and where it is needed, and adjusting the kind of intervention to coordinate with different stages of the conflict and different styles of the negotiators (Susskind and Babbitt 1992).

There are three issues concerning strategy and tactics that warrant special mention. The first is that most international mediators are themselves representatives of governments or organizations that have constituencies. This may provide benefits to the mediator, in the form of standing or leverage described in the preceding section. It also may constrain the mediator, in that certain strategies may not be endorsed by his/her own constituency and therefore may not be possible to employ. In some cases, this may hamper the mediator's effectiveness.

The second issue is that, even though the mediator and the negotiators in any international dispute are representatives of larger groups, there is a profound interpersonal dimension to these negotiations not unlike the interpersonal dynamics in any negotiation. International mediators must be attuned to the personality clashes, jealousies, competition, needs for recognition and understanding, and countless other "people" issues that a good mediator in any domestic mediation must manage.

Finally, there are many ways in which international mediation is different in degree but not in kind from any domestic public-policy dispute. Most are multiparty (even bilateral disputes involve multiple factions on each side that have to be included in the negotiation); multi-issue; are highly visible, with the media looking on at every turn; multicultural; extend over long periods of time; and occur alongside other forums in which the disputing parties have contact with each other. This is particularly true as international mediation moves into the environmental and economic policy arenas. Much can therefore be learned by drawing from the experience of consensus building used in domestic policy dialogues and similar decision-making processes.

The differences in degree, however, mean that international mediators need to make use of a more diverse set of strategies and tactics. For example, an international negotiation may involve an exceedingly complex array of issues and information. In some cases, such information may be hard to obtain as it touches on the internal security of a country. The international mediator must have good information sources and be able to have access to such information in a timely manner. Further, international disputes may go on for years rather than months and so the mediator must keep reassessing his/her information about parties' interests and alternatives to be sure this information is current.

Likewise, the cross-cultural issues may be more pronounced in an international conflict. The opportunities for misperception and misunderstanding are great, especially in disputes where the parties have historically had little or no contact with each other.

The consequences of no agreement in a domestic dispute may be a lawsuit; in an international dispute it may be war. Often, the disputing parties are fighting at the same time as they are negotiating. These more dangerous extremes in international conflict may not require different mediation strategies, but may put the international mediator under more public pressure to produce a settlement.

There are those international mediators who focus on the issues in dispute, and those mediators who work instead with the underlying needs of the parties. These two "frames" are sometimes differentiated by their perceived objectives: the first aims for "settlement" of a dispute, the second for "resolution" (Burton, in this volume). The implication is that settlement is a temporary respite in an otherwise ongoing conflict, whereas resolution deals with the basic causes and changes the fundamental way in which the parties relate to each other.

The mediators who operate within the "settlement" frame are looking for formulas that are workable, creative approaches to meeting a variety of interests that the disputing parties can accept without losing face at home. For example, Chester Crocker's mediation of the dispute between South Africa and Namibia is now famous for its "linking" of South African withdrawal from Namibia to Cuban withdrawal from Angola (Crocker 1992).

Mediators interested in "resolution" frame the negotiations differently. They want to identify the underlying needs that drive a conflict, and their purpose in the mediation process is to help the disputing parties to understand and acknowledge each other's needs and thereby transform the relationship between the parties. For example, dialogue groups between Israelis and Palestinians focus on their mutual needs for recognition, identity, and security (Kelman 1993). Similarly, many church groups seek to bring disputing parties together by virtue of their shared spiritual beliefs.

Social-construction theory also provides interesting insight into international conflict. Until very recently, many decision makers in the international community saw the world only in terms of the superpower conflict; everything was framed in the context of East versus West and whether the disputants in a conflict were part of the United States or Soviet sphere of influence. Another aspect of this frame of reference was the notion of "realpolitik," that the dynamic driving the behaviors of all states is the competition for military power and dominance.

The fall of the Soviet Union, the resulting changes in central and Eastern Europe, and the attendant changes in the international system have radically altered this frame of reference. The rise of Japan and Germany as economic competitors to the United States has also introduced the importance of economic as well as military capability into the calculation of strength and leverage in the international community.

International mediation will now be conducted in the context of this new, post–cold war mentality. Regional and ethnic conflicts will take center stage, as will conflicts in developing countries over scarce resources and environmental degradation. This may call for different strategies, and maybe even different kinds of mediators, than were used previously.

Now, as the world shifts dramatically, with the old systems being called into question on a daily basis, the quest for innovation in all spheres takes on greater importance. Hopefully the use of international mediation as an alternative to violence or stalemate will increase, and the practice of international mediators will continue to be enhanced by the insights of domestic mediation theory.

REFERENCES

Amy, D. 1987. *The Politics of Environmental Mediation.* New York: Columbia University Press.

Aubert, V. 1965. "Competition and dissensus: Two types of conflict and conflict resolution." *Journal of Conflict Resolution* 7:26–35.

Babbitt, E. F. 1993. "Beyond neutrality: the use of leverage by powerful states as mediators in international conflict." Ph.D. Diss., Massachusetts Institute of Technology, Cambridge, MA.

———. 1994. "The power of moral suasion: A profile of Jimmy Carter." In D. M. Kolb & Associates, eds., *When Talk Works: The Profiles of Master Mediators,* 375–94. San Francisco: Jossey-Bass.

Berger, P. L., and T. Luckman. 1966. *The Social Construction of Reality.* New York: Doubleday.

Black, D., and M. P. Baumgartner. 1983. "Toward a theory of the third party." In Boyum and Mather, eds., *Empirical Theories of Courts.* New York: Longman.

Buckle, L. G., and S. R. Thomas-Buckle. 1986. "Placing environmental mediation in context: Lessons from 'failed' mediations." *Environmental Impact Assessment Review* 6:55–72.

Burton, J. W. 1990. *Conflict: Resolution and Provention.* New York: St. Martin's Press.

Carnevale, P. J. D. 1986. "Strategic choice in mediation." *Negotiation Journal* 2:41–56.

Carnevale, P. J. D.; D. E. Conlon; K. Hanisch; and K. L. Harris. 1989. "Experimental research on the strategic choice model of mediation." In Kressel and Pruitt, eds., *Mediation Research.* San Francisco: Jossey-Bass.

Carnevale, P. J. D., and R. Pegnetter. 1985. "The selection of mediation tactics in public sector disputes: A contingency analysis." *Journal of Social Issues* 41:65–83.

Cobb, S., and J. Rifkin. 1989. "The social construction of neutrality in mediation." Paper presented at the annual meeting of the Society of Professionals in Dispute Resolution, October, Washington D.C.

———. 1991. "Practice and paradox: Deconstructing neutrality in mediation." *Law and Social Inquiry,* 16(1):35–62.

Crocker, C. A. 1992. *High Noon in Southern Africa: Making Peace in a Rough Neighborhood.* New York: W. W. Norton.

Deutsch, M. 1973. *The Resolution of Conflict.* New Haven, CT: Yale University Press.

Dingwall, R. 1987. "Empowerment or enforcement: Some questions about power and control in divorce mediation." In Dingwall and Eekelaar, eds., *Divorce Mediation and Legal Processes.* London: Oxford University Press.

Donahue, W. 1989. "Communicative competence in mediators." In Kressel and Pruitt, eds., *Mediation Research.* San Francisco: Jossey-Bass.

Douglas, A. 1962. *Industrial Peacemaking.* New York: Columbia University Press.

Druckman, D. 1975. "The influence of situation in interparty conflict." *Journal of Conflict Resolution* 19:69–82.

Emerson, R. M., and S. L. Messinger. 1977. "The micropolitics of trouble." *Social Problems* 25:121–34.

Evans, G. W., and C. M. Crumbaugh. 1969. "Effects of prisoner's dilemma format on cooperative behavior." *Journal of Personal and Social Psychology* 3:486–88.

Fisher, R., and W. L. Ury. 1981. *Getting to YES.* Boston: Houghton Mifflin.

Folberg, J., and A. Taylor. 1984. *Mediation.* San Francisco: Jossey-Bass.

Folger, J., and S. Bernard. 1985. "Divorce mediation: When mediators challenge the divorcing parties." *Mediation Quarterly* 10:5–24.

Forester, J. 1989. *Planning in the Face of Power.* Berkeley, CA: University of California Press.

Friedman, R. 1987. "Organization change and cultural analysis: Redefining labor-relations at international harvester." Ph.D. Diss., University of Chicago.

Frohman, L. A., and M. D. Cohen. 1970. "Compromise and logrolling: Comparing the efficiency of two bargaining processes." *Behavioral Science* 15:180–83.

Galanter, M. 1974. "Why the 'Haves' come out ahead: Speculations on the limits of legal change." *Law and Society Review* 9:95–160.

Goffman, E. 1959. *The Presentation of Self in Everyday Life.* New York: Doubleday.

———. 1974. *Frame Analysis.* New York: Harper & Row.

Goldberg, S.; E. Green; and F. E. A. Sander. 1985. *Dispute Resolution.* Boston: Little, Brown.

Greenhalgh, L. 1987. "Relationships in negotiations." *Negotiation Journal* 3:235–45.

Harrington, C. 1985. *Shadow Justice: The Ideology and Institutionalization of Alternatives to Court.* Westport, CT: Greenwood Press.

Hiltrop, J. 1985. "Mediator behavior and the settlement of collective bargaining disputes in Britain." *Journal of Social Issues* 41:83–101.

———. 1989. "Factors associated with successful labor mediation." In Kressel and Pruitt, eds., *Mediation Research.* San Francisco: Jossey-Bass.

Hiltrop, J., and J. Z. Rubin. 1982. "Effects of intervention mode and conflict of interest on dispute resolution." *Journal of Personality and Social Psychology* 42:665–72.

Ito, K. 1985. "Ho'oponopono, to make right: Hawaiian conflict resolution and metaphor in the construction of family therapy." *Culture, Medicine, and Psychiatry* 9:201–17.

Janosik, R. 1987. "Rethinking the culture-negotiation link." *Negotiation Journal* 3:385–97.

Jones, T. 1988. "Phase structures in agreement and no-agreement mediation." *Communication Research* 15:470–95.

Kelman, H. C. 1993. "Creating coalitions across conflict lines." In S. Worchel and J. Simpson, eds., *Conflict Between People and Groups.* Chicago: Nelson-Hall.

Kochan, T., and T. Jick. 1978. "The public sector mediation process." *Journal of Conflict Resolution* 22:209–41.

Kolb, D. M. 1983. *The Mediators.* Cambridge, MA: MIT Press.

———. 1985. "To be a mediator: Expressive tactics in mediation." *Journal of Social Issues* 41:11–27.

———. 1987. "Corporate ombudsman and organization conflict resolution." *Journal of Conflict Resolution* 31:673–91.

———. 1989a. "Labor mediators, managers, and ombudsmen: Roles mediators play in different contexts." In Kressel and Pruitt, eds., *Mediation Research.* San Francisco: Jossey-Bass.

———. 1989b. "How existing procedures shape alternatives: The case of grievance mediation." *Journal of Dispute Resolution,* 59–87.

———. 1992. "Women's work: Peacemaking behind the scenes." In Kolb and Pruitt, eds., *Hidden Conflict in Organizations: Uncovering Behind-the-scenes Disputes.* Newbury Park, CA: Sage.

Kolb, D. M., and Associates. 1994. *When Talk Works: Profiles of Mediators.* San Francisco: Jossey-Bass.

Kolb, D. M., and B. H. Sheppard. 1985. "Do managers mediate, or even arbitrate?" *Negotiation Journal* 1:379–88.

Kressel, K. 1972. *Labor Mediation: An Exploratory Survey.* Albany, NY: Association of Labor Mediation Agencies.

———. 1985. *The Process of Divorce: How Professionals and Couples Negotiate Settlements.* New York: Basic Books.

Kressel, K., and D. G. Pruitt. 1985. "Themes in the mediation of social conflict." *Journal of Social Issues* 41:179–99.

———. 1989. "A research perspective on the mediation of social conflict." In Kressel and Pruitt, eds., *Mediation Research.* San Francisco: Jossey-Bass.

Kriesberg, L. 1987. "Timing and the initiation of de-escalation moves." *Negotiation Journal* 3:375–85.

Lewicki, R., and B. Sheppard. 1985. "Choosing how to intervene: Factors influencing the use of process and outcome control in third party dispute resolution." *Journal of Occupational Behavior* 6:49–64.

Lovell, H. 1952. "The pressure lever in mediation." *Industrial and Labor Relations Review* 6:20–30.

McEwen, C., and R. J. Maiman. 1984. "Mediation in small claims court: Achieving compliance through consent." *Law and Society Review* 18:11.

Maggiolo, W. 1971. *Techniques of Mediation in Labor Disputes.* Oceana, NY: Dobbs Ferry.

Merry, S. E. 1982. "The social organization of mediation in nonindustrial societies." In Abel, ed., *Politics of Informal Justice.* New York: Academic Press.

———. 1987. "Cultural frameworks of mediation." Wellesley College, Wellesley, MA.

Merry, S. E., and M. Rochleau. 1985. *Mediation in Families: A Study of the Children's Hearings Project.* Cambridge, MA: Cambridge Children and Family Services.

Moore, C. 1986. *The Mediation Process: Practical Strategies for Resolving Conflict.* San Francisco: Jossey-Bass.

Murnighan, J. K. 1986. "The structure of mediation and intravention." *Negotiation Journal* 2:351–57.

Nader, L., and H. F. Todd, eds. 1978. *The Disputing Process—Law in Ten Societies.* New York: Columbia University Press.

Pearce, W.; S. L. Barnett; and J. Rifkin. 1987. "Communication in dispute mediation sessions: Institutional and interactional analyses." Unpublished paper.

Pruitt, D. G.; N. B. McGillicuddy; G. Welton; and W. R. Fry. 1989. "Process of mediation in dispute settlement centers." In Kressel and Pruitt, eds., *Mediation Research.* San Francisco: Jossey-Bass.

Rubin, J. Z., ed. 1980. *Dynamics of Third Party Intervention: Kissinger in the Middle East.* New York: Praeger.

Sarat, A. 1988. "The new formalism in disputing and dispute processing." *Law and Society* 21:695–717.

Schon, D. A. 1983. *The Reflective Practitioner.* New York: Basic Books.

Shapiro, D.; R. Drieghe; and J. Brett. 1985. "Mediator behavior and the outcome of mediation." *Journal of Social Issues* 41:101–15.

Sheppard, B. 1983. "Third party conflict intervention: A procedural framework." In

Staw and Cummings, eds., *Research in Organizational Behavior* 6. Greenwich, CT: JAI Press.

Sheppard, B.; K. Blumenfeld-Jones; and J. Roth. 1989. "Informal thirdpartyship: A program of research on everyday conflict intervention." In Kressel and Pruitt, eds., *Mediation Research.* San Francisco: Jossey-Bass.

Silbey, S. S., and S. E. Merry. 1986. "Mediator settlement strategies." *Law and Policy* 8:7–32.

———. 1987. "The problems shape the process: Interpreting disputes in mediation and court." Paper presented at the Law and Society Conference, Washington, DC.

Silbey, S. S., and A. Sarat. 1988. *Dispute Processing in Law and Legal Scholarship: From Institutional Critique to the Reconstruction of the Judicial Subject.* Madison: University of Wisconsin Institute for Legal Studies.

Simkin, W., and N. Fidandis. 1986. *Mediation and the Dynamics of Collective Bargaining.* Washington, DC: The Bureau of National Affairs.

Stevens, C. 1963. *Strategy and Collective Bargaining Negotiations.* New York: McGraw-Hill.

Susskind, L., and E. Babbitt. 1992. "Overcoming the obstacles to effective mediation of international disputes." In Bercovitch and Rubin, eds., *Mediation in International Relations: Multiple Approaches to Conflict Management.* London: MacMillan/St. Martin's Press.

Susskind, L., and J. Cruikshank. 1987. *Breaking the Impasse.* New York: Basic Books.

Susskind, L., and C. Ozawa. 1983. "Mediated negotiation in the public sector." *American Behavioral Scientist* 27:229–55.

Touval, S., and I. W. Zartman. 1986. *International Mediation in Theory and Practice.* Boulder, CO: Westview Press.

———. 1989. "Mediation in international conflicts." In K. Kressel and D. Pruitt, eds., *Mediation Research.* San Francisco: Jossey-Bass.

Ury, W. L.; J. Brett; and S. Goldberg. 1988. *Getting Disputes Resolved.* San Francisco: Jossey-Bass.

Vidmar, N. 1985. "An assessment of mediation in small claims court." *Journal of Social Issues* 41:127–45.

Wall, J. 1981. "Mediation: An analysis, review, and proposed research." *Journal of Conflict Resolution* 25:157–81.

Wall, J., and D. Rude. 1985. "Judicial mediation: Techniques, strategies and situational effects." *Journal of Social Issues* 41:47–65.

Welton, G., and D. G. Pruitt. 1987. "The mediation process: The effects of mediator bias and disputant power." *Personality and Social Psychology Bulletin* 13:123–33.

Zartman, I. W., and S. Touval. 1985. "International mediation: Conflict resolution and power politics." *Journal of Social Issues* 41:27–47.

CHAPTER 4

Applications and Misapplications of Conflict Resolution Ideas to International Conflicts

Louis Kriesberg

Ideas about how to resolve one kind of conflict often can be usefully applied to many other kinds of conflicts. However, sometimes such applications can result in mistakes, and the perpetuation or even escalation of conflicts. Correctly transferring conflict resolution ideas from one conflict to another necessitates accurately judging that the conflicts are similar in relevant ways. In this chapter, I first consider the ways international conflicts are and are not like other kinds of conflicts. Then basic conflict resolution ideas are mapped out before considering how they can be and have been applied in efforts to mitigate adverse aspects of international conflicts.

Before proceeding, I wish to make one general observation about the advocacy of particular concepts rather than others in social science and in policy debates. Advocates often argue vigorously about the meaning of a concept or the validity of a proposition; currently, for example, there is controversy about the meaning of the term *security* (Stephenson 1988). Advocates urge acceptance of particular concepts for at least two major reasons.[1] First, most of us usually assert that we urge others to adopt specific propositions or concepts because we believe them to be more accurate reflections of reality than are alternative ones. If people work with appropriate abstractions, they will be more effective in their undertakings than if they use concepts that distort reality. For example, if people accurately regard social conflicts as an inherent aspect of social life, they will act more effectively than if they mistakenly believe that conflicts are a product of only a particular social system or of inadequate socialization.

The second reason is particularly relevant for this topic. Many of us, at times, promote specific propositions or concepts because we believe that if people will accept them, they will behave better. For example, if human nature is understood to be basically loving and cooperative, then people will act more on trust and themselves be more trustworthy. In the application of conflict resolution ideas to international conflicts, many of us are promoters. The danger of such promotion is that it is guided by wishful thinking. In this chapter, I will try to discuss conflict resolution propositions on the first ground, avoiding wishful thinking as much as possible.

Comparing International and Domestic Conflicts

The traditional distinction between domestic and international conflicts is readily made and important differences between them are assumed. After noting them, I will question whether or not they always distinguish one domain from another. Three kinds of differences are important; they pertain to the characteristics of the adversaries, to the system of which the adversaries are a part, and to the issues in contention and the means used to advance them (Kriesberg 1982).

First, the adversaries in international conflicts are generally clearly bounded entities, governments, with representatives who can speak and commit the party to a course of action. In domestic conflicts, however, the contending parties are often not clearly bounded, and who can speak for them is consequently unclear.

Furthermore, the adversaries in international conflicts are very large, highly differentiated entities; their leaders must attend to a variety of constituencies; they include specialists in fighting, negotiating, and other activities; and they contain many groups, each with its special interests. Domestic adversaries are generally much smaller and less differentiated.

Second, international conflicts occur within a world system without an overarching political-legal authority. Domestic conflicts, on the other hand, occur within a social system that has such an authority. In addition, adversaries in international conflicts are relatively autonomous, while in domestic conflicts, the parties are highly interdependent with each other and with many other actors.

Finally, some characteristics of the issues in international conflicts and how the conflicts are conducted generally are different than is true for domestic conflicts. Issues in contention in international conflicts often involve fundamental cultural, ideological, and ethnic identities and values. Large-scale organized violence is often used or threatened in international conflicts, but less frequently in domestic ones.

Exceptions to these differences, however, are so many and great that the distinctions between international and domestic conflicts should be questioned. That is consistent with the conflict resolution approach to social conflicts, which assumes that conflicts in one domain are not wholly different from ones in other domains.

First, consider the characteristics of the adversaries. Even in international conflicts, the adversaries sometimes are not clearly bounded and unitary; they may be religious, ethnic, or ideological communities or social-movement organizations. Furthermore, some international conflicts are waged by one or more adversaries who are not large and highly differentiated, for example, an organization engaged in hostage taking as a means of struggle. On the other hand, many adversaries in domestic conflicts are highly organized, for example, in industrial conflicts in many countries.

Considering the sociopolitical context, we must recognize that in many international conflicts a significant shared authority exists, for example, in conflicts between allies or about matters that the adversaries have agreed to handle through negotiations, adjudication, or arbitration. In addition, the global system is becoming increasingly integrated and interdependent. Economic, human rights, and ecological issues are increasingly global, so that governments are no longer able to be autonomous, if they ever were. On the other hand, in some domestic conflicts an overarching political-legal authority does not exist; for example, in revolutionary periods. Furthermore, some domestic adversaries can effectively leave the relationship with one another and establish new relationships with other actors.

Finally, as the world becomes more highly integrated, international conflicts increasingly take on the character of disputes in which many shared interests are involved. With the end of the cold war and the lessened ideological character of many world conflicts, international disputes are likely to become more narrow and focused. These developments have relevance for how international conflicts are waged. In many international conflicts, violence has not been considered a real option for a long time; for example, among allies and even among adversaries in regard to nonvital issues. On the other hand, violence is used or threatened in many large-scale domestic fights, such as in revolutions and in wars of secession.

This discussion should make it clear that domestic conflicts are not homogenous and different from a homogenous set of international conflicts. Conflicts differ in many ways, and most of these differences are variations along several dimensions. For example, the existence of a superordinate authority is a matter of degree, not a dichotomous distinction. Applying conflict resolution ideas and practices from the domestic domain to the international domain, then, should take into account the specific ways in which particular conflicts are similar and dissimilar.

In principle, therefore, drawing insights about resolving one kind of conflict can be usefully applied to other kinds of conflict. Inferences from struggles among any entities with leaders and constituencies are possibly relevant for international conflicts. Which conflict resolution practices are and are not transferable depends upon particular relevant similarities.

Conflict Resolution Ideas and Practices

Conflict resolution ideas have been drawn from efforts to mitigate the worst aspects of international, as well as domestic, conflicts and from traditional negotiation experience. In this analysis I stress the conflict resolution ideas that have recently been developed and especially note those propositions significantly derived from domestic experiences, whose relevance for international conflict resolution warrants consideration.

In the past, several conflict resolution ideas, domestically derived, have been argued as pertinent to international conflict. This has been most evident in the efforts to apply practices relating to law and political structures, discussed by Johnson (in this volume). Many analysts have promoted the creation of international law as a way of controlling international conflicts. They have sometimes seemed to regard international law or world law as domestic law, writ large. In addition, lessons learned from particular domestic-conflict domains were sometimes regarded as relevant and their transfer advocated. This has been the case, for example, with ideas about controlling international conflicts on the basis of experiences with labor-management collective bargaining (Jackson 1952).

Recent developments in conflict resolution ideas and practices and their possible application to international conflicts are stressed here. The practices and interpretations of them are based on general theories about the nature of social conflicts. Admittedly, however, all conflict resolution analysts and practitioners do not share the same views of social conflict. I give most attention to the generally expressed viewpoints and the ones I believe to be most valid.

General Assumptions

Most conflict resolution theorists and practitioners assume that social conflicts are inherent in social life. Inequalities in the possession of goods and access to resources that are desired and that are scarce is one major source of conflicts. Even differences about what is desirable, if one party seeks to impose its preferences on another, is a source of ideological or value conflicts. In either case, social groups frequently come to believe that getting another party to act differently is worth insisting upon, even against the wishes of that other party. A social conflict will then erupt.

Second, conflict resolution theorists and practitioners generally also assume that conflicts are important and sometimes essential ways to advance widely shared interests (Wehr 1979). It is not the struggle itself that is to be condemned, but how it is waged. Advocates of conflict resolution methods often favor nonviolent and regulated ways of conducting a social conflict, so that it is constructive and not destructive.

Thirdly, an assumption is often made that each specific conflict has a life course, moving through several stages. A conflict is not viewed as moving inexorably from one stage to another; rather, the idea is best treated as a metaphor. I note eight stages, relevant to conflict resolution: (1) a latent stage where the underlying conditions for a social conflict are present; (2) an emergence stage in which the adversaries come to view themselves as in a struggle with each other; (3) an escalation stage in which the intensity and/or extent of the conflict grows, for example, to include the use of large-scale violence; (4) a turnaround stage that may entail a stalemate, a defeat of one party, or a reframing of the conflict; it may also entail a crisis that leads to further escalation or to de-escalation; (5) a de-escalation stage in which moves are made to reduce the level and/or extent of struggle; (6) a settlement stage in which the adversaries seek to reach an agreement ending at least some aspects of the dispute; (7) an outcome stage in which, with or without an agreement, the conflict appears to have been terminated; and (8) a postconflict stage in which the outcomes of the conflict provide the bases for a new conflict or for reconciliation, and have other consequences.

A fourth basic assumption held by many theorists and practitioners of conflict resolution is that each specific conflict is embedded in a multifaceted relationship among the adversaries, and the conflict is interlocked with many other conflicts (Kriesberg 1980). Changes in other aspects of the adversary relationship or in the salience of other conflicts will affect the course of the specific conflict that is the focus of attention.

A final idea is critical. Conflicts often can be settled or resolved so that the outcome is mutually beneficial; there is a win/win outcome (Pruitt and Rubin 1986). In many ways, this is counterintuitive. Conflicts break out because parties believe they have incompatible goals; they believe that they are in a zero-sum relationship so that what one gains is at the expense of the other.

A conflict that appears to be zero-sum can be reframed to have a possible positive sum outcome in several ways (Kriesberg, Northrup, and Thorson 1989). First, the parties may be suffering from a misunderstanding, and with better communication they may recognize that their conflict has been unrealistic. Second, they may reframe or redefine their conflict so that common interests become more salient, perhaps at the expense of other parties. For example, a labor-management conflict may be settled at the expense of consumers. Third, the adversaries, perhaps with the aid of intermediaries, may find additional resources so that they can easily divide a larger pie. Fourth, the adversaries may recognize that the costs of waging the struggle have risen to be out of proportion to the goals sought and that a settlement would be beneficial. Finally, the adversaries may reframe their conflict as a problem and in seeking a common solution discover an option that provides each adversary with the essentials of what it seeks. This may be possible because of trade-offs among differently values preferences or by changing the set of negotiating partners (Raiffa 1982). An actual conflict, in which adversaries believe they are in a zero-sum struggle, may be modified by a combination of the possibilities listed above. What is likely to be effective depends on the nature of the specific conflict and on its social context.

Note also that each specific conflict is embedded in larger, longer-term conflicts and itself encompasses a series of shorter-term disputes. These longer-term and shorter-term disputes have their own course of development. Various kinds of conflict resolution methods are appropriate for different stages of a conflict and for different contexts in which a specific dispute is located.

Specific Conflict Resolution Methods

Conflict resolution methods will be discussed in relationship to several of the conflict stages listed above. Most work in the field is focused on the negotiation stage and I give that stage most attention, but the others also warrant examination.

Prevention. The conflict resolution perspective suggests several ways in which conflicts can be prevented from emerging, in addition to the traditional method of suppression. One method is to reduce the underlying bases for conflict; this may mean reducing inequalities and/or differences in values. Another way is to increase the level of integration among the potential adversaries; as a consequence, the mutual benefits of cooperation would make the emergence of conflict very costly. A third way is to develop regulations for managing conflicts that become so institutionalized that a conflict is experienced as routine and takes on a game or sport quality; electoral politics is sometimes such a procedure.

Limit escalation. In domestic conflicts, superordinate authorities are often available to limit conflict escalation. As noted earlier, this possibility is much less likely to be available in international conflicts. A much greater reliance must be placed on limits established by the adversaries themselves. Traditionally, this has been attempted by threat, by deterrence. However, this method may lead to mutual threat and arms races that are escalating (Patchen 1988).

A conflict resolution approach suggests taking into account the interests and perceptions of the adversary so that what is intended to be defensive is not interpreted as offensive. In international relations, this includes means of defense that are not provocative; for example civilian-based, nonviolent defense or military means that are not capable of rapid forward deployment and use. It also includes closer integration between adversaries and possibilities of mutual gain such that the relationship's disruption, as a result of conflict escalation, would be costly (Fisher 1984).

Some advocates of nonviolent action as a means of struggle argue that it empowers the weaker party, but in a way that facilitates finding a mutually satisfactory outcome (Bondurant 1965). This presumes that peace and justice will be better served when adversaries are relatively equal and the means of struggle recognize the other side's humanity.

Prenegotiation. Most of the work in conflict resolution has been focused on negotiations and mediation. In the last few years, however, increasing attention has been given to understanding how adversaries get to the point of entering negotiations (Stein 1989). The conditions that make adversaries ready to move toward settlement are increasingly being examined. One idea is that the adversaries are in a hurting stalemate (Touval and Zartman 1985).

Whatever the conditions may be, the adversaries must believe that a mutually acceptable settlement is possible and preferable to continuing the struggle and trying to intimidate the adversary. Such beliefs may involve a redefinition of the conflict, and that may be aided by intermediaries presenting new options. Finding a formula that holds out the possibility of an agreement that is mutually acceptable, then, is often critical.

A strategy to bring adversaries to view the conflict as having a mutually acceptable outcome involves making choices. These pertain to the selection of the parties to be involved in the conflict resolution effort, the issues to be negotiated about, and the inducements to be used (Kriesberg 1992). In selecting parties for de-escalation, it may be useful to include intermediaries who can fulfill a variety of mediating functions, including offering suggestions, facilitating communication, and adding resources. Among the many parties to a dispute, only those amenable to a settlement may be included, excluding the intransigents. On the other hand, care must often be taken that those who can disrupt a settlement (sometimes the intransigent ones) be included in negotiating a settlement.

In selecting issues, at an early de-escalating stage or at the transition stage, narrow issues that do not affect vital interests are best undertaken. Such confidence-building measures can then lead to negotiations about more central issues. In selecting inducements, conciliatory actions can be useful signals at the point of seeking de-escalation. Coercive actions are usually not productive at that stage. An important component of the prenegotiation stage is to signal the other side that movement toward a settlement is possible. It is important to indicate readiness without appearing vulnerable, risking inviting the other side to increase its demands.

Problem-solving negotiations. Many techniques have been developed to increase the chances that adversaries will redefine their conflict to be a problem to which there may be a mutually satisfactory or even beneficial solution. A basic method is by training disputants in this approach. Presumably, if the adversaries believe that integrative outcomes are possible, they will act in such a way as to find them. They would not if they believed that such an outcome was not possible.

There are many specific suggestions about how to conduct negotiations to find such solutions, discussed, for example by Bush (in this volume) and Fisher (in this volume). These suggestions include separating the person from the problem; focusing on interests, not positions; and inventing options for mutual gain (Fisher and Ury 1981). There are suggestions, too, about shifting the levels of the negotiating teams, of fractionating a dispute, or of linking issues to facilitate trade-offs.

Considerable emphasis in the conflict resolution field is placed on the contributions that intermediaries can make in facilitating problem-solving negotiations. Most attention is given to the activities performed by persons playing the social role of mediator. Those functions may be grouped into four categories: formulating options, increasing costs of not reaching an agreement, providing compensations that facilitate reaching an agreement, and providing a setting for the adversaries to negotiate (Carnevale 1986).

These functions may be served by a person or group recognized by the disputants as a mediator. That actor may be an official or nonofficial person or group. Sometimes the functions are served by elements in one of the adversary units. Such people are acting as quasi mediators; they do not have the same possibilities or constraints that those playing the social role of mediator have (Kriesberg 1991).

Mediators (and to some extend quasi mediators) can help formulate new options for settlement by constructing possible bridging proposals or combinations of trade-offs (Pruitt and Rubin 1986). Mediators can press for a settlement by setting time limits, by threatening withdrawal and publicly attributing intransigence to one or more of the negotiating sides, or by giving legitimacy to one of the party's proposals. Such kinds of pressure are more likely to be tried and proven effective in domestic than in international settings. Mediators can offer compensation by adding resources to make the settlement possible, including compensating one or both sides for the losses entailed in the settlement. Mediators can provide a setting in which interaction between the adversaries is encouraged and even facilitated, but with little or no direct or substantive intervention by the mediator.

Intermediary roles extend beyond mediator roles, ranging from arbitrator to consultant. Arbitration is rare in international conflicts. Consultation in the form of problem-solving workshops has been conducted by several scholars;

for example, Herbert Kelman (1972) and John Burton (1990). As Ronald Fisher (in this volume) points out, which roles and strategies are appropriate is contingent on the conflict phase as well as other features of the conflict.

Reaching high-quality agreements. Several ideas may contribute to reaching enduring accords that foster reconciliation and integration among the former adversaries. Parties with important stakes in the outcome of a conflict should be included in negotiating an agreement. The participation of intermediaries often helps ensure that diverse interests are taken into account in reaching a settlement. Furthermore, the participation of intermediaries increases the vested interests in sustaining the agreement.

Agreements that include procedures for monitoring and interpreting the agreement can often be helpful. Some agreements can have features that foster the development of organizations and groups that will have a vested interest in the growth and sustenance of the settlement (Kriesberg 1992).

Illustrative Applications

To have appropriate, effective application of conflict resolution ideas to a particular struggle, it is important to analyze the nature and phase of that conflict. Then the suitable conflict resolution method can be selected, depending on the goal. I will discuss a few actual uses of the ideas mapped out earlier, without arguing that the persons conducting those activities were consciously applying such ideas.

Prenegotiation

The application of several kinds of conflict resolution ideas can be illustrated in the conduct of international conflict de-escalation. The role of nonofficial intermediaries and the use of unilateral conciliatory gestures are stressed in this contribution.

Intermediaries. In recent years, considerable attention has begun to be given to nonofficial channels of communication and diplomacy, called variously, Track II, supplementary, citizen, or people-to-people diplomacy (Berman and Johnson 1977; McDonald 1991). In addition, in recent years, increased use is being made of problem-solving workshops (Kelman 1972). These forms of intermediary action are probably most effective in the early stages of de-escalating efforts, when the possibilities of getting to the negotiating table are explored (Earle 1991).

De-escalating negotiations are entered when the adversaries believe that the time is right to do so. Intermediaries, as well as groups within one or more of the adversary parties, may try to help convince the leaders of the adversary sides that the time is ripe to move toward settlement. They can help reframe the conflict so that an outcome that is mutually preferable to continuing the struggle seems possible. For example, many informal, sometimes covert, meetings were held over many years between Israeli Jews and Palestine Liberation Organization (PLO) members and supporters. These meetings improved each side's understanding of the other and fostered trustworthy interpersonal links so that when the circumstances were conducive for official de-escalating probes, success was made more likely.[2]

Unilateral conciliatory gesture. Osgood (1962) and others have argued for the use of unilateral conciliatory gestures in order to reduce tensions and begin de-escalating movement. President John F. Kennedy's June 1963 speech at American University has been pointed to as an example of such initiatives, as has President Sadat's visit to Jerusalem in November 1977 (Etzioni 1967; Kriesberg 1981; Kelman 1985).

Such events, however, are not simply manifestations of interpersonal social psychological mechanisms. When considering de-escalation at the international level, constituency considerations are very important. The events are staged to affect the constituencies of the adversary or a wider audience.

In addition, if conducted without prior, confidential communications, even major conciliatory gestures may be dismissed as propaganda. In actuality, unilateral actions are often prepared by confidential meetings. For example, prior to President Kennedy's American University speech, Norman Cousins (1972) had been invited to meet with General Secretary Khrushchev. Norman Cousins reported to President Kennedy that Nikita Khrushchev wanted some signal that he could use to move ahead on the nuclear weapons test and other issues. The speech was part of a series of events to win support for de-escalating moves.

How effective such gestures are depends to a significant degree on the context, especially on the stage of the conflict. For example, in the late 1950s, Nikita Khrushchev did make many gestures, including large-scale reductions in the Soviet armed forces. In the context of the cold war, and mixed with what the West perceived as Soviet threats, however, these gestures were not effective in quickly de-escalating the conflict.

Problem-Solving Negotiations

In discussing the application of conflict resolution methods to de-escalating negotiations, I give particular attention to strategic choices in negotiation, to the methods of negotiation, and to mediation.

Strategy of negotiation. Negotiation strategy involves choices about the parties in the negotiations, the issues to be discussed, and the inducements to be used. Choosing which parties should participate in de-escalating negotiations should not be done without reflection. Three competing principles can be readily stated. First, include all the parties with a stake in the conflict and its outcome. Second, do not exclude parties with the power to prevent reaching an agreement. Third, select those parties who are ready to reach a settlement and exclude the intransigents.

It is easy to point to cases where the failure to follow each principle contributed to the failure to reach an agreement or to reaching an inadequate agreement. Thus, the exclusion of parties with a vital stake in the conflict can lead to an agreement that is quite unfair to them; as was the case with the Munich agreement of 1938. Excluding parties with the capacity to disrupt an agreement can prevent an agreement from being actualized; for example, when Syria was excluded from the U.S.-mediated treaty between Israel and Lebanon in 1983, the treaty was never ratified (Young 1987). Including intransigents may prevent or greatly delay reaching an agreement, as it did, for example, in the Middle East. Conversely, excluding the intransigents has sometimes sped de-escalation; for example, note that in ending the Cuban Missile Crisis, the Cuban government was essentially ignored.

Negotiation methods. A basic recommendation of the conflict resolution approach is for negotiators to be open to learning the other side's underlying interest. One should not enter the negotiations with fixed positions. There is evidence in support of this approach as a way to maximize mutual gain. For example, in the SALT II negotiations, a major issue was determining when a modification of one missile launcher should be characterized as the development of a new one. At one point in the negotiations, the Soviets asked that a decrease in weight of 10–12 percent be considered a modification of a missile, not a new launcher. The U.S. negotiators suspected that the Soviets wanted to develop a more compact successor to their ICBMs. It took a long time to discover that the underlying interest had to do with reducing the fuel load in order to test the missiles within Soviet territory (Talbott 1984, 261–62).

In complex international negotiations with large bureaucracies on each side, however, entering without positions and clear priorities can lead to confusion and the failure to reach any agreement. Being flexible can mean being ill-prepared and that too has problems; for example, see accounts of the U.S.-Soviet summit in Reykjavik (Scowcroft, Deutch, and Woolsey 1987). That case also illustrates the creativity that can occur when detailed positions have not been worked out in advance of a meeting.

Mediation. As noted earlier, the idea of an intermediary providing mediating services is an important one in the conflict resolution approach. There is considerable discussion about the attributes of a mediator and of the way in which the role should be played. The degree of neutrality and activism of the mediator is much discussed. In the North American alternative dispute resolution model, the neutrality and the facilitative character of the role is usually stressed. The mediator should not attempt to impose or even suggest his or her own solution.

In actual international conflict mediation, when government representatives serve as mediators, particularly if they are from great powers, they generally are very active and seem to be expected to be so. Under certain circumstances and when conducted by nonofficials or representatives of small powers, the mediators primarily provide facilitative services.

In the early phases of de-escalation, in the prenegotiation stage, transmitting information is particularly important. Mediators are critical in providing channels of communication between parties who do not recognize each other, for example in the Arab-Israeli conflict (Touval 1982).

During this prenegotiation phase of de-escalation, intermediaries can also help formulate new options for possible agreements. Nonofficials can help provide the opportunities for creating options and for devising strategies about who the parties to negotiation should be. This may be done through a variety of channels, as indicated by the history of indirect exchanges between the PLO and the Israeli government before their mutual recognition in September 1993. There is increasing recognition of the value of supplementary or Track II diplomacy (McDonald 1991). In addition, in recent years, increased use is being made of problem-solving workshops.

International nongovernmental organizations (INGOs) also can provide the forums in which possible de-escalating solutions can be explored. Many of these are organized around occupational interests and provide mediating services only informally and indirectly (Kriesberg 1972). Some INGOs are focused on particular issues that are matters of international contention, and provide significant opportunities to discuss options that are then transmitted to the respective governments of the participating INGO members; this is true for the Pugwash and Dartmouth conferences (Rotblat 1967; Pentz and Slovo 1981).

At the negotiation stage, mediators in international conflicts often are very active, and some of them add considerable resources that may facilitate reaching an agreement. This is particularly true when the mediator is the representative of a major government. This has been particularly notable, for example, in the roles played by U.S. Secretary of State Henry Kissinger and by President Jimmy Carter in Israeli-Egyptian negotiations (Touval 1982).

In mediating the Israeli partial withdrawals from the Sinai, Henry Kissinger could offer U.S. guarantees and military personnel to monitor the Israeli-Egyptian agreements. In mediating the negotiations for an Israeli-Egyptian peace treaty, Jimmy Carter could offer Israel aid to build new airfields to compensate for those lost by returning all of the Sinai to Egypt.

Different forms of mediation and of mediating activities are effective at different stages of de-escalation. Relatively informal, nonofficial, facilitative mediation is likely to be more effective at the early, prenegotiation stage than at the negotiation stage. Exploratory probing is often best done when officials can deny full responsibility.

Reaching Equitable and Enduring Settlements

To reach equitable settlements, conflict resolution analysts generally contend that it is necessary to take into account the underlying interests of the parties to the conflict. There is certainly evidence that the failure to resolve a conflict in that sense has led to renewed conflicts later. Conflicts, however, are rarely fully resolved, and never all at once. Accommodation takes a long time and follows many partial settlements.

Agreements are more likely to endure insofar as their enactment generates vested interests in their survival and in their expansion. This was the case for the European Coal and Steel Community and the European Economic Community.

Conclusions

This discussion leads to several conclusions. First, long time periods should be used in de-escalating international conflicts. It is also useful to recognize that adversaries share the same globe; they cannot escape each other. Consequently, ongoing relations are critical, and that is why problem-solving conflict resolution methods are especially valuable.

Second, this discussion indicates that some generalization across domains is useful. International conflicts are not a unique, homogeneous set of conflicts. General concepts about social conflicts are possible and can be helpful for effectively de-escalating international conflicts. Thus, it is useful to consider the life course of conflicts and of conflict resolution efforts. Different methods are appropriate for different phases of each, and their appropriate application depends on the particular international conflict.

Third, whether or not conflict resolution methods should be applied, even whether or not the *concepts* should be applied, depends in part on one's values. When the time is right to seek a settlement and when a conflict should be escalated in order to gain a settlement that advances a particular party's interests is a policy choice, guided at least partly by preferences (Kriesberg 1987).

Finally, ideas about conflict help shape reality, as well as being shaped by the realities of conflict. The ideas of conflict resolution are powerful and influential. If adversaries believe that they are in a struggle that can only offer the options of victory or defeat, the way they conduct that struggle will be different than if they regard themselves as in a relationship in which their conflict poses a problem to be solved.

In the last years of the Soviet Union, and in its successor states, interest in conflict resolution ideas has grown rapidly (Kremenyuk 1988). In the past, conflicts were viewed as manifestations of the inequalities in capitalist societies; they did not exist in socialist societies. Conflicts between classes in capitalist societies or between socialist and capitalist elements were struggles between right and wrong, progress and reaction, the future and the past. Finding a win/win solution in that circumstance made no sense. As a conflict resolution perspective becomes influential, it challenges fundamental ideas about the nature of all societies and social relations. It contributed to Mikhail S. Gorbachev's "New Thinking" (Dragsdahl 1989), which was critical in the transition leading to the dissolution of the Soviet Union (Kriesberg 1992).

Relying on traditional thinking had damaged the Soviet Union. It had relied too much on coercion and military power. We may ask whether or not overreliance on such traditional thinking has not also damaged the U.S. role in the world and whether continued reliance on such thinking further damages the United States (Agnew 1987).

The fundamental question is to what extent one mode of thinking or another shapes the world, or whether it reflects it more or less accurately. The discussion here suggests that the way we think about social conflicts does affect the chances of settling a dispute or resolving a conflict, but that there is an important interaction between experience with the conflict conditions, at a given time, and the ideas about them.

NOTES

1. There are other reasons as well. Sometimes people argue for particular propositions or interpretations of concepts because acceptance of their views will give them influence, status, or power. For example, advocates of the significance of racial differences may be seen as advancing the interests of their racial category.

2. The agreement signed between the PLO and the Israeli government in September 1993 did require a set of conducive circumstances. Those conditions were created by the end of the cold war and by the war driving Iraq out of Kuwait. However, the implications of those conditions were evident in 1991, and yet they alone were not sufficient to produce an agreement. What was also necessary were experiences between the adversaries that could make such an agreement seem conceivably feasible and trustworthy. Alternative routes had to appear as worse. It was also necessary to construct a formula that gave each side some of what it wanted at a cost that it could bear. The agreement about Gaza and Jericho and the mutual recognition were critical components in that formula.

REFERENCES

Agnew, J. 1987. *The United States in the World Economy.* Cambridge University Press.
Berman, M., and J. Johnson, eds. 1977. *Unofficial Diplomats.* New York: Columbia University Press.
Bondurant, J. R. 1965. *Conquest of Violence: The Gandhian Philosophy of Conflict.* Rev. ed. Berkeley and Los Angeles: University of California Press.
Burton, J. 1990. *Conflict: Resolution and Provention.* New York: St. Martin's Press.
Carnevale, P. 1986. "Strategic choice in mediation." *Negotiation Journal* 2:41–56.
Cousins, N. 1972. *The Improbable Triumvirate.* New York: Norton Press.
Dragsdahl, J. 1989. "How peace research has reshaped the European arms dialogue." In *The Annual Review of Peace Activism, 1989,* 39–45. Boston, MA: The Winston Foundation for World Peace.
Earle II, R. 1991. "Private intervention in public controversy: Pros and cons." In L. Kriesberg and S. Thorson, eds., *Timing the De-escalation of International Conflicts.* Syracuse, NY: Syracuse University Press.
Etzioni, A. 1967. "The Kennedy experiment." *Western Political Quarterly* 20:361–80.
Fisher, D. 1984. *Preventing War in the Nuclear Age.* Totowa, NJ: Rowman & Allanheld.
Fisher, R., and W. Ury. 1981. *Getting to YES.* Boston: Houghton Mifflin Co.
Jackson, E. 1952. *Meeting of Minds: A Way to Peace through Mediation.* New York: McGraw-Hill.
Kelman, H. C. 1972. "The problem-solving workshop in conflict resolution." In A. L. Merritt, ed., *Communication in International Politics,* 168–204. Hobson, IL: University of Illinois Press.
———. 1985. "Overcoming the psychological barrier: An analysis of the Egyptian-Israeli peace process." *Negotiation Journal* 1:213–34.
Kremenyuk, V. A. 1988. "The emerging system of international negotiations." *Negotiation Journal* 4:211–20.
Kriesberg, L. 1972. "International non-governmental organizations and transnational integration." *International Associations* 24:521–24.
———. 1980. "Interlocking conflicts in the Middle East." In Louis Kriesberg, ed., *Research in Social Movements, Conflicts and Change, Vol. 3,* 99–118. Greenwich, CT: JAI Press.
———. 1981. "Noncoercive inducements in U.S.-Soviet conflicts: Ending the occupation of Austria and nuclear weapons tests." *Journal of Political and Military Sociology* 9(Spring): 1–16.
———. 1982. *Social Conflicts.* 2d ed. Englewood Cliffs, NJ: Prentice Hall.
———. 1987. "Timing and the initiation of de-escalation moves." *Negotiation Journal* 3:375–84.
———. 1991. "Formal and quasi mediators in international disputes: An exploratory analysis." *Journal of Peace Research* 28:19–27.
———. 1992. *International Conflict Resolution: The U.S.-USSR and Middle East Cases.* New Haven, CT: Yale University Press.

Kriesberg, L.; T. Northrup; and S. Thorson, eds. 1989. *Intractable Conflicts and Their Transformation.* Syracuse, NY: Syracuse University Press.

McDonald, J. 1991. "Further explorations of track II diplomacy." In L. Kriesberg and S. Thorson, eds., *Timing the De-escalation of International Conflicts.* Syracuse, NY: Syracuse University Press.

Osgood, C. E. 1962. *An Alternative to War or Surrender.* Urbana: University of Illinois Press.

Patchen, M. 1988. *Resolving Disputes between Nations: Coercion or Conciliation?* Durham, NC: Duke University Press.

Pentz, M., and G. Slovo. 1981. "The political significance of Pugwash." In W. M. Evan, ed., *Knowledge and Power in a Global Society,* 175–203. Beverly Hills: Sage Publications.

Pruitt, D. G., and J. Z. Rubin. 1986. *Social Conflict.* New York: Random House.

Raiffa, H. 1982. *The Art and Science of Negotiation.* Cambridge, MA: Harvard University Press.

Rotblat, J. 1967. *Pugwash: The First Ten Years.* New York: Humanities Press.

Scowcroft, B.; J. Deutch; and R. J. Woolsey. 1987. "A way out of Reykjavik." *The New York Times Magazine* (January 25): 40–42, 78–84.

Stein, J. G., ed. 1989. *Getting to the Table.* Baltimore and London: The Johns Hopkins University Press.

Stephenson, C. M. 1988. "The need for alternative forms of security: Crises and opportunities." *Alternatives* 13:55–76.

Talbott, S. 1984. *Deadly Gambits.* New York: Alfred A. Knopf.

Touval, S. 1982. *The Peace Brokers.* Princeton, NJ: Princeton University Press.

Touval, S., and I. W. Zartman, eds. 1985. *International Mediation in Theory and Practice.* Boulder, CO: Westview Press.

Wehr, P. 1979. *Conflict Regulation.* Boulder, CO: Westview Press.

Young, R. J. 1987. *Missed Opportunities for Peace—U.S. Middle East Policy 1981–1986.* Philadelphia: American Friends Service Committee.

CHAPTER 5

The Psychology of Social Conflict and Its Relevance to International Conflict

Dean G. Pruitt

This chapter focuses on the psychology of social conflict. Conflict occurs when one party makes remarks or takes actions that are opposed by remarks or actions from the other. Most of the principles presented here are based on theory and research concerning individuals in conflict. However, there is reason to believe that many of these principles apply more broadly; hence, speculative extensions will be made to international relations.

Antecedents of Conflict

Relative deprivation and group identification. Interpersonal conflict ordinarily arises out of actual or anticipated relative deprivation. One's achievements or expected achievements fall short of one's goals or standards. This is distressing—especially if one feels that the deprivation is illegitimate because important principles (e.g., principles of fairness) are involved (Crosby, Muehrer, and Loewenstein 1986). If another party seems to be the source of the distress, the seeds of conflict are sown, though actual conflict does not always occur.

Intergroup conflict (and by extension international conflict) also arises out of relative deprivation. However, (contrary to Gurr's 1970 speculations) it is group deprivation rather than individual deprivation that matters. Individual distress is not an important antecedent of intergroup conflict, but the shared sense that one's group is actually or potentially being wronged can be quite explosive (Dube and Guimond 1986).

To develop a sense of group deprivation, it is necessary to identify with one group in contrast to another. There is evidence that such identifications per se can contribute to intergroup conflict. People become convinced that their group is better than the other group, even when there are minimal objective differences between the groups; they are then prone to discriminate in favor of members of their own group (Tajfel and Turner 1979). Such attitudes and behavior are very likely to frustrate members of the other group, causing them to feel relative group deprivation and hence encouraging conflict. One cure for this phenomenon is to blur the psychological boundaries between the groups, for example, by having individuals belong to two or more crossed groupings, such as Democrats and Republicans from the North and South (Vanbeselaere 1987).

Strategic choice. There are various strategies for dealing with actual or expected relative deprivation, including the following (Rubin, Pruitt, and Kim 1994):

Inaction—doing nothing.

Yielding—reducing one's goals or standards to suit the other party.

Problem solving—seeking a formula that will satisfy both parties' goals and standards. The ideal form of problem solving involves a discussion between the two parties, but one party can engage in problem solving alone.

Contending—trying to bend the other to one's wishes. Threats and other hostile actions are common elements of a contentious strategy.

Choice among these strategies determines the nature of the conflict that ensues. Problem solving encourages the development of win-win agreements. Contending can produce failure to reach agreement and escalation, though it is sometimes a precursor to effective problem solving by clarifying the relative power of the parties and hence the outer boundaries of a possible agreement. Unilateral yielding leads to a one-sided victory; bilateral yielding produces a compromise, which is often inferior to a win-win agreement.

Conflict style and the dual-concern model. What determines the choices people make among these strategies? Part of the answer is conflict style, an element of personality. Self-administered scales have been devised for determining which of the four styles a person prefers (Kilmann and Thomas 1977; Rahim 1986). However, situational forces are undoubtedly more important than stylistic preferences, especially when groups instead of individuals are in conflict.

Multidimensional scaling of a number of data sets suggests that conflict style is a function of two independent dimensions: concern for self and concern for others (Van de Vliert and Kabanoff 1990). The approximate location of these strategies in the space formed by these dimensions is shown in figure 1. Contending involves high concern for self and low concern for others, problem solving involves high concern for self and others, yielding involves high concern for others and low concern for self, inaction involves low concern for both self and others. Rubin, Pruitt and Kim (1994) call this the dual-concern model of strategic choice.

The dual-concern model is also useful for predicting the impact of *envi-*

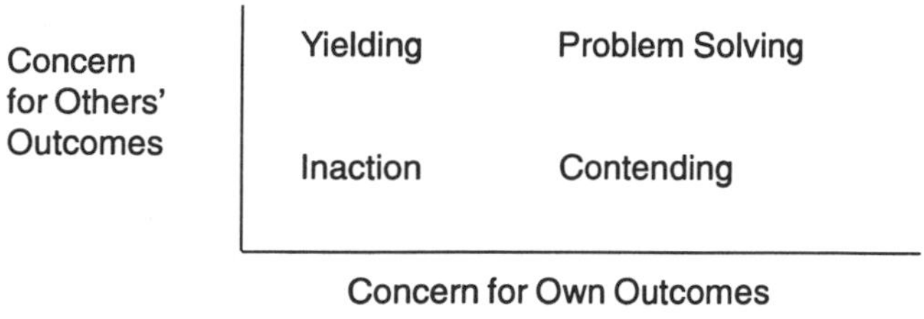

Concern for Others' Outcomes	Yielding	Problem Solving
	Inaction	Contending

Concern for Own Outcomes

Fig. 1. The dual-concern model of strategic choice

ronmental forces on strategic choice. For example, a good mood tends to encourage a concern for others, while high aspirations encourage a concern for the self. It follows that high aspirations alone should produce contending, good mood alone should encourage yielding, but the combination of the two should encourage problem solving. Evidence from one of our experiments supports these predictions (Pruitt, Carnevale, Ben-Yoav, Nochajski, and Van Slyck 1983). Of course, aspirations can be too high, precluding agreement. However, if they are within the realm of the possible, keeping them high on both sides increases the likelihood of achieving a win-win agreement, provided that the parties have a concern for one another's outcomes.

Another experiment in the same series looked at the relationship between negotiators and their constituents. Earlier findings (Pruitt 1981) had shown that highly accountable negotiators (those with low power in their own organizations) tend to have a high concern for their organization's outcomes and to be contentious in their approach. We (Ben-Yoav and Pruitt 1984) were able to show that this effect is quite different when there is concern for the other party's outcomes induced by future dependence on the other party. When high accountability was coupled with future interdependence, the result was a choice of problem solving and the development of win-win solutions. The practical message from this study is that a negotiation system is most effective when the negotiators on both sides are highly accountable back home but also have a continuing relationship with each other. This arrangement forces them to seek solutions that bridge both parties' interests. This message should be as applicable to international negotiation as it is to domestic negotiation.

Sources of contentious behavior. Research on the antecedents of individual aggression (Baron and Richardson 1994; Geen 1989) is relevant to people's decisions about contending. The stronger their impulse to aggress, the more likely they are to adopt a contentious approach, and the more extreme will be the contentious tactics they adopt. Hence, the greater will be the chances of escalation. Highlights of the findings on aggression are as follows:

Relative deprivation encourages anger and the impulse to aggress. The greater the deprivation and the more important the goals and standards that are frustrated, the stronger is this impulse. (Whether this impulse will be acted upon, and contentious behavior actually enacted, depends on the strength of inhibitions to be discussed below.) This anger is stronger and aggression more likely when relative deprivation is accompanied by:

1. A perception that the source of the frustration has acted intentionally and maliciously (i.e., not under the pressure of understandable environmental pressures). This point seems applicable to international relations; those who saw the Russian invasion of Afghanistan as a precursor of aggression against the West were more upset than those who attributed it to the impending collapse of the Communist government in Afghanistan.
2. Physiological arousal. In laboratory studies, arousal—produced by exercise, noise, or crowding—tends to summate with relative deprivation, producing a more extreme aggressive response. This suggests that aggressive reactions are more likely to occur in fast-moving international crises when it is not possible for decision makers to relax long enough to think things over coolly.
3. Aggressive cues—elements of the environment that remind people of aggression. This suggests that one should not hold an international conference in a room that has a mural of the Rape of the Sabine Women on the wall. Neutral, soothing colors would be better.
4. Aggressive models—other people who engage in aggression. This helps explain why protest movements often spread so fast—each group becoming a model for the next.

Research has also discovered conditions under which contentious and aggressive impulses tend to be *inhibited* and conciliation to be encouraged. These include:

1. Positive moods, due to humor, good food, and so on. Peters (1955), a labor negotiator and mediator, suggests that agreements are often reached in a pleasant relaxed atmosphere, such as a restaurant that is far from the formal negotiation setting. Parallels can be found in international negotiation.
2. Empathy toward the other party. A conciliatory spirit often ensues when one gains an understanding of the sources of the other's positions and actions (Johnson 1971a).
3. Individuation of the other party. Interpersonal aggression is easy when the other party is viewed as a group member—a type of person rather than an individual. Aggression is much more difficult when the

other seems unique (Worchel and Andreoli 1978). This implies that it will be harder to aggress against groups whose members stand out as individuals than groups that look like uniform sets of people. This argues for intercultural contact, though care must be taken to avoid culture shock and intergroup friction in such contacts (Kelman 1963).

4. Positive relations with the other party. These can result from positive feelings, or simply the desire for a working relationship in anticipation of future dependence on the other party.

5. Fear of retaliation from the other party (Baron 1971).

6. Incompatible activities. Many activities are incompatible with aggression, such as, in international relations, the manufacture of consumer goods and trade and finance with the other country. These should inhibit contending and aggression to the extent that they are important in a country's thinking.

7 The availability of other means of redressing relative deprivation. Research shows that aggression is more likely when frustrated people see no peaceful way to solve their problem.

The Quality of Relationships

Positive relationships between parties discourage the use of heavy contentious tactics and encourage problem solving or yielding. Problem solving, in turn, encourages the development of win-win solutions. Yielding can produce the same result in the long run, if practiced by both sides over a series of issues with each side yielding on issues where the other's interests are stronger. Negative relationships make agreements hard to reach and encourage escalatory spirals.

An important feature of relationships is that they tend to be stable over time. Positive relationships usually persist despite the occurrence of disagreement; negative relationships usually persist despite efforts to repair them. Four psychological mechanisms that account for this persistence have been spelled out by Cooper and Fazio (1979; see also Rubin, Pruitt, and Kim 1994). These mechanisms cause attitudes toward and perceptions of the other party to be self-reinforcing. They are:

1. The self-fulfilling prophecy (see Rosenthal and Jacobson 1968). People tend to be aggressive toward others they view as hostile, which encourages the others to retaliate, thus confirming the view of them as hostile. Likewise, people tend to behave positively toward others they trust, which encourages the others to reciprocate, thus demonstrating that they are worthy of trust.

2. Selective perception. People tend to notice things that fit in with

preconceptions (provided that they are not too divergent from what is expected) and ignore things that don't fit in (Hastorf and Cantril 1954).

3. Biased information search. When information must be sought, there is a tendency to ask questions that will elicit evidence supporting existing views (Snyder and Swann 1978).

4. Biased attribution. When other parties behave the way we expect, we tend to attribute that behavior to their inner dispositions, reinforcing our view of what they are really like. When they behave differently from expectation, we tend to attribute this behavior to environmental pressures and assume that it tells us nothing about what they are really like (Regan, Straus, and Fazio 1974). This effect has been demonstrated for distressed and nondistressed married couples (Holtzworth-Munroe and Jacobson 1988). Holsti (1962) has shown the same effect in international relations in a study of John Foster Dulles's perceptions of the Soviet Union. When the Russians behaved contentiously, Dulles announced that it confirmed their aggressive nature. When they behaved in a conciliatory fashion, however, he explained their behavior as due to circumstances, such as military weakness. In this way, he was able to maintain a stable view of the Soviet Union as a country bent on world domination.

These four mechanisms have the effect of prolonging good relations with another party while making bad relations hard to change. In intergroup and international relations, these mechanisms are supplemented by group norms, which make it hard to voice views that are opposed to the general consensus.

Conflict Resolution

Lessons learned. What can be learned about resolving conflict from the points made so far? A number of practical ideas emerge from this psychological perspective:

1. Blurring intergroup boundaries. One can try to develop cross-cutting group memberships or to show each side that they are similar to the other—especially in the realm of attitudes and values (see Byrne 1971).

2. Encouraging perceived common ground. When people have goals that require cooperation or depend on each other for future favors, they are less likely to aggress against each other. The effect is likely to be even stronger if they actually engage in cooperation (see Johnson, Johnson, and Maruyama 1984).

3. Encouraging individuation of and empathy toward the other party. The image of Gorbachev in a Western-style hat traveling around the world with a wife in designer clothes did wonders for softening perceptions of the Soviet Union during the Reagan administration.

4. Encouraging activities that are incompatible with aggression—for example, manufacturing consumer goods, trade, and foreign investment.

5. Encouraging a good mood in potentially hostile interchanges.

6. Diminishing psychological arousal during periods of interpersonal and intergroup tension. Decision makers in these settings need time out to rest and think clearly.

7. Encouraging the other party to believe that its basic goals can be accomplished by means other than contending. For example, in negotiation, it is often wise to demonstrate concern for the other's interests and flexibility about the shape of the final agreement. If this stance is combined with a clear and firm dedication to one's own basic goals, the result is likely to be problem solving rather than contending on the other side (Rubin, Pruitt, and Kim 1994).

Unilateral conciliatory initiatives. When relationships are heavily strained, as a result of much prior escalation, the self-reinforcing mechanisms described earlier make them hard to change. The parties seem doomed to continuing or worsening struggle. Every issue, however minor, becomes a new battleground. How can such a situation be turned around?

Osgood (1962) has suggested the value of a series of unilateral conciliatory initiatives from one of the parties. These should be designed to cut through the thickets of distrust that characterize such relationships. They should be unexpected and dramatic, so as to counteract selective perception and encourage the other side to rethink the relationship. Such rethinking is particularly likely if these initiatives continue over time and involve apparent risk to the actor taking them. Examples of such initiatives in international affairs include Sadat's trip to Jerusalem (Kelman 1985) and the series of unilateral actions Gorbachev took to end the cold war.

There is evidence that unilateral initiatives work best when they come from powerful parties whose behavior cannot be interpreted as a simple sign of weakness (Lindskold and Bennett 1973).

Hurting stalemate. Contentious conflicts, in which the parties are trying to win, tend to de-escalate when a hurting stalemate arises—that is, when both parties perceive that further gains are not possible and that costs are persistent or rising (Touval and Zartman 1989). Hurting stalemates encourage unilateral initiatives as well as receptivity to these initiatives. They also encourage receptivity to third-party intervention. Hence, third parties are often well advised to wait for the development of a hurting stalemate before trying to intervene.

One source of a hurting stalemate is a "power balance" such that neither side has the capacity to force its will upon the other or take the other for granted. A historical effort to arrange such a balance can be seen in Kissinger's intervention to prevent Israeli destruction of the Egyptian army at the end of the October War. With the Egyptian army intact, Israel had to fear Egypt just as Egypt had to fear Israel. This action paved the way for subsequent mediated negotiation and for Sadat's later unilateral initiatives and Israeli receptivity to them.

Negotiation. Negotiation involves verbal interchange aimed at reaching agreement to resolve a conflict. All four of the strategies described earlier are possible in the arena of negotiation, but contending tends to be relatively mild (for example, military initiatives are less likely when negotiations are going on) and problem solving is encouraged.

There is large literature on negotiation including both practical (Fisher and Ury 1981; Zartman and Berman 1982) and theoretical (Druckman 1977; Pruitt 1981; Pruitt and Carnevale 1993; Rubin and Brown 1975; Walton and McKersie 1965; Zartman 1978) contributions. Some of this literature has a solid empirical base, but it mainly consists of informed speculation. Parts of this literature seem useful for understanding international negotiation, including the following.

1. Research on reflective (active) listening. Reflective listening involves solid attention to what the other party is saying coupled with efforts to accurately verbalize the other's positions and feelings. This strategy has several virtues (Johnson 1971a). It allows one to gain valid information about the other's position, while reassuring the other about one's interest and concern. However, a negotiator must be careful not to seem too warm in reflecting the other's position, because this may be interpreted as a sign of weakness (Johnson 1971b). What is needed is a cool but accurate summary of the other's viewpoint. As a result, the other is likely to see one as concerned about both parties' needs, encouraging the other to switch to problem solving.

2. When issues become complex, a formula-detail sequence is often useful (Zartman 1978). First a relatively succinct agreement in principle is developed, providing a sketch of the high points in the final agreement. This formula is usually developed by the top negotiators. The details of the agreement are then worked out in the context of this framework, often by subordinates.

3. A typology of win-win agreements has been developed, as a checklist,

by Rubin, Pruitt, and Kim 1994. The types are: expanding the pie, compensation, cost cutting, logrolling, and bridging. These authors suggest refocusing questions that can be posed to help discover each type of agreement.

4. Negotiators are more likely to make concessions that imply giving up gain rather than incurring loss (Neale and Bazerman 1991). This suggests the value of redefining issues in terms of relative degrees of gain.

5. There has recently been considerable interest in second-chance negotiation. Agreement is first reached and then the negotiation is reopened in an effort to improve on that agreement. In the second phase, it is understood that either party can insist on the first agreement. The value of this procedure is that the second phase encourages a trusting atmosphere, since neither party can force the other to accept an unfavorable agreement (Ury, Brett, and Goldberg 1988).

6. The discovery of win-win solutions is aided by a careful analysis of the interests and assumptions underlying both parties' positions. Computer-assisted procedures are now available for such purposes.

Third-party Functions. A literature on the psychology of mediation has also recently developed (Kressel and Pruitt 1989). For example, research on mediator tactics in domestic settings shows the following:

1. Mediator empathy encourages joint problem solving and results in high-quality agreements (Zubek, McGillicuddy, Peirce, Pruitt, and Syna 1992).

2. Sharpening issues and developing agendas also encourages high-quality agreements (Carnevale, Lim, and McLaughlin 1989; Zubek et al. 1992).

3. Mediators should modulate their interventions to the progress made by the disputants. If disputants are moving toward agreement, they should keep quiet; if not, they should intervene (Donohue 1989).

This research is in its infancy, but is making good progress.

Challenges for the Future

Psychological theory of the kind just described has two limitations in its application to international conflict. One is that it largely concerns dyads—the relations between two parties. Yet international diplomacy often involves larger groupings, such as multilateral conferences. The other is that it ignores collective decision making—the political and bureaucratic processes that go on within groups, organizations, and countries as they generate strategies for dealing with each other.

To remedy these deficiencies, we probably need a systems model that views the parties as segments of a larger communication network that is seeking a general consensus (Pruitt 1994). To develop such a model, it would make sense to do a broad study of communication and decision making in and around a multilateral international conference. The study would involve periodic interviews with diplomats from several key countries and the people they deal with back home. A multidisciplinary, multinational team of scholars should do this study. I sense a readiness for such a study among scholars both here and abroad.

REFERENCES

Baron, R. A. 1971. "Magnitude of victim's pain cues and level of prior anger arousal as determinants of adult aggressive behavior." *J. Personality and Social Psychol.* 17:236–43.
———. 1994. *Human Aggression.* 2d ed. New York: Plenum.
Ben-Yoav, O., and D. G. Pruitt. 1984. "Accountability to constituents: A two-edged sword." *Organizational Behavior and Human Performance* 34:282–95.
Byrne, D. 1971. *The Attraction Paradigm.* New York: Academic Press.
Carnevale, P. J. D.; R. G. Lim; and M. E. McLaughlin. 1989. "Contingent mediator behavior and its effectiveness." In K. Kressel, D. G. Pruitt, and Associates, *Mediation Research,* 213–40. San Francisco: Jossey-Bass.
Cooper, J., and R. H. Fazio. 1979. "The formation and persistence of attitudes that support intergroup conflict." In W. G. Austin and S. Worchel, eds., *The Social Psychology of Intergroup Relations,* 149–59. Monterey, CA: Brooks/Cole.
Crosby, F.; P. Muehrer; and G. Loewenstein. 1986. "Relative deprivation and explanation: Models and concepts." In J. M. Olson, C. P. Herman, and M. P. Zanna, *Relative Deprivation and Social Comparison,* 17–32. Hillsdale, NJ: Erlbaum.
Donohue, W. A. 1989. "Communicative competence in mediators." In K. Kressel, D. G. Pruitt, and Associates, *Mediation Research,* 322–43. San Francisco: Jossey-Bass.
Druckman, D. 1977. *Negotiations: Social Psychological Perspectives.* Beverly Hills: Sage.
Dube, L., and S. Guimond. 1986. "Relative deprivation and social protest: The personal-group issue." In J. M. Olson, C. P. Herman, and M. P. Zanna, *Relative Deprivation and Social Comparison,* 201–16. Hillsdale, NJ: Erlbaum.
Fisher, R., and W. Ury. 1981. *Getting to Yes: Negotiating Agreement without Giving In.* Boston: Houghton Mifflin.
Geen, R. G. 1989. *Human Aggression.* Milton Keynes, England: Open University Press.
Gurr, T. R. 1970. *Why Men Rebel.* Princeton, NJ: Princeton University Press.

Hastorf, A. H., and H. Cantril. 1954. "They saw a game: A case study." *J. Abnormal and Social Psychol.* 49:129–34.

Holsti, O. R. 1962. "The belief system and national images: A case study." *J. of Conflict Resolution* 6:244–52.

Holtzworth-Munroe, A., and N. S. Jacobson. 1988. "An attributional approach to marital dysfunction and therapy." In J. E. Maddux, C. D. Stoltenberg, and R. Rosenwein, eds., *Social Processes in Clinical and Counseling Psychology*, 154–70. New York: Springer-Verlag.

Johnson, D. W. 1971a. "Role reversal: A summary and review of the research." *International Journal of Group Tensions* 1:318–34.

———. 1971b. "The effects of warmth of interaction, accuracy of understanding, and the proposal of compromises on the listener's behavior." *J. Counseling Psychol.* 18:207–16.

Johnson, D. W.; R. Johnson; and G. Maruyama. 1984. "Goal interdependence and interpersonal attraction in heterogeneous classrooms: A metanalysis." In N. Miller and M. B. Brewer, eds., *Groups in Contact: The Psychology of Desegregation*, 187–212. New York: Academic Press.

Kelman, H. C. 1963. "The reactions of participants in a foreign specialists seminar to the American experience." *Journal of Social Issues* 19:61–114.

———. 1985. "Overcoming the psychological barrier: An analysis of the Egyptian-Israeli peace process." *Negotiation Journal* 1:213–34.

Kilmann, R. H., and K. W. Thomas. 1977. "Developing a forced-choice measure of conflict-handling behavior: The 'MODE' instrument." *Educational and Psychological Measurement* 37:309–25.

Kressel, K., D. G. Pruitt, and Associates. 1989. *Mediation Research.* San Francisco: Jossey-Bass.

Lindskold, S., and R. Bennett. 1973. "Attributing trust and conciliatory intent from coercive power capability." *J. Personality and Social Psychol.* 28:180–86.

Neale, M. A., and M. H. Bazerman. 1991. *Cognition and Rationality in Negotiation.* New York: Free Press.

Osgood, C. E. 1962. *An Alternative to War or Surrender.* Urbana, IL: University of Illinois Press.

Peters, E. 1955. *Strategy and Tactics in Labor Negotiations.* New London, CT: National Foremen's Institute.

Pruitt, D. G. 1981. *Negotiation Behavior.* New York: Academic Press.

———. 1991. "Strategies and negotiation in international negotiation." In V. A. Kremenyuk, ed., *International Negotiation: Analysis, Approaches, Issues.* San Francisco: Jossey-Bass.

———. 1994. "Negotiation between organizations: A branching chain model." *Negotiation Journal* 10, no. 3(July): 117–30.

Pruitt, D. G., and P. J. Carnevale. 1993. *Negotiation in Social Conflict.* Pacific Grove, CA: Brooks/Cole.

Pruitt, D. G.; P. J. D. Carnevale; O. Ben-Yoav; T. H. Nochajski; and M. R. Van Slyck. 1983. "Incentives for cooperation in integrative bargaining." In R. Tietz, ed., *Aspi-*

ration Levels in Bargaining and Economic Decision Making, 22–34. Berlin: Springer-Verlag.

Rahim, M. A. 1986. *Managing Conflict in Organizations.* New York: Praeger.

Regan, D. T.; E. Straus; and R. Fazio. 1974. "Liking and the attribution process." *J. Experimental Social Psychol.* 10:385–97.

Rosenthal, R., and L. F. Jacobson. 1968. *Pygmalion in the Classroom.* New York: Holt, Rinehart and Winston.

Rubin, J. Z., and B. R. Brown. 1975. *The Social Psychology of Bargaining and Negotiation.* New York: Academic Press.

Rubin, J. Z.; D. G. Pruitt; and S. H. Kim. 1994. *Social Conflict: Escalation, Stalemate, and Settlement.* 2d ed. New York: McGraw-Hill.

Snyder, M., and W. B. Swann, Jr. 1978. "Behavioral confirmation in social interaction: From social perception to social reality." *J. Experimental Social Psychol.* 14:148–62.

Tajfel, H., and J. Turner. 1979. "An integrative theory of intergroup conflict." In W. G. Austin and S. Worchel, eds., *The Social Psychology of Intergroup Relations,* 33–47. Monterey, CA: Brooks/Cole.

Touval, S., and I. W. Zartman. 1989. "Mediation in international conflicts." In K. Kressel, D. G. Pruitt, and Associates, *Mediation Research,* 115–37. San Francisco: Jossey-Bass.

Ury, W. L.; J. M. Brett; and S. B. Goldberg. 1988. *Getting Disputes Resolved: Designing Systems to Cut the Costs of Conflict.* San Francisco: Jossey-Bass.

Vanbeselaere, N. 1987. "The effects of dichotomous and crossed social categorization upon intergroup discrimination." *European J. Social Psychol.* 17:143–56.

Van de Vliert, E., and B. Kabanoff. 1990. "Toward theory-based measures of conflict management." *Academy of Management J.* 33:199–209.

Walton, R. F., and R. B. McKersie. 1965. *A Behavioral Theory of Labor Negotiations.* New York: McGraw-Hill.

Worchel, S., and V. A. Andreoli. 1978. "Facilitation of social interaction through deindividuation of the target." *J. Personality and Social Psychol.* 36:549–56.

Zartman, I. W. 1978. *The Negotiation Process.* Beverly Hills: Sage.

Zartman, I. W., and M. R. Berman. 1982. *The Practical Negotiator.* New Haven, CT: Yale University Press.

Zubek, J. M.; N. B. McGillicuddy; R. S. Peirce; D. G. Pruitt; and H. Syna. 1989. "Short-term success in mediation: Its relationship to disputant and mediator behaviors and prior conditions." *J. of Conflict Resolution* 36:546–72.

CHAPTER 6

Conflict Provention as a Political System

John W. Burton

"Provent" is included in dictionaries to mean provant, or food, and is a term no longer in use. "Pro" has the connotation, moving ahead of, as in progress. Provent is reinvented for our purposes as a means of distinguishing decision-making processes aimed at merely "preventing" conflicts by coercive means, such as police in the streets, from those that seek to eliminate the causes of conflicts by looking ahead and dealing with their sources. In this article it is argued that there is a logical extension of conflict resolution processes to *pro*ventive decision making at all social levels, including the political.

Societies, universally, are experiencing the failure of authorities to preserve law and order and, thereby, to ensure an absence of conflict, domestically and internationally. What are the reasons for failure of systems and within systems? Does an extension of conflict analysis and resolution, as it has now evolved, offer the basis of a *pro*ventive system to replace the traditional authoritative, and now failing, *pre*ventive system?

Tradition

Philosophers have, almost unanimously, given support to the view that "the notion of authority is that some person is entitled to require the obedience of others regardless of whether those other persons are prepared to find the particular order or rule enjoined upon them as acceptable or desirable or not ..." (Lloyd 1964).

This notion of authority was to be applied, of course, only where there was a recognized and legitimate authority, as in the family, in social and industrial institutions and in political systems. It was not intended to apply to the international system of independent nation-states, there being no central authority entitled legitimately to require and to enforce obedience.

The empirical evidence is now that this notion of a legal authority, that assumes both wisdom and the power to apply it despite objections, is a philosophical invention that is impractical not only in international relations but also in domestic relations at all social levels: the assumption seems no longer to be valid that that which is not acceptable or desirable can be enforced.

Whether this is so because recent developments in communications and the availability of modern weapons have made resistance more effective and because of some recent deterioration in social and moral values or whether it is due to some more fundamental error that was present in traditional thinking that should now be identified needs to be answered before any practical options can be explored.

The Separation of National and International

The philosophical position outlined by Lloyd justified the making of a clear distinction between national and international politics. There was domestic law and order provided by an obligation to obey an authority with a monopoly of enforcement powers and an international system that rested on the relative economic and military power of its members along with some measure of agreed norms in shared functional activities, such as transport and communications. National and international politics were separate studies with different norms and assumptions.

The League of Nations was, after World War I, an attempt to establish an international system that would at least promote functional agreements, but it fell far short of being an authority in the Lloyd sense. With the outbreak of World War II went the hope that a central coordinating organization could be a means of promoting law and order. The lawyer Hans Morgenthau had held this belief, but with the outbreak of war he became the author of the dominating text of the time, *Politics among Nations: The Struggle for Power and Peace* (1948). In this book, by contrast, he canvassed the view that what order there might be in the international field could be due, in the absence of a central authority with enforcement powers, only to power balances plus perhaps some functional agreements of universal convenience. While law and order prevailed in the sovereign state (and its colonies), in the international system there was no controlling authority, making domestic and international politics two distinctly different types of system.

International relations was researched, taught, and practiced in this political power frame with a focus on strategic studies and decision making at an international level, with little attention given to domestic politics. There were anomalies that are now surfacing. The nation-state was, and is still, assumed to be a relevant autonomous unit even when comprised of different ethnic groups. Majority government within a nation-state was, and still is, assumed to be "democratic" even when its authority rules over such ethnic and other nonrepresented minorities. On the other hand, ethnic, geographical, or other political units, previously included within such a nation-state, having gained their independence over time by defying authoritative controls, have in many cases achieved the status of a nation-state, thereby freeing themselves of unacceptable authoritative controls.

This anomaly is a special feature of the postcolonial era. Given population distributions and boundaries determined by past colonial aggressions, the trend toward independent autonomies will continue. It can continue by violence or, alternatively, the inevitable could be brought about by processes that lead all concerned to acknowledge mutual advantages in a nonviolent transition.

The Assumption That Deterrence Deters

This anomaly, freedom acquired by defying authorities that claim a legal right to require the obedience of others and by coercion if they object, exposes an assumption that is hidden away in philosophies and underpins both the notion of legitimate authorities and of power balances as a means of political control. This is the assumption that deterrence deters.

So much was this a consensus that the United Nations Charter was drafted on the assumption that the domestic system of authority was the ideal: it entailed an enforced law and order. Those who were responsible for the Dumbarton Oaks draft of the charter sought to apply this ideal system to the international level.

There were only fifty or so sovereign states at the time, and the balance of power in the post–World War II era was clearly with those nations that drafted the charter, provided that they operated as a combined force. Unlike the League of Nations, the United Nations was to have a Security Council that would control world affairs as a legitimized authority. Each would have a veto to ensure that they worked together. At no session at the Charter Conference at San Francisco was the idea of this central authority, relying on enforcement capabilities, questioned. Neither was it questioned in academic studies at that time.

The sponsoring powers failed to work together, and the cold war set in. But even had they worked together they would have failed in their task. Korea and Vietnam, among other situations, were in due course to suggest that the basic, but unstated, assumption of this philosophical power approach—that authority prevails and deterrence deters—was false, at least at the international level. The widely accepted "power politics" approach to international relations was undermined.

In present times, of course, it is difficult to argue that the conventional view expressed by Lloyd, implying that deterrence deters, applies at the domestic level either. The causes of crime, aggressions, and violence in relationships at all levels are up for exploration. The separation of that which is domestic from that which is international on law and order grounds is no longer tenable, for deterrence has not been seen reliably to deter at either level.

If this is so, and if societies truly wish to avoid violence and conflict generally, the questions to be posed are why authoritative deterrence does not always deter, and how can *pro*vention be introduced nationally and internationally so as to avoid the need for what seems to be failed authoritative coercion?

Shifts in Thinking

It is useful to trace out the main stages in changes in thinking that were brought about by the observation of these realities. When the observation was first made in the early 1960s that deterrence does not necessarily deter, there was turmoil. The international relations community feared that all of its texts and teaching notes, reflecting very much the power political "realities" of Morgenthau, were being questioned. There were personal confrontations at special national meetings of international relations teachers. Those who were questioning the power politics frame were challenged to make a case study, and to come up within twelve months with an alternative that could be examined.

The case study chosen was the then contemporary conflict between Indonesia, Malaya, and Singapore. Official nominees of the parties were brought together in London before a group of eight or so international relations teachers. The intention was merely to learn more about the nature of conflict and why, in particular, power balances had not deterred. What transpired was a major surprise to all the academics in that the parties saw this meeting as a means of resolving their conflict and, indeed, did so.

This direct contact with parties to a conflict, themselves also for a first time in a direct face-to-face relationship, was a revealing experience for all concerned. International relations was no longer seen to be about relationships between states with different power capabilities. There were people involved! These people were not just representatives of institutions called "states": they were people who had strong feelings about minorities, competing cultures, foreign interventions, and other conditions that gave rise to domestic insecurities and fears for the future, leading to armed conflicts with neighbors. Ethnic identities were clearly a source of security and had to be preserved. Migrant communities and their external affiliations were a concern. A human element had been introduced into international power politics!

All disciplines had their own abstract construct so they could be more precise, quantitative, and "scientific." Sociology, like law, had a construct that was malleable and could be coerced into conformity. Morgenthau had given international relations a construct, "Aggressive Man": man is aggressive, therefore, the state is aggressive. But these experiences of direct interaction by and with parties to a conflict introduced real persons in off-the-record, exploratory, analytical, and facilitated discussions.

Introducing Conflict Resolution

From here on the academic participants became interested in "conflict resolution" rather than international relations as such: how to deal with situations when the deterrence strategies do not work. More importantly, why do they not work? Other conflicts were examined by the same processes with the help of U.S. and other scholars.

Johan Galtung was making clear his concerns about "structural violence," suggesting that conflict was not necessarily because "man is aggressive" as Morgenthau had us believe (1969). These conflict resolution exercises confirmed this and led to insights into structural reasons for conflict. While, however, the parties concerned were able to reperceive and redefine their relationships and arrive at resolutions of their problems, there was still no explanation as to why and in what circumstances deterrence did not deter. There was, therefore, no basis for a theory of conflict or conflict resolution, or any guide to preventive policies.

There was already disquiet in some of the academic community about the unreal nature of separate disciplines and their constructs. In 1979 there was a conference in Berlin of scholars from many countries, attended also by Galtung, at which an attempt was made to delve beneath separate disciplinary constructs and to find just what was the nature of this human being that had been so much a victim of "structural violence" and who could, it was thought, be deterred and made to conform. Their approach, published in 1980 (edited by Lederer) was called "Needs Theory."

Several Centers for Conflict Analysis and Resolution had been established in different countries, one of which was at George Mason University, Virginia. These had a focus on process but no theoretical frame, giving an impression of "do-gooders" rather than making a serious attack on a major problem. In 1988 the Berlin group was invited to meet with the George Mason Conflict Resolution group, and their papers were published in 1990 (Burton 1990). This conference had far-reaching consequences for conflict resolution, both in theory and in practice.

Needs Theory

Before outlining some of these consequences it is as well to explain needs theory. It is a theory of behaviors that challenges the widely accepted assumption that human behaviors are wholly malleable. It is no more than an attempt to put into the various disciplines, and especially conflict analysis, a real person rather than an abstract construct. It draws attention to those ordinary and well-recognized needs, such as for personal identity and recognition, that are so often frustrated by institutions and political structures, leading to aggressive responses. Maslow and many psychoanalysts have postulated needs, from physical to relationship needs. In most cases the assumption persisted that such needs were malleable, that "social consciousness" and "morality" can by choice and, indeed, should, lead to self-control and social conformity.

Needs theory was intended merely to go one step further and to argue that the empirical evidence is there are some fundamental needs, such as individual and identity groups needs, that are compulsive and *will* be pursued regardless of cost.

This implies that, if conflicts are to be resolved and provented, institutions may sometimes have to be adjusted to human needs rather than the other way around. Clearly, there is no precise definition of needs, only an assertion that there are some behaviors that cannot, in certain circumstances of structural violence, be controlled by threat or coercion. Added must be the observation that while such behaviors may have been suppressed in the past for periods of time by slavery and conditions giving rise to apathy, with universal communications and the availability of means of violence this is no longer possible.

So, some thirty years after the assertion was made that deterrence does not reliably deter, there was now some explanation. It had far-reaching consequences.

Disputes and Conflicts

First, it was now clearly necessary to make a distinction between "disputes" and "conflicts," that is, situations that could be dealt with by coercion, or by negotiation and compromise, on the one hand, and those in which there could not be compromise and that had to be treated as a problem to be resolved to the total satisfaction of all the parties concerned. Disputes involve negotiable interests and roles, conflicts involve inherent needs. Authorities could impose certain controls affecting interests. But the person could no longer be treated as though behavior were wholly malleable: there were limits to the capacity of the individual or identity group to accommodate to authoritative demands.

Translated into real life this means that unemployed youths, denied a role in society, are likely to join street gangs and find their own role by violence with others or in other ways, and no controls can prevent such behaviors. Other opportunities have to be created. It means that ethnic minorities will not, and probably cannot, accept a minority role and will seek separate autonomies. It means that a great power cannot by threat or by the employment of force suppress independence movements or even coerce changes in the policies of other nations.

A Challenge to Legal Processes and Its Alternatives

Second, this analytical approach was an immediate challenge to the then growing "peace studies" community, interested mainly in arms control and disarmament, and to others who took the idealistic view that merely with goodwill many conflicts could be resolved. It was also a challenge to the growing dispute settlement school of thought that sought to develop alternatives to legal processes. These still included bargaining and negotiation but paid little attention to hidden fears and motivations that could not be revealed in a power negotiation as this would be a sign of weakness. These different schools of thought are yet to be brought together in some commonly accepted frame.

Breaking through System Levels

A third consequence of needs theory was that it drew attention to the similarities of conflict and its sources at all system levels, from the family to the international. Offering significant aspects of the real person to replace separate constructs was a means of cutting through the boundaries of disciplines. Leadership problems, probably the most serious sources of many ethnic conflicts, are no different, in a needs perspective, from personal problems in management and in family relations. Ethnic conflicts relate to street gang warfare as a means of recognition and identity.

Furthermore, there are revealed the relationships between different problem areas. Unemployment is an economic problem, but it is no less a social problem for it deprives individuals of their role and identity, leading to violence within a community as anger is transferred. Limited educational opportunities can be justified on financial grounds, but when the longer-term social consequences are costed, revisions are seen to be required. It is only when needs are identified and their frustrations taken into account that policies in any field are likely to shift from dealing with specific problems in isolation.

The Spillover of Domestic Politics to the International

A fourth consequence was the realization that behaviors were not only the same domestically and internationally but that international relations were very much the result of domestic problems, including problems of leadership. Conflicts were the consequence of trading policies being forced on others by more economically powerful states, of leadership behaviors designed to acquire electoral support, and of other such domestic problems. Studying international relations, including strategic studies, as a separate specialization and focusing only on the *results* of such domestic power politics behaviors, was clearly taking the separation of the domestic from the international to an extreme.

Toward Provention

But there were in needs theory even wider implications for conflict resolution. Conflict resolution commenced as a process by which a particular conflict might be analyzed and resolved. But given "structural violence," resolving one conflict would not provent others occurring. Dealing with one case of crime due to poverty, or one international conflict due to a leadership or an ethnic problem, would not provent many others occurring. Conflict resolution of this order was a limited contribution. To make a significant contribution it would have to enter into the decision making field at all social and political levels. It would have to provide a substitute for the power or we-they adversarial institutions that have evolved over time and that persist in legislatures, legal systems, in industry, and at all social levels.

Conflict Resolution as a Costing Process

Power political realists tend to react to conflict resolution as merely another form of idealism. But this misses the main thrust of conflict analysis as a process. There is no morality or ideology involved or even wishful thinking. The analytical conflict resolution process introduces another realism: it is essentially a costing process. It enables the parties to a conflict to perceive more accurately the issues that are usually hidden in a power bargaining situation. There can be a wage dispute, but underlying it there can often be found recognition and identity issues, wage demands being a form of protest and unlikely to resolve the problem. So it is with international disputes and conflicts. The Greek Cypriots assumed that the Turkish Cypriots sought union with Turkey, while Turks thought Greeks sought union with Greece. Interacting together in London in 1965 they discovered that both sought independence (Burton 1969).

In a limited way international corporations are beginning to do some costing. They are the most powerful of organizations in the emerging global economy. They must look to the future. Already they are giving thought to their role in environmental pollution and related problems, knowing full well that in the longer term these could be costly to corporations. This is the reason for the formation of the World Business Academy in California and Business for Social Responsibility in Washington, D.C. Even at the personal and small group levels conflict resolution processes rest on costing: reperceptions, reassessments of motivations, insights into behaviors, giving rise to reconsideration of policies and structures.

This costing element eliminates the power factor in the conflict resolution process. Parties, powerful and relatively weak, are able to reassess their policies in the light of new information. If such a process had been undertaken before the Vietnam war, for example, there would have been a reassessment in the light of what was discovered: that postcolonial Vietnam, like the nonaligned countries of Asia, no less regarded as Communist influenced by the United States, sought their real independence and would not be an agent of China. It took a lost war to provide an assessment of the widespread support given to those who were prepared to defy attempts by any foreigners to limit independence.

Costing is a usual process in decision making. But it has been limited within the power frame because of the assumption that, with sufficient power, submission can be achieved. There are, of course, still those in the strategic studies area who would argue that Korea and Vietnam could have been "won" if more force had been used. Winning, however, is difficult to assess. Wars can be won, and the peace can be lost. Japan lost the war, but it is far from clear that the cost to Britain was in the longer term worth the gains from the depression policies that excluded Japan from colonial markets that brought it into the war. What conflict resolution seeks to do is to enable direct and facilitated analysis of relationships—impossible within a traditional power politics frame. An important element in this costing is the introduction of behavioral dimensions that are excluded in power approaches.

In short, far from idealism, the attempt is made to bring together two apparently conflicting realisms: the realism of power politics leading to structural violence and the realism of the costs of the consequences of structural violence.

Conflict Resolution and Decision-Making Theory

Some element of idealism remains, however, unless, in addition to arriving at conflict resolution processes, and the discovery of viable options in the particular case, there can be consensus processes of change that remove sources of conflict, nationally and internationally.

What needs theory suggests is an approach to conflict of all kinds that *pro*vents conflict by eliminating the violence of structures, by eliminating the circumstances that give rise to crime and conflict. Conflict resolution thus becomes part of decision-making theory and practice. It is in this decision-making context that conflict resolution should now be assessed. It has the potential to fill a void. Power politics, domestically and internationally, have failed. Crime, violence, ethnic and leadership conflicts, large-scale corruption, and ecological disasters are a feature of national and global relations. There are fallback positions taken by military dictators and by governments that opt out and hand over to market forces. The desperate search is for a viable institutional and decision-making frame.

Decision-making theory was a core course in international relations during the 1960s. In retrospect it was the link between the power politics past and the future of the study. It has since not been a major interest, except perhaps in management studies. Yet it probably is the most important study in contemporary conditions. If there is to be consensus change toward a problem-solving system, then consensus change must be a *continuing* part of decision-making processes within all institutions, public and private. All systems have their faults. In changing circumstances in which reliable prediction is impossible, continuing reassessments of relevance are required. This requires consultative and informed decision making, not just top leadership initiatives within some traditional power frame.

Decision-making theory altered dramatically thirty years ago when Karl Deutsch published *The Nerves of Government* (1963), a book still within a power frame but a significantly modified one. His model was the war-time invention of electronic devices by which pilots could be made aware of clouds or obstacles ahead and divert around them, thus avoiding problems. This "feedback" mechanism became a central feature of his models. Rather than a simple stimulus-response model of decision making, in which power is employed to carry out a response policy, he introduced a preliminary or trial response so that there could be feedback from the target. Then there could be a reconsidered response.

Conflict resolution processes are of this order but going much further in the same direction. In a particular situation they provide facilitation by a third party to ensure a continuing interaction between parties in conflict, delving into perceptions and motivations more deeply than would be possible merely by diplomatic or short-term and emergency responses.

Domestic Institutions

It can be deduced that fundamental changes are required in our traditional we-they, adversarial decision-making institutions, taking conflict resolution into the field of political decision making and institutional change.

This is a field still to be explored. Clearly the ideal would be leaderships who were facilitators, legislatures that were nonadversarial and problem solving, legal processes that were analytical of behaviors, and industries that were less we-they in management and more participatory. These are, of course, just the changes that electorates are demanding. But what must be the directions of change, and by what processes can there be consensus and acceptance by those whose roles and interests would seem to be threatened?

The Global System

These considerations now must be made within an evolving global system that is significantly altering domestic politics. The sovereign state is no longer sovereign in the sense that term was employed before a global system emerged. No longer can a central national authority determine employment levels, establish minimum wage levels, provide social security, health, and educational benefits, without having in mind the competitive nature of global markets and the transfer of routine labor to undeveloped countries.

Fascism, the corporate state, evolved in Italy before World War II. The corporate state is now widespread not merely nationally but internationally. There will be no going back to the free market notion of competition. Oligopolies and monopolies dominate, with clusters of fragile small businesses supplying some local services. The global system is now fascism. It has its positive attributes, including cheaper production costs, and even opportunities for undeveloped economies to make some limited progress. It can cater to the requirements of a large proportion of industrial labor, perhaps providing desired securities. But it is in no position to cater to the needs of that 15 to 20 percent of people who are left as long-term unemployed in developed countries and of unemployed youth who normally seek routine jobs before finding a career opportunity. Fascism in Italy left a large proportion of the labor force with no option but to join the army, and a role had to be found for it. Nation-states within this emerging global economy are being faced with the same problem. So far it has not been tackled except by greater and greater reductions in welfare, health, and education expenditures, and increased numbers of police and jails. It is still less in a position to do anything about conditions of tribalism and poverty in the underdeveloped world.

The traditional adversarial institutions of government cannot cope with this emerging economy. Far more serious and analytical discussion is required than emerges in party political systems. A conflict resolution problem-solving frame is one in which reassessments of the relevance of separate institutions can take place.

The United Nations

The United Nations has been the main casualty of this separation of the international from the domestic. It still operates mainly as the means of preserving sovereign states and their inherited boundaries, all resisting demands for separate autonomies. Its means are peacekeeping and peace en-forcement. It has no professional facilitators who could assist in resolving problems. Indeed, whether it be Cyprus or Sri Lanka there would be resistance to such facilitation within the frame of the United Nations for fear it might lead to separate autonomies.

The United Nations commenced as an organization of fifty or so nation-states. The postcolonial era has led to this number being more than trebled. Many, perhaps a majority, are defending, sometimes at great cost in lives and resources, boundaries and their discriminatory institutions. This is especially so of members of the Organization of African Unity. These domestic prob-lems are the source of much international conflict, and to provent conflict they have to be resolved. In the best of circumstances the postcolonial adjust-ment will be a prolonged and costly process. But a major contribution could be made by the United Nations facing up to the problem and actively antici-pating ethnic and related conflicts, and facilitating problem-solving processes. Peacekeeping and peacemaking are no solution. Already they and the relief services necessary once conflict occurs are beyond the willing capacities of other member states.

Probably there must be established a nongovernmental organization (NGO) for these purposes, available, not just to the United Nations but more importantly to parties in conflicts that would be prepared to meet informally, preferably secretly, to explore options in this problem solving and costing mode. (The processes that such an NGO would follow, deduced from conflict resolution theory and practice, have been spelled out in some detail in a handbook *Resolving Deep-Rooted Conflict* and reprinted as an appendix in *Conflict: Practices in Management, Settlement and Resolution* (Burton 1987, 1990).

The Future of Conflict Resolution

Perhaps it could be argued that the final goal of conflict resolution as a study is to phase itself out as the human dimension is included in separate speciali-zations. In a sense this is happening. Quite different disciplines are teaching the subject. Not only could conflict resolution be phased out in this way but so could international relations as a separate discipline. Michael Banks has contributed an article, "The International Relations Discipline: Asset or Li-ability for Conflict Resolution" (1986). It raises an even more important question, whether international relations as a study is an asset or liability in helping to analyze and to resolve pressing domestically triggered international problems.

A Challenge to the Academic Community

Conflict resolution has the potential to be a viable option to an inherited and failed power political system. It has the potential both to help eliminate the structural violence that is the consequence of a history of power politics and to offer alternatives to the adversarial systems that are an inherent part of power politics.

One must conclude that there is now a tremendous challenge to the academic community to give a lead toward less adversarial institutions nationally and internationally and to promote problem solving as a process. Education along these lines has commenced at the primary school level but as yet has not advanced much further. Appropriate texts, lectures, courses, radio discussions, media articles, and even works of fiction are required for families, students at all levels in all studies, police, administrators, lawyers, industrial managers, and a threatened middle and upper "class." An insecure public awaits such a lead.

REFERENCES

Banks, M. 1986. "The International Relations Discipline: Asset or Liability for Conflict Resolution." In E. Azar and J. Burton, eds., *International Conflict Resolution*. Brighton: Wheatsheaf.

Burton, J. W. 1969. *Conflict and Communication: The Use of Controlled Communication in International Relations*. New York: Free Press.

———. 1987. *Resolving Deep-Rooted Conflict. A Handbook*. Latham, MD: University Press of America.

———, ed. 1990. *Conflict: Human Needs Theory*. New York: St. Martin's Press.

Burton, J. W., and F. Dukes. 1990. *Conflict: Practices in Management, Settlement and Resolution*. New York: St. Martin's Press.

Deutsch, K. 1963. *The Nerves of Government*. New York: Free Press.

Galtung, J. 1969. "Violence, Peace and Peace Research." *Journal of Peace Research* No. 3.

Lederer, K., ed. 1980. *Human Needs: A Contribution to the Current Debate*. Cambridge, MA: Oelgeschlager, Gunn and Hain.

Lloyd, D. 1964. *The Idea of Law*. London: Pelican.

Morgenthaw, H. 1948. *Politics among Nations: The Struggle for Power and Peace*. New York: Knopf.

Part 3

Conflict Resolution in the
Global Arena: Opportunities
and Obstacles

CHAPTER 7

Why Global Conflict Resolution Is Possible:
Meeting the Challenges of the New World Order

John A. Vasquez

As the Berlin Wall came down, pulled apart by individual hands with the powers that be looking on, a host of issues that had dominated the history of a generation in the East and the West went off the global agenda. Gradually in their place new issues have captured the world's attention—some, intractable struggles of the past, like the civil war in Yugoslavia and the ethnic disputes in Armenia and Azerbaijan, and others, the effects of local ongoing rivalries, like the Persian Gulf War. The end of the cold war has provided a new opportunity for peace and consensus among the strongest states in the system. At the same time, this change in the global order has made for new violence among states that are less powerful and has given rise to nationalist claims. Can conflict resolution, its practice and theory, provide any insights and guidance for this new global era? This chapter argues that it can and identifies those aspects of theory and research that are most relevant.

Applying conflict-resolution techniques has both political and intellectual obstacles that must be overcome. Many of the political obstacles, such as the rivalry of the superpowers that encouraged and supported conflict between states and factions, particularly in the third world, have come to an end with the end of the cold war. That rivalry was the real reason there was so little use of conflict-resolution techniques in the past thirty years; the superpowers were not committed to ending conflict in a particular area—such as Angola, Cambodia, or Central America—but to winning at the expense of the other side. Such an environment is clearly not conducive to the application of conflict-resolution approaches.

With that obstacle pushed aside, this chapter will look at the most important intellectual obstacles facing the use of conflict-resolution approaches in global politics. The chapter has three purposes. First, to examine and refute realist objections that conflict resolution cannot be applied to global problems because international politics is fundamentally different from domestic politics and what has worked in the context of a society ruled by a formal government will not work in the context of a global anarchy. Second, to develop a theoretical framework for analyzing the dynamics of conflict that can explain conflict in either the domestic or global context. Third, to identify the most pressing issues for maintaining peace in the post–cold war era and show how conflict resolution can address those issues in a manner that helps to both prevent and mitigate war.

The Unrealism of Realist Objections to Conflict Resolution

Strange as it may seem, the most fundamental objection to the use of conflict resolution in global politics has been conceptual. The argument usually made by realists is that conflict resolution is not feasible and will not work. Hence, there is little use in yet another idealistic effort to apply techniques developed in the context of a domestic political system to the anarchy of global politics. The failure of the League of Nations, the realist argument goes, should have put an end to all that nonsense.

Within intellectual circles, particularly in the United States, attempts to apply conflict resolution to global politics have often been cavalierly dismissed because proponents of these techniques are often seen as naively believing that the fundamental struggle for power underlying international politics can somehow be ameliorated. Most objections to global conflict resolution are based on the assumption that world politics is fundamentally different from all other politics and will, unless radically changed, remain an arena inhospitable to attempts to apply conflict-resolution techniques to all but the most routine issues. Both classical realists, like Hans Morgenthau (1960), and neorealists, like Kenneth Waltz (1979), maintain that a struggle for power is inherent in international politics, because it is an anarchy—that is, there is no overall government to prevent states from doing whatever they please. Given the pernicious nature of humanity, politics, which is always a struggle for power (Morgenthau 1960, 27), becomes at the global level a deadly game in which nothing can prevail against force as effectively as force. There is no higher court of appeal, no government of overwhelming force that can protect the weak from the strong. In this context, each state can rely only on itself. To survive, power must be met with power, or in the technical parlance of neorealism, the system encourages states to either balance power or be crushed (Waltz 1979).

This description of what the world would look like without government is a Hobbesian view. As with Hobbes, each individual member of a system (in this case states) is seen as self-seeking. For Morgenthau (1960, 31–35) states are motivated by some sort of drive for power; for Waltz (1989) they are motivated by the fear of insecurity and a drive to survive. In either case, the assumption is made that states respond primarily to power and, in the absence of the kind of overwhelming power embodied in government, there can be no regulation of acts of force, coercion, and violence. The absence of government, technically defined as anarchy, means a Hobbesian state of nature where each member is at each other member's throat, and life is indeed nasty, brutish, and short.

This assumption is inherent in the logic of both Hobbes and realists, and without it, much of their political theory is hard to derive. The absence of government (defined as anarchy), however, does not logically entail the violence and chaos of the Hobbesian state of nature (also defined as anarchy). Whether absence of government entails violent chaos is not something that can be determined by the meaning of words, but is something that must be ascertained on the basis of an empirical examination of the evidence. The realist case appears persuasive in light of its view of human nature because it takes two distinct referents of the word, *anarchy*—absence of government and violent chaos—and collapses them into a cause-effect relationship.

Yet even the simplest and most cursory view of history does not reveal anything like a constant Hobbesian state of nature. To be sure, there are wars and many nasty things that occur in global politics, but wars, revolutions, violent crimes, and many other nasty things also occur in the realm where formal government reigns. The presence of government does not ensure the absence of nasty things; nor does the absence of government ensure the presence of nasty things.

Kenneth Waltz (1979, 102), the contemporary thinker most associated with deriving an explanation of international politics from the image of anarchy, assumes that the absence of hierarchical government means a violent chaotic Hobbesian state of nature. Lack of formal government, however, does not necessarily mean lack of order (chaos)—for order can and does emerge without the presence of government. Waltz's (1979, 88–93, 119–121) own speculations on the balance of power explain how anarchy produces a pattern of behavior in which states automatically balance each other.

If one kind of order can emerge out of chaos, why can't another? I, along with other nonrealists, have two major disagreements with Waltz on this question. The first is to deny that the kind of balance of power order Waltz sees as emerging automatically actually does emerge and work in the lawlike fashion Waltz describes. The second is to deny that only one kind of order can or does emerge in the modern global system from 1495 to the present. Unlike most realists, I assume that the global system is, in part, a social construction in which beliefs, norms, and practices can under certain conditions come to constitute a global culture that patterns behavior, giving it an order.

Realists do not lend much credence to the role of rules and institutions in producing peace because they see the heart of international politics as consisting of a struggle for power within anarchy. Waltz's (1979) reformulation of classical realism, in particular, places great emphasis on the structural anarchy of the system as an explanation of behavior. Yet, is the global system fundamentally anarchic? If one means by anarchy the absence of hierarchical domestic-type government, then it is; but if one means the absence of all governance and order, then it is not (see Bull 1977). Despite the analogy to domestic government, most realists, including Waltz, use the term *anarchy* to mean not simply the absence of hierarchical government, but the presence of a Hobbesian state of nature.

In the modern global system since 1495, anarchy, while present at times, has not been as pervasive as Waltz would have us believe. Global society does not permit states to go to war for just any reason; it identifies either through law or intellectual argumentation the casus belli and legitimate reasons for war (see Johnson 1975, 1981, in this volume). One of the reasons Waltz underestimates the amount of order in the system is that he treats the anarchy/order distinction as a dichotomy, when it is better seen as a continuum. Major wars have given rise to world orders (although not world governments) and most wars are not fought in conditions of anarchy, but within a regional or global order that shapes the way in which the war is fought (see Doran, in this volume). The kind of anarchy Waltz and Hobbes talk about only emerges with the complete breakdown of a political system, and this can occur at either the domestic or the international level, a point Waltz (1979, 102–4) is willing to grant. When it occurs at the domestic level, the result is civil war or social revolution; when it occurs in the global system, the result is world war.

To place great emphasis on global anarchy is to obscure the existence of important pillars of order in the global system. As Campbell (1989, 104) astutely observes, the defining characteristic of the international system since the sixteenth century has been capitalism, not anarchy. Capitalism is not anarchic in the sense of being chaotic and without order, nor does it survive very well in a violent Hobbesian world. The emergence of capitalism gradually produced a world economy (see Wallerstein 1974). Also beginning in 1495, there evolved a political structure of independent modern nation-states that was legally institutionalized in the Peace of Westphalia (1648) and for which realism provided an ideology. These historical events substantiate the claim that the interstate system is a constructed and contingent condition founded at a specific period of history and with changing characteristics. The presence of nation-states in a capitalist world economy demonstrates that the absence of government does not mean the absence of order.

Nor does the absence of government make for inevitable violence or a constant state of war. Despite realist claims to the contrary, peace is possible in the global system. Peter Wallensteen (1984) has shown that there are distinct periods of peace between 1816 and 1976, during which war did not occur between the strongest states in the system—1816–48, 1871–95, 1919–32, and 1963–76. More interestingly, he determines that what distinguishes these periods of peace from periods of war is the attempt by major states to develop rules of the game to guide their relations. This finding is consistent with the notion that peace is something that is learned and constructed, not something that simply happens.

Finally, the absence of (formal) government does not mean the absence of governance. Government is only one way of making authoritative decisions. International actors have developed other forms of organization and informal "decision games" (see Mansbach and Vasquez 1981, 282–87) for resolving issues. Sometimes these involved important security issues or what is called "high politics." The most obvious example of this is the Concert of Europe (1815–48 or so), which served as a way by which the elite made important political decisions through a process of consensus building, bargaining, and compensation. In our day, the G-7 has often served as a way of governing aspects of the world economy. The GATT provided a more formal mode of governance for trade.

If the objection to conflict resolution is that techniques at the domestic level cannot be adopted at the global level because the international structure is anarchic, then this objection does not apply because the contemporary international system does have an order to it. It cannot be assumed, as realists often do, that the boundary between anarchy and hierarchy is coterminous with the boundary between domestic politics and international politics. This can be seen to be the case, since many domestic states often break down into anarchy, even though they still have a formal government. Some domestic societies, like Lebanon, Northern Ireland, and even El Salvador in the 1980s more exemplify the kind of Hobbesian anarchy realists assume than the international system does. Indeed domestic systems, in part because there are so many more of them, more frequently break down than does the international system. Thus, it should come as no surprise that the number of civil wars and cases of civil strife has exceeded the number of interstate wars.

None of this means that conflict-resolution techniques will not work better in a system that has a number of channels and practices for resolving disputes, as well as norms limiting violence.[1] If a society has a firm legal structure implanted and that structure decrees that certain kinds of cases not be handled by the court, but by professional mediators or arbitrators, then these channels will be more widely used than if the structure simply makes them available to interested parties (see Bush, in this volume). Likewise, a structure like nineteenth-century America, which outlawed attempts by labor to organize or to employ any tactics like strikes that would allow them to gain their ends, will encourage the adoption of violent means. Conversely, the creation of new channels that had not previously existed, such as collective bargaining, legalized unions, the National Labor Relations Board (NLRB), can do much to end management-labor strife and violent class conflict. Structure is important, but not fixed. It can change.

The main task is to discuss how system structure can offer both incentives and barriers to conflict resolution. This is a much better way of conceptualizing the problem rather than seeing the international system as fundamentally different. This is a task that both Johnson and Doran in the next two chapters will address.

The major conceptual problem is not transferring techniques and theory from the domestic to the global level, but applying knowledge of and experience with interpersonal relations to intergroup relations. Differences between individuals and collectivities is a subject of inquiry that has attracted considerable attention in some disciplines and is an area that those studying conflict resolution need to explore further (see Pruitt, in this volume). However, since domestic and global conflict resolution both deal with *intergroup* conflict, the problem of transferring knowledge about individuals to collectivities does not frequently present itself.

The realist focus on anarchy has obscured the real reason why conflict-resolution techniques did not enjoy wide currency in the cold war. The rivalry between the superpowers generally prevented them from working together to either resolve intractable disputes, as in the Middle East, or to impose settlements on weaker clients. Instead of trying to resolve issues, both superpowers exploited issues in the periphery for their own purposes as their weaker clients exploited the superpowers to prevent defeat. Once the cold war ended, Russia was no longer willing to support expensive allies either economically or diplomatically, so a number sued for peace. Through this process, peace broke out all across the system (see Rosenau 1991).

The above analysis suggests that, in order for conflict resolution to work, it must rely on the strong to intervene in disputes or at least for the strong to support third-party intervention rather than provide continued support to the combatants. Current cooperation between not only Russia and the United States, but among all major states, including China, provides a basis for a new historic consensus on the rules of the game. Such rules will evolve rather than being rationalistically constructed. Nevertheless, as they evolve, conflict-resolution techniques can be expected to provide an important diplomatic tool for resolving disputes among states. The specific areas in which these techniques can be expected to play a significant role will be addressed in the final section of this chapter.

While a number of traditional and time-tested techniques, like the creation of buffer states and the holding of international conferences, are now possible because of a consensus among major states, this book seeks to explore the development and adaptation of new techniques. Learning to improve the way we make peace involves improving our knowledge of conflict processes and making better use of that knowledge in the way in which conflict resolution is applied and practiced. Before turning to the challenges posed by attempting to create a new world order, the next section looks at the importance of conflict theory for the practice of conflict resolution. It points out the need for a common framework that can deal with the dynamics of both domestic and global politics, and outlines one framework to illustrate the feasibility of applying social psychological approaches (used in domestic conflict resolution) to interstate relations.

Toward a Unified Theory of Conflict

The analyses presented in the previous chapters were a result of a series of multidisciplinary seminars in which the participants discussed the various ways that conflict resolution is conducted and studied in different contexts. All of the participants agreed that, in order to conduct conflict resolution successfully, it was necessary to have some knowledge about the causes and dynamics of conflict, as well as the factors that would promote settlement and resolution. Yet, it became clear that there was no single guiding theoretical approach and that some efforts were more informed by theory and research than others.

This multiplicity provides an important opportunity for learning, particularly since some disciplines, especially social psychology and sociology, seem to have a more comprehensive and developed theory of conflict resolution than do others, especially law, international relations, and history. There are important exceptions to these tendencies, in that legal training within the United States has begun to give some attention to conflict resolution, although often with an emphasis on practice rather than theory. Also, international relations inquiry has seen calls for a paradigm shift away from realism (Burton et al. 1974; Burton, in this volume; Vasquez 1983a; Banks 1985), and important work on interstate conflict resolution (Patchen 1988; Mitchell and Webb 1988), negotiation, and bargaining (Raiffa 1982) has been conducted, even if it has been at the margins of the discipline. International relations, law, and history would benefit greatly from a systematic exposure to and integration of the more developed theories of conflict and conflict resolution within psychology and sociology.

Popular discussion of highly salient domestic and interstate disputes is often conducted in terms of broad, sweeping claims about human nature without much knowledge of the social science research (or biological research) on human behavior in the last fifty years (see Masters 1989). Sometimes this extends to academic disciplines. The traditional realist belief that domestic politics is fundamentally different from international politics, for example, has blinded many scholars to the possibility that a unified scientific theory of conflict may be possible. Theory and research on conflict, particularly the escalation of conflict to violence, in psychology, sociology, and international relations suggest that the dynamics of conflict and the ways in which it can be resolved are not so different that they cannot be explained by a single theory with the proper caveats.

It is possible to learn from each other and develop a common framework for studying such questions as: What are the sources of conflict and how do they vary by context? How and why does conflict unfold and escalate to violence? What types of issues are associated with violence? What structural factors inhibit the use of violence and encourage the use of other mechanisms or techniques for resolving conflict? What are the characteristics of peaceful systems? What psychological processes are associated with the use of violence? Once collective violence erupts, how can it be limited or ended? How can crises that are prone to escalation to violence be prevented from arising or, failing that, how can they be managed once they emerge? What role can negotiation and third-party intervention play in these processes?

Despite the extensive work done on conflict resolution and conflict theory, there has been surprisingly little analysis of the concept of conflict itself. Here some of the theoretical work in international relations on the relationship between conflict and cooperation may be of help. A growing body of research on interstate interactions suggests that the dynamics of conflict are separate from the dynamics of cooperation (Rummel 1972; Ward 1982). This means that conflict should not be seen as simply the opposite of cooperation. The research also implies that the factors producing conflict are not just the opposite of the factors that produce cooperation. Learning how to avoid conflict, then, does not mean that we will automatically learn how to cooperate or make peace. Avoidance or prevention of conflict may be but a prerequisite to learning how to live peacefully. More importantly, the fact that conflict and cooperation are separate and uncorrelated dimensions means that conflict need not be abolished in order to have cooperation. Conflict can occur within the context of a cooperative relationship and cooperation can occur within the context of conflict (see Axelrod's [1984, chap. 4] discussion of cooperation among soldiers on the Western front in World War I).

Although such a conceptual distinction may seem obvious, it can have important implications. For example, it is often charged that conflict resolution assumes a harmony of interests and fails to understand that, in politics, conflict is inherent and can never be eliminated because there will always be fundamental conflicts of interest (see Carr 1939). Peace, however, does not require the elimination of conflict, it only requires that the conflict be resolved nonviolently or with minimal force.

If conflict and cooperation are multidimensional concepts that are separated, it is necessary to identify the different dimensions and suggest how they might interact. The work of Mansbach and Vasquez (1981, chap. 7) on global conflict and cooperation provides a framework for doing this. We argue that cooperation and conflict consist of three dimensions that refer to distinct aspects of behavior and that need to be untangled before they can be recombined to see how conflict is related to cooperation. These dimensions are: (1) agreement versus disagreement (a similarity or difference in *opinion* or, more technically, in the issue position of actors), (2) positive versus negative acts (*behavior* that is seen as either desirable or undesirable), and (3) friendship versus hostility (*attitudes* reflecting psychological affect).

One of the benefits of this framework is that it permits a theory of the dynamics of conflict that is informed by social psychology to be applied at the interstate level so that it is possible to tell whether a unified theory might have any plausibility. Making this kind of case is essential if the conceptual barriers between social psychology and international relations theory are to be broken down. The remainder of this section will outline a theory that can analyze the dynamics of conflict and cooperation across levels of analysis and thereby help move discourse toward a common framework by integrating the insights from a variety of approaches.

Mansbach and Vasquez (1981, chap. 7) argue that how the three dimensions of conflict and cooperation interact is crucial for deciphering how a *relationship* emerges out of contention. It is important to understand what shapes and changes relationships because most theorists believe that the underlying relationship between disputants is the key for resolving conflict (see Burton 1984; Burton, in this volume). It is assumed that differences in opinion (agreement-disagreement) shape behavior (i.e., the pattern of positive and negative acts), and behavior determines psychological affect (friendship and hostility). One of the great ironies of human interaction, pointed out by Coplin and O'Leary (1971, 9), is that conflictive (i.e., negative) acts are intended to change issue positions, but instead change affect. Typically, if an actor tries to resolve a disagreement on a salient issue by punishing another actor, this will generate hostility rather than any shift in issue position.

Spirals of conflict or cooperation occur when all three dimensions reinforce each other over time. In a conflict spiral, disagreement leads to the use of negative acts, which in turn produces hostility. The presence of hostility encourages more disagreement, which, if it persists, leads to a vicious cycle of disagreement, negative acts, and hostility. One should not try to explain the pattern of negative and positive acts, but how "normal" interactions give rise to cooperative or conflictive spirals, and the effects these spirals have on determining the overall relationship between two actors. This underlines the point that *behavior* is something that comes out of and shapes a relationship.

Actors do not simply behave conflictively or cooperatively; they *relate* to each other in conflictive or cooperative ways. A relationship involves all three dimensions—a pattern of agreement and disagreement, a pattern of exchanging positive and negative acts, and the residual attitude of friendship or hostility generated by the previous two patterns.

Mansbach and Vasquez (1981, chap. 7) use this conceptual analysis to develop a theory of conflict and cooperation that delineates how each of the dimensions of conflict affects how actors contend over issues. It is important to keep in mind that the pattern of friendship and hostility that emerges out of the pattern of agreement/disagreement and positive/negative acts has a tremendous impact on how the disputants define the issues dividing them. The underlying perceptual foundation of an issue (or technically the *issue dimension* that links stakes together [see Mansbach and Vasquez 1981, 60]) can run the gamut from an extreme actor dimension, where the emphasis is on who is getting what with the focus on enemies and friends, to an extreme stake dimension, where the focus is on what is at stake and there are no permanent friends or enemies.

Contenders that link stakes together on the basis of an *actor dimension* will have a large number of stakes in a few issues. Conversely, issues that are defined on the basis of a *stake dimension* will consist of a relatively small number of stakes that are brought together on the basis of some obvious substantive focus and/or geographical location (arms control in Europe, trade {or monetary] questions among OECD states). The hallmark of intractable conflict, whether it be at the interpersonal, intergroup, or interstate level, is that issues are defined on the basis of an actor dimension. Indeed, as conflict intensifies, all issues may be collapsed and linked into a single grand issue— us versus them.

According to this theory, whether an actor dimension or a stake dimension is present has profound effects on how issue positions are determined, the types of stakes that are discussed, the kinds of proposals that are made for the disposition of these stakes, and the general pattern of cooperation and conflict that emerges in contention. The issue position an actor takes can be said to be a function of the decision-making calculus the actor employs for determining whether it is for or against a given proposal. There are three such calculi: (1) a *cost-benefit* calculus, in which actors determine whether they are in favor of or opposed to a proposal on the basis of the costs and benefits they would accrue if the proposal were adopted; (2) an *affect* calculus, in which actors determine whether they are in favor of or opposed to a proposal on the basis of whether their friends or enemies are in favor of it: and (3) an *interdependence* calculus, in which issue positions are determined on the basis of what effect the position on this issue will have on *other* issues on the agenda (see Mansbach and Vasquez 1981, 191–97 for elaboration). Those involved in intractable conflict usually adopt a negative affect calculus rather than a cost-benefit or interdependence calculus. Individuals that employ a negative affect calculus favor any position that will hurt their opponents and oppose any position that will help their opponents.

A relationship that is characterized by a consistent use of the negative affect calculus over time will lead each actor to link more and more stakes into a single issue, since the issue is being defined simply as what hurts one's opponent. As a result, the type of stakes under contention changes, with concrete stakes becoming infused with symbolic and transcendent importance. As actors become increasingly concerned with relative gain and loss, stakes that may have had comparatively minor value are now seen as having great importance because they represent a commitment to larger stakes. Thus, West Berlin in the 1960s became worth risking a nuclear war, because it was symbolic of America's defense of Europe. Eventually, the contention between the two actors may take on the characteristics of a titanic struggle between two ways of life or even between good and evil, particularly if leaders of a group find it necessary to rationalize their policies with a higher purpose in order to mobilize domestic actors to make sacrifices for the coming struggle. Thus, when parties involved in negotiation speak publicly they often resort to name calling and make little progress. (Similar effects may occur in interpersonal disputes where an audience is present.) When such highly moralistic and/or ideologically sharp language is introduced, then the contention can be seen as involving transcendent stakes.

As one moves from concrete to symbolic to transcendent stakes, issues become more intangible and hence less divisible. What little research there has been on issues shows that the more tangible an issue, the greater the likelihood of eventual resolution, while the more intangible, the more contentious and conflict-prone an issue is (Vasquez 1983b; Henehan 1981, 13). Because some types of stakes are inherently more resolvable, the type of stakes over which actors contend will have an important effect on their interactions. Concrete stakes, because they are tangible and divisible, are more likely to permit compromise. Symbolic stakes make actors less flexible and more willing to stand firm because their symbolic nature leads to fears about losing a reputation for credibility or of establishing a bad precedent, if they entertain concessions necessary to bring about a compromise. Issues involving transcendent stakes are the most difficult to resolve, because they reflect fundamental differences over values, norms, and/or rules of the game.

Contention that focuses primarily on symbolic and transcendent stakes will tend to be intractable. A relationship that is dominated by them will produce conflict that tends to fester and escalate. In order to resolve issues, actors indicate how they would like the stakes under contention to be distributed. Proposals for the disposition of stakes can be analyzed in terms of the way in which they propose to distribute costs and benefits between the contending parties. Initially, in any contention, a side may suggest that it get most, if not all, of the benefits and the opponent bear most of the costs. Actors that contend over symbolic and transcendent stakes will not move from their initial issue positions because of the feeling that "my claims are just and yours are not." Negotiation may be further hampered when proposals of both sides take on the characteristics of a zero-sum game.

The key to whether a proposal will produce agreement and a resolution of the issue or foster disagreement and stalemate is how it assigns costs and benefits. Table 1 shows that there are four ways in which costs and benefits can be distributed—each side shares equally in the costs and the benefits (cell I); each side gets equal benefits, but one side bears more of the costs (cell II); or the reverse, each side shares the costs equally, but one side gets more benefits (cell III); and finally one side gets most of the benefits and the other bears most of the costs (cell IV). Proposals that are most apt to give rise to protracted disagreement are those in cell IV, because they call for a severely disproportional distribution of costs and benefits, with zero-sum proposals being but the most extreme of this type.

Transcendent and symbolic stakes usually give rise to type-IV proposals. Successful negotiation and attempts to find win-win solutions typically entail transforming initial type-IV proposals to one of the other types. Some kinds of issues are more amenable to such a move than others—depending on the salience (importance) of the issue, the type of stakes that compose it, and the variety and number of stakes linked in an issue. Those issues that link a large number of stakes that are infused with symbolic and transcendent significance are highly unlikely to be the subject of serious negotiation without being fundamentally redefined (i.e., defused of their emotional content and delinked from each other). Since this is often inherently difficult and politically infeasible, some issues simply cannot be negotiated, but must be fought out.

If this theory is correct, the key to nonviolently resolving such issues is either to have a procedure that can impose a settlement, like a court order, or, if that is not possible, then to get the parties to stop suggesting type-IV solutions and get them to propose more equitable solutions. It is in such a situation that mediation or problem solving (see Fisher, in this volume) by a

Table 1. Types of Proposals for Disposing of Stakes

Distribution of benefits	Distribution of costs	
	Equal	Unequal
Equal	I	II
Unequal	III	IV

Source: Vasquez and Mansbach 1984, 427.

third party may help move negotiation along or provide a way for disputants to come to a solution that their hostility and domestic commitments (if groups are involved) prevent them from proposing (see also Kolb and Babbitt, in this volume). A conceptual analysis of this sort makes it clear that it is the proposals about how to resolve the issue and not necessarily the issues themselves that are zero-sum. Both theoreticians and practitioners are finding that, for many disputes and deep-seated conflicts, win-win solutions can be developed, although table 1 makes it clear that some may win more than others.

The above analysis illustrates that if we have a theory about the dynamics of conflict, it will facilitate attempts to resolve intractable conflicts. Although there is no single scientifically corroborated theory, the construction and testing of such theories do inform practice and increase our understanding. The only point here is that such efforts will be more useful if they build on each other and, in particular, if their theorizing and research is more fully integrated with the work in social psychology. The work in that area has been significant, and one of the main tasks that needs to be done is to see how and whether theory and research in social psychology can be applied to other disciplines and contexts. Such efforts are best initiated through multidisciplinary discussion and collaborative research.

Preventing and Mitigating War in an Era of New Nationalism and Ethnic Conflict

As we enter a new historical era, the prospect for peace among the major states is quite high. The dangers to peace lie not in major-state confrontation, but from wars among less powerful states, ethnic disputes, and rising nationalism. In a new era when rules have changed, theory is one of the few guides available, and if it is a good theory it will not only be able to identify the major issues facing conflict resolution, but also offer solutions. The closing section of this chapter will identify the major challenges facing conflict resolution in the new world order and outline some of the ways conflict-resolution theory can help practitioners meet those challenges, especially that of preventing and mitigating war.

The issue politics theory of conflict outlined in the previous section demonstrated how a number of conflict resolution techniques outlined by Kolb and Babbitt, Kriesberg, Pruitt, and Burton (all in this volume) can be of use in the global arena. A theory of conflict, however, is not a theory of war. A theory of conflict does not distinguish between conflict that may end in war, like that preceding World War I, and conflict that does not, like Soviet-American conflict in the cold war. Because conflict resolution has not developed a theory of war, its basic strategy has been to prevent or end war by reducing the underlying conflict. Such an approach, although necessary, is very arduous and imprecise, because not all conflict may have the same potential for violence and because the variables that convert conflict into violence have not been specified.

Elsewhere (Vasquez 1993, chap. 4), I have argued that of all the issues over which humans could logically fight, territorial issues seem to predominate. In fact, most issues do not give rise to interstate wars unless they are linked with territorial claims. Thus, it is probably not an accident that research has found that most interstate wars start between neighbors.[2] Similarly, although there has not been any systematic research on the question, many internal wars are over the control of territory by certain ethnic or regional groups.

Not all territorial disagreements, however, become protracted disputes that result in war. Much depends on how states learn to handle territorial issues and the underlying needs that motivate claims. This provides an opening for conflict-resolution theories to apply their insights and techniques within a broader understanding delineated by peace research on war.

If this analysis is correct, then *conflict resolution should place a special emphasis in its research and practice on territorial issues*—why they arise, the underlying needs they represent, the kinds of norms that govern their disposition, how they become linked with other issues, and the extent to which they are susceptible to different social constructions—in short, how they are handled and the relationship between how they are handled and peace and war.

The existing theoretical understanding about the relationship between territory and war is that all other factors being equal, states or other sovereign groups, like tribes, will use aggressive displays to demark boundaries. This process does not have to result in war, but for many nation-states in the modern global system it usually has at some point in their history. Once boundaries are established by being accepted as legitimate by both sides, then war or the threat of war need not dominate the relationship of the two sides (see Kocs forthcoming, for evidence). Indeed, the explanation postulates that the threat of war goes way down even if the two neighbors have sharp disagreements over other issues, so long as those issues are not linked to territorial claims (see Vasquez 1993, chap. 4 for elaboration). This is a much more optimistic view of global politics, comparatively speaking, than the realist view, which sees international politics as a constant struggle for power (cf. Morgenthau 1960; Waltz 1979).

The recognition that boundaries are an important source of conflict has not been lost on practitioners. International law has recognized the importance of borders, and there is a fairly substantial body of laws governing this subject (see von Glahn 1976, chaps. 15–16). The presence of this body of law in the contemporary era has been useful and has helped frame conflict and put specific disagreements within a legal context (see Johnson, in this volume). This in turn constrains the circumstances and the rationale for the use of force.

While this has helped mitigate conflict and perhaps prevented some use of violence, it has done so mostly in disputes that are relatively minor and/or have already experienced some use of force already. Bikash Roy (1995) has shown in a series of case studies of North America, Russia, and the Indian subcontinent, that one of the major factors that separates territorial disputes that give rise to recurrent war and those that do not is the presence of ethno-national links in the disputed territory with one or both of the contending sides. He finds that the presence of those ties of identity transform the issue into a transcendent stake (as defined by Mansbach and Vasquez 1981, 62). This makes the stake very salient in the domestic politics of each side, helping to support the position of hard-liners.

On the basis of Roy's (1995) initial research, one would suspect that the ethno-national ties help produce the kind of conflict spirals delineated by the Mansbach-Vasquez explanation of conflict presented in the previous section. Once initiated, the conflict becomes self-amplifying. Thus, the presence of a transcendent stake leads to proposals to dispose of the stake in a zero-sum manner. This, of course, produces persistent disagreement, which in turn leads over time to a reliance on negative acts to force a change in the issue position of the other side. Negative acts among relative equals lead to an increase in psychological hostility rather than a shift in position. This in turn makes both sides define the relationship in terms of an actor dimension rather than a stake dimension, which encourages each side to link all the issues under contention between them into one overarching issue of us versus them, good versus evil. Further disagreement produces a vicious circle in which the issue reaches the highest levels of salience, infused with all kinds of transcendent significance, and becomes a powerful symbol in domestic political contention.

What the theory of war adds to these insights is that when the issue under contention involves a territorial stake, then the probability of a conflict spiral's eventually resulting in war goes way up. What makes the probability of war go up is how the territorial issue is handled by each side. A number of findings in peace research show that when relatively equal states adopt the practices of power politics to deal with issues, this leads to a series of steps that eventually produce a crisis that escalates to war. Each step brings the parties closer to war by making it more difficult for them not to take the next step toward war because of either the logic of the interaction and/or the domestic political reactions (Vasquez 1993, chaps. 5, 6). Nevertheless, there are many exits from the road to war and this provides conflict resolution with many openings to intervene and steer leaders and publics off that road and onto an exit.[3]

One of the great challenges for conflict resolutionists is to develop strategies of effective intervention at each of the critical junctures. Here the work of Fisher (in this volume), as well as Pruitt (in this volume) and Kolb and Babbitt (in this volume) are particularly relevant. Although such an analysis is beyond the scope of this chapter, by way of illustrating what is required, the following can be said: The primary goal of conflict resolutionists will be to break the vicious circle of spiraling conflict and reverse it to develop self-amplifying feedback in the direction of cooperation. This will be no mean feat, but at some point the dynamics of the model will push the parties forward and make the effort easier. The difficult task will be the initial change in direction.

Here research on previous transformations can provide guidance. For example, in terms of trying to thaw the cold war or of bringing about a Sino-American rapprochement, the strategy used by diplomats was to let the most salient disagreement become dormant and concentrate on defusing hostility by finding issues of moderate salience on which both sides could agree. This in turn generated some agreement and some positive acts. It also permitted issues to be de-linked, so that the more tractable could be negotiated on the basis of proposals that were not zero-sum. The de-linking of issues allowed concrete stakes to emerge and drain some of the symbolic and transcendent qualities from other stakes, but not all. This helped create a constituency for accommodation, while simultaneously reducing the influence of hardliners.

Of course, at some point the de-escalation process will involve internal political battles on each side, so that conflict resolution will remain an art and not a science (as witnessed by Jimmy Carter's recent efforts in North Korea and Haiti), but that does not mean that it cannot be informed by the findings of scientific research (as Carter's have been). The previous chapters in this book provide a number of insights on how to reduce hostility, find common ground on issues of moderate salience, and drain some of the transcendent and symbolic qualities from stakes.

While the conflict theory points to strategies for turning around the direction of a relationship, the theory of war underlines the importance of norms that govern the holding and transferring of territory. Since whether territorial issues will become resolved by the use of force depends on how they are handled, the presence and nature of norms on territory hold the key to preventing war, at least from a theoretical point of view. There is some research to support this theoretical deduction. It has been found that the presence of ambiguous norms provides openings for the use of force and violence.

Norms can be ambiguous in two ways—because a situation arises that is not covered by the norm or because competing norms emerge. Luard (1986,

87, 110) shows that when each of these situations occurred in Western history, wars were more likely. Thus, until the rise of nationalism in Europe, most territorial transfers were guided by principles of dynastic succession. So long as a son was the clear inheritor of the sovereign, there was little conflict over succession and the transfer of territory. This norm was recognized by all the sovereigns, including neighbors who may have coveted a particular parcel. If, however, the norm was ambiguous in a certain area, for example when no son was present and only a daughter was available to inherit, as was the case with Maria Theresa (empress of Austria), or there were multiple legitimate heirs, then war could break out (Luard 1986, 87). Likewise, if a new norm should arise to challenge the old norm, then all kinds of territorial disputes could break out because no single norm would be accepted as legitimate. This is precisely what happened with the rise of nationalism. Nationalism challenged the norm of dynastic succession, which gave rise to numerous territorial claims and wars to settle those claims (see Luard 1986, 110). Because of this outcome, war was able to sustain the norm of nationalism as governing the holding and transferring of territory.

As a norm, nationalism maintains that any given nation (defined as a people of common origin, language, culture, and/or identity) is entitled on the principle of self-determination to govern itself, which means to have its own sovereign state. This norm has been so ingrained in modernity that it is taken as a natural ethical principle and rarely examined critically. If the territorial explanation of war is correct, however, the new nationalism of the post–cold war era raises important questions about this norm, in terms of its overall ethical consequences.

This is because the principle of nationalism, if carried to its logical conclusion, would render asunder a number of states and generate a host of new states. Given the fact that there are upward of 5,000 "distinct communities" in the world (Gurr and Scarritt 1989, 375), if even a fraction of them claimed territory, this would put the world in great turmoil. The ethnic conflict in the former Soviet Union and in the former Yugoslavia underline the dangers of the norm. The new nationalism increases territorial disputes and the prospect for war in two ways—first it sets up territorial issues within states, and second, once those states achieve some kind of independence, it increases the total number of states in the system.

One of the firm scientific findings uncovered by peace research is that there is a strong relationship between the number of states in the system and the number of wars and militarized confrontations in the system (Small and Singer 1982, 130, 141; Gochman and Maoz 1984, 592–93; Maoz 1989, 202). This relationship holds because new states must secure their boundaries with their new neighbors. The new states may not be satisfied with their new boundaries, because of ethno-linguistic ties to people living in neighboring states and/or because older states may not accept the boundaries of the new state. One of the greatest challenges facing the new world order is that the existing norms of nationalism and self-determination are fragmenting states. This will lead to civil and interstate wars because the norms disrupt the legitimacy of existing boundaries and generate territorial disputes.

Once this challenge is theoretically understood, it is possible to develop solutions that have a chance of actually working to solve the underlying causes of violence. Three obvious solutions suggest themselves: First, contest the norm of nationalism as the foundation for holding territory, because following it out to its logical conclusion will create smaller and smaller states, one for every identity. Second, develop procedures for dealing with ethnic conflict and territorial disputes that can address the needs and interests of contending parties and produce peaceful change; that is, procedures and rules that can resolve conflict and/or settle disputes (Burton, in this volume). This will help prevent some wars, but more importantly provide ways of mitigating and limiting wars so that they do not become a fight to the finish. Third, work in the long term to "de-territorialize" identity, as a way of both de-linking it from violence-prone territorial issues and contesting the norm of nationalism. Each of these solutions will be examined briefly.

It behooves scholars to take a critical look at the norm of nationalism in terms of the practical effects of logically applying it across the board and in terms of its purported consequences and the reasons for adopting it in the first place. Clearly, the claims for national unity that all people of the same nationality should have the right to govern themselves stirred people in the nineteenth century and created an emotional bond among people who spoke the same language yet were divided by state boundaries, such as Italians and Germans. In some areas, such as Italy, this claim had an extra force, because parts of the nationality were governed by foreigners—for example, the Austrians. Connected with the latter was the idea that self-government would mean justice not only in the intrinsic sense of self-determination, but also in terms of social justice and economic well-being.

Claims for the new nationalism can be challenged on two grounds. First, in the postmodern world of philosophy as opposed to the modern world of the Enlightenment, the very idea of nationality no longer holds the intellectual force it once did. All identity, including nationality, is now seen as a social construction. People, and sometimes even groups, are seen as having multiple identities. The question of identity is no longer a question of birth or biology, but a question of choice. Second, it is not clear, as the globe has moved to a single world economy, just what kind of sovereignty and political and economic cohesion the proliferation of a number of small states would engender. In the world economy, even fairly strong states like France, Italy, Britain, Chile, India, and Nigeria, have difficulty making all the decisions that will have a major impact on their economy and standard of living—decisions on inflation and employment, for example. Weaker states are often at the mercy of the IMF and World Bank, or G-7. There is a distinct tension between the new nationalism and the historic forces of global economic integration and regional political integration. This is illustrated in the bittersweet Serbian quip that in the year 2025 there will be only seven states in Europe, the EC and the six former republics of Yugoslavia.

Given the short-term negative impacts of extending the norm of nationalism so that more and more states are created (and here we are probably talking about decades), scholars should rethink the legitimacy of the norm of nationalism. An alternative norm is that adopted by the Organization of African Unity, which froze all colonial borders despite their artificial nature. This norm has probably prevented many an interstate war, although not always internal wars, which often have tribal and ethnic roots. Adoption of this norm globally or in as many regions as possible would have certain obvious benefits in mitigating current conflict and preventing future wars. If war is associated with territorial claims and the number of states in the system, then freezing borders and the number of states obviously can prevent war, *if this new norm is accepted as legitimate* by political actors, or at least those that have a certain amount of power. Therein lies the rub.

The rub, however, poses a challenge to conflict resolutionists to make the new norm and its benefits more acceptable. What is wrong with imposing a new norm is that it creates a tension between the status quo and social change. Those who benefit from the status quo will like the norm; those who want their own state, like the Kurds, will not; and those who find themselves in new states, like Russian minorities and other groups in the new successor states of the former Soviet Union, will be wary.

This is the age-old problem in world politics of how to bring about fundamental change. One of the main functions of war has been to bring change and make binding decisions. Peace requires functional equivalents for both, if it is not to be hopelessly ideologically biased in favor of the status quo (see Bush, in this volume). The freezing of borders will not work, because those most hurt by it will not accept it, and without that acceptance war may not be prevented. To work, the freezing of borders must provide some procedure for peaceful change; thus what is really frozen is the use of force to change borders. International law can provide general rules, but these do not fit every instance. Here, the practices of conflict resolution, because they are various and informal, can be applied to the needs and political requirements of the individual case. In the end, the incentives to use nonviolent means are twofold: First, there is the frustration and suffering resulting from the failure of violence to achieve the ends of the groups that have used that approach, from Kurds to Basques. Second, a regional consensus on the norm of freezing borders supported by a global concert of power would provide political incentives and, potentially, punishments for violating the norm.

This suggests, of course, that the practices of conflict resolution must work within the larger context of the peace structure of the global system. A structure based on a kind of concert of power (see Kupchan and Kupchan 1991; Rosecrance 1992; Vasquez 1994) would probably be both the most effective and feasible for the new world order, particularly if it were legitimized by the United Nations as a whole. Nevertheless, there will be limits to the kind of punishment strong states will be motivated to impose. In addition, resorting to war to prevent war, to which collective security arrangements are always prone (see Betts 1993), seems both contradictory and self-defeating.[4]

A better and more feasible solution is simply to permit war to be used and then focus on limiting it both in terms of the way in which it is fought and its territorial scope, and the amount of aid, arms, and diplomatic support that will be provided by outside parties. Since it is difficult to eliminate all war, the emphasis should be on making war more like a boxing match and less like a fight to the finish.

Some of the most important rules to impose would be on limiting human atrocities, like those that occurred in the Bosnian war, and greater enforcement on treatment of refugees and prisoners of war. In terms of preventing such atrocities in the future, it would not be too far-fetched to have such rules and norms worked out among those in disputes beforehand. Part of the mitigation of war would basically involve a bargain between strong states and belligerents that they would not intervene if the war were fought according to preexisting rules; in other words, the war would be fought out on the basis of the strength of the protagonists. One thing strong states would not want to do would be to try to level the playing field or engage in other acts that would extend the length of the war and the human suffering involved in it. It would be much better if they would stand ready to impose the equivalent of diplomatic TKOs to end protracted wars where one side has clearly lost yet retains a viable military force.

In the long run, the best solution to prevent war from arising from ethnic disputes is to separate ethnic identity from territoriality. There is no logical reason why identity has to be attached to territory. Indeed, in the premodern era in Western history, identity and territory were not linked. Most empires did not require one to give up one's identity in order to live in a particular territory. In the most stable pluralist societies, like the United States, ethnicity is not associated with particular territories (regions) within a state. De-linking identity from territory would help reduce the probability of war. If it is the case that territorial issues are more prone to war than other issues, then one of the ways of reducing ethnic war is to separate identity issues from questions of territory; that is, to "de-territorialize" identity issues.

De-territorialization of identity issues would immediately reduce the zero-sum nature of many ethnic conflicts. When identity is linked with territory, the dispute more easily takes on a zero-sum quality because if one ethnic group gains a piece of territory, the rival group is seen as losing that territory for its own group. When identity is not linked with territory, no such inference need be made. The fact that I am an Italian need not diminish or rival the fact that you are Irish. Herein lies a role for problem-solving workshops. They can bring together individuals in ethnic conflicts to examine to what extent their identity need be threatened by the other's.

Even though identity is a social construction and it has not always been linked to territory in history, recent tradition and nationalist mythmaking, as well as existing norms, will make it difficult to de-territorialize identity issues. Yet the prospect of so many wars provides a rational basis for combatting these tendencies. The first step in that process is for scholars to critically examine the benefits of nationalism and the necessity of a territorial foundation of identity. Ultimately, however, as Burton (in this volume) tells us, any solution will work only if it truly resolves the conflict in a way that meets the fundamental needs of all sides. This will be no less true of the attempt to de-territorialize identity. Only if control of territory does not provide greater advantages—economic, social, political and cultural—for the group that controls the territory, will identity be able to be de-territorialized. In the interim, traditional diplomatic practices, like the creation of buffer zones, can help ameliorate the situation.

These suggestions should make it clear that not only is conflict resolution possible in global politics, but that it can offer specific solutions and strategies for dealing with some of the most intractable problems facing the new world order—nationalism and ethnic war.

NOTES

My thanks to Marie T. Henehan for valuable comments and suggestions.

1. This does not mean conflict resolution cannot emerge or work in the context of war. Much depends on whether the combatants have grown sick of the violent way they have been trying to resolve the issues that divide them. Zartman's (1989) conception of a hurting stalemate is based on the premise that there are only certain times in a violent conflict that are ripe for the use of conflict-resolution techniques.

2. Approximately 90 percent of the interstate wars fought since 1648 have involved neighbors, usually as initiators (see Vasquez 1993, table 4.2, 134).

3. There is more than one path to war, but the path identified here is seen as the typical one by which equal states who are the strongest in the system have gone to war. Wars between unequal states would be expected to follow some other path (see Vasquez 1993, 48–50).

4. Nevertheless, as recently illustrated by Jimmy Carter's negotiation in Haiti, conflict resolution techniques can be used in the presence of coercion to avoid war while enforcing the actions of a U.N.-based concert of power.

REFERENCES

Axelrod, R. K. 1984. *The Evolution of Cooperation.* New York: Basic Books.

Banks, M. 1985. "The Inter-Paradigm Debate." In M. Light and A. J. R. Groom, eds., *International Relations: A Handbook of Current Theory,* 7–26. London: Frances Pinter.

Betts, R. K. 1993. "Systems of Peace as Causes of War? Collective Security, Arms Control, and the New Europe." In J. Snyder and R. Jervis, eds., *Coping with Complexity in the International System,* 265–301. Boulder, CO: Westview.

Bull, H. 1977. *The Anarchical Society.* New York: Columbia University Press.

Burton, J. W. 1984. *Global Conflict: The Domestic Sources of International Crisis.* Brighton, Sussex: Wheatsheaf.

Burton, J. W.; A. J. R. Groom; C. R. Mitchell; and A. V. S. de Reuck. 1974. *The Study of World Society: A London Perspective.* Occasional Paper No. 1. Pittsburgh: International Studies Association.

Campbell, D. 1989. *Security and Identity in United States Foreign Policy: A Reading of the Carter Administration.* Ph.D. Diss., Australian National University.

Carr, E. H. 1939. *The Twenty Years' Crisis.* 1964, Reprint. New York: Harper & Row.

Coplin, W. D., and M. K. O'Leary. 1971. "A Simulation Model for the Analysis and Explanation of International Interactions." Paper presented at the annual meeting of the International Studies Association, San Juan, Puerto Rico.

Glahn, G. von. 1976. *Law among Nations.* 3d ed. New York: Macmillan.

Gochman, C. S., and Z. Maoz. 1984. "Militarized Interstate Disputes, 1816–1976: Procedures, Patterns, and Insights." *Journal of Conflict Resolution* 28 (December): 585–616.

Gurr, T. R., and J. R. Scarritt. 1985. "Minorities Rights at Risk: A Global Survey." *Human Rights Quarterly* 11:375–405.

Henehan, M. T. 1981. "A Data-based Evaluation of Issue Typologies in the Comparative Study of Foreign Policy." Paper presented at the annual meeting of the International Studies Association, Philadelphia, March.

Johnson, J. T. 1975. *Ideology, Reason, and the Limitation of War.* Princeton: Princeton University Press.

———. 1981. *Just War Tradition and the Restraint of War.* Princeton: Princeton University Press.

Kocs, S. A. forthcoming. "Territorial Disputes and Interstate War, 1945–1987." *Journal of Politics* (1995).

Kupchan, C. H., and C. A. Kupchan. 1991. "Concerts, Collective Security, and the Future of Europe." *International Security* 16 (Summer): 114–61.

Luard, E. 1986. *War in International Society.* New Haven: Yale University Press.

Mansbach, R. W., and J. A. Vasquez. 1981. *In Search of Theory: A New Paradigm for Global Politics.* New York: Columbia University Press.

Maoz, Z. 1989. "Joining the Club of Nations: Political Development and International Conflict, 1816–1976." *International Studies Quarterly* 33 (June): 199–231.

Masters, R. D. 1989. *The Nature of Politics.* New Haven: Yale University Press.

Mitchell, C. R., and K. Webb, eds. 1988. *New Approaches to International Mediation.* Westport, Conn.: Greenwood Press.

Morgenthau, H. J. 1960. *Politics among Nations.* 3d ed. New York: Knopf.

Patchen, M. 1988. *Resolving Disputes between Nations: Coercion or Conciliation.* Durham, N.C.: Duke University Press.

Raiffa, H. 1982. *The Art and Science of Negotiation.* Cambridge, Mass.: Harvard University Press.

Rosecrance, R. 1992. "A New Concert of Powers." *Foreign Affairs* 71 (Spring): 64–82.

Rosenau, J. N. 1991. "Interdependence and the Simultaneity Puzzle: Notes on the Outbreak of Peace." In C. Kegley, Jr., ed., *The Long Postwar Peace,* 307–29. New York: HarperCollins.

Roy, B. A. 1995. *In Bondage to Borders: Territorial Claims and Prospects for Peace between Neighboring States.* Ph.D. Diss., Rutgers University.

Rummel, R. J. 1972. "U.S. Foreign Relations: Conflict, Cooperation, and Attribute Distances." In B. Russett, ed., *Peace, War, and Numbers,* 71–113. Beverly Hills: Sage.

Small, M., and J. D. Singer. 1982. *Resort to Arms: International and Civil Wars, 1816–1980.* Beverly Hills: Sage.

Vasquez, J. A. 1983a. *The Power of Power Politics: A Critique.* New Brunswick, N.J.: Rutgers University Press.

———. 1983b. "The Tangibility of Issues and Global Conflict: A Test of Rosenau's Issue Area Typology." *Journal of Peace Research* 20 (no. 2): 179–92.

———. 1993. *The War Puzzle.* Cambridge: Cambridge University Press.

———. 1994. "Building Peace in the Post–Cold War Era." In M. Midlarsky, J. Vasquez, and P. Gladkov, eds., *From Rivalry to Cooperation: Russian and American Perspectives on the Post–Cold War Era,* 208–18. New York: HarperCollins.

Vasquez, J. A., and R. Mansbach. 1984. "The Role of Issues in Global Cooperation and Conflict." *British Journal of Political Science* 14 (September): 411–33.

Wallensteen, P. 1984. "Universalism vs. Particularism: On the Limits of Major Power Order." *Journal of Peace Research* 21 (no. 3): 243–57.

Wallerstein, I. 1974. *The Modern World-System: Capitalist Agriculture and the Origins of the European World Economy in the Sixteenth Century.* New York: Academic Press.

Waltz, K. N. 1979. *Theory of International Politics.* Reading, Mass.: Addison-Wesley.

———. 1989. "The Origins of War in Neorealist Theory." In R. Rothberg and T. Rabb, eds., *The Origin and Prevention of Major Wars,* 39–52. Cambridge: Cambridge University Press.

Ward, M. D. 1982. "Cooperation and Conflict in Foreign Policy Behavior: Reaction and Memory." *International Studies Quarterly* 26 (March): 87–126.

Zartman, I. W. 1989. *Ripe for Resolution: Conflict and Intervention in Africa.* Updated ed. New York: Oxford University Press.

CHAPTER 8

International Law and the Peaceful Resolution of Interstate Conflicts

James Turner Johnson

The purpose embedded in international law is to establish structural incentives and constraints to regularize and regulate intercourse among states, a purpose that includes the regulation and resolution of interstate conflicts. By contrast with the relationship between dispute resolution and law in the domestic sphere—which as Robert A. Baruch Bush (in this volume) makes clear is one of some tension, with alternative dispute resolution (ADR) having developed as a means to deal with disputes *outside* of formal legal processes—the relation between conflict resolution and law in the international sphere is one of interdependence and complementarity. The structure of order by which international law provides for peaceful interaction among states and other actors in the international arena constitutes an overarching framework within which diplomatic and other efforts to avoid and resolve conflicts may proceed. International law depends on such activity, as it develops, to add depth and texture to existing formal and customary structures of order among states; similarly, such activity may generate new law. Conflict resolution in the international sphere thus does not represent an *alternative* to law; rather, it presupposes such law and serves to generate a richer and more inclusive network of law.

The full range of elements constitutive of contemporary international law includes the positive law of treaties, conventions, and other international instruments such as the United Nations Charter (what is called "black-letter law"); the conceptions of states regarding customary international law and their actions on the basis of these conceptions; the reflections of jurists and other theorists concerned with identifying the underlying principles of international law in the relations among states; and conceptions of *lex ferenda* (proposals for what ought to be added to the positive law) of states, international lawyers, jurists, and others. An important feature of international law, then, is that it does not consist of the "black-letter law" alone, but includes these other elements. (On the nature of international law see further Best 1980, 16–22; Falk and Mendlovitz 1966, 1–3).

As regards conflict between states, the development of international law has taken two somewhat different, though related, approaches. The first and oldest approach assumes that conflict between states is inevitable and seeks to regulate and control it to the mutual benefit of the conflicting parties and the general international system. On this understanding, international conflict follows from the disparate interests of individual states and the fact that states have no superiors able to adjudicate disputes arising from the pursuit of those interests. Lacking such superiors, states have the right to use their own resources, up to and including armed force, to secure the ends sought. Armed conflict, then, from this perspective is not an international aberration but the result of inherent competition among states over their interests. Resolving a dispute means allowing the conflict to play itself out. At the same time, however, it is recognized that an armed conflict may itself be the source of new disputes, both between the parties engaged and potentially involving others who might be affected by the contest between them. International law developed according to this understanding thus does not seek to eliminate armed conflict but to hold it within limits designed to minimize the injustices that might lead to new disputes.

The result of this approach to dealing with international conflict is the law of war, which is devoted to regularizing and restraining the conduct of armed hostilities between states. With a history reaching back through just war tradition to the roots of Western culture, this approach to dealing with international disputes has generated a powerful body of customary law, precedent, and principle. Beginning in the latter part of the nineteenth century it has also generated a significant body of positive international law in the form of the work of the two Hague Conferences, the various Geneva Conventions and Protocols, and associated agreements. This positive law of war (or, in the contemporary term, law of armed conflicts) is a major element within the corpus of positive international law (on the law of war/armed conflicts see Friedman 1972; Roberts and Guelff 1989; Schindler and Toman 1973; on other elements of international law in relation to it see Black and Falk 1972).

The second approach to international conflict developed within international law seeks to restrict the resort to force by states as a way of settling disputes between them. It does this through the creation of a collective international order, to which member states voluntarily cede some of their rights, including that of resort to force to settle disputes with other states. At the same time, the new collective international representative body provides for alternative means of resolving disputes that protect the interests of the member states and of the collective as a whole: means including neutral third-party arbitration, judicial settlement, enforced cooling-off periods, enforced sanctions short of military force against recalcitrant states embroiled in disputes, interposition of neutral peacekeeping forces, and the threat of overwhelming international action by force in case of denial of the terms of settlement by one or more of the parties to a dispute. At the extreme, then, while this approach does not deny the role of force in the settlement of disputes, it moves the right to resort to force to a higher level, that of the international collective body, and it interposes between disputing parties a new range of alternatives, options, and incentives for choosing them while providing impediments and disincentives for the parties to use force instead. With its roots in the Enlightenment-era "perpetual peace" movement, this approach to international law has in the twentieth century produced the League of Nations, the International Court of Justice, the Pact of Paris, the United Nations, and a growing body of associated practice, precedent, and related international agreements.

Finally, both of these approaches to dealing with international conflicts through international law must be measured in the contemporary context not only by the degree to which they function as intended to dampen, prevent, or resolve conflicts between states but also by their adaptability to the many contemporary conflicts (e.g., civil wars, ethnic conflicts, terrorism, covert warfare) that fall outside the range of the established parameters of the law and its supporting system.

The plan of this chapter is defined by the issues I have summarized. First I will discuss the historical and thematic roots of international law, giving special attention to the implications there for regulating and resolving conflicts among states. Next I will look at the problem of regulation of violence as an effort to establish such resolution. Then I will turn to the considerable effort expended in twentieth-century international law toward de-legitimizing resort to force and toward providing alternative means toward regulation and resolution of interstate conflicts. Finally, I will conclude with some reflections on the usefulness of international law as a means of conflict resolution in noninternational conflicts (i.e., those between sub- or transnational groups over ethnic, tribal, religious, or ideological differences).

Historical and Thematic Roots of International Law

The origins of modern international law can be located for practical purposes within the century bounded by Franciscus de Victoria's *De Indis* and *De Jure Belli* (1532) on the one hand and Hugo Grotius's *De Jure Belli ac Pacis* (1625) on the other (Victoria 1917; Grotius 1949; on the origin of international law see Scott 1934). Victoria, a professor of theology at the University of Salamanca in Spain, is the benchmark figure for understanding the way in which ideas from a medieval cultural consensus that was still largely moral and political were reshaped into a modern form that could provide the foundation for a new conception of international law (see further Scott 1934, vol. 1; Johnson 1975, chap. 3).

The historical context for Victoria's reflections was the Spanish experience in the New World and particularly the encounter with the cultures of the Indians (hence the title *De Indis,* "Of the Indians"), who knew nothing of the dictates of Christian religion or the assumptions and habits of European politics. In response to this encounter Victoria turned to natural law, which he believed accessible to both Indians and Spanish through reason, as the basis for regulating the interrelationship between these cultures.

A pressing issue was whether the Spanish had the right to use force against the Indians to prevent practices deemed immoral and to spread Christian religion, and in turn whether the Indians had the right to defend themselves against such use of force. Victoria addressed this issue, appealing to natural law, by finding balancing rights on both sides: he denied the right to spread religion by force of arms, allowing the Indians the right to defend themselves against such forceful attempts at conversion; yet he insisted that in the natural law the right of free passage required that the Indians allowed Spanish missionaries to come among them to preach and seek converts.

While the bloody and dominating historical record of Spanish colonial treatment of Indian polities and cultures shows that Victoria and his circle did not prevail in their own time, several important principles of later international law can be recognized here. First, each of the parties in the interaction is conceived as having rights and a formal equality with the other. The goal is peaceful interaction between them. The Spanish cannot use armed force against the Indians without just cause, and the Indians are entitled to defend themselves by force against unjust attacks. In turn, the Indians may not aggress against the Spanish, and the Spanish also possess the right of self-defense. Among the reasons that may justify use of armed force the claimed superiority of Christian religion does not count, as Victoria states baldly: "Difference of religion is not a cause for just war" (Victoria, *De Jure Belli,* sec. 10).

Roughly a hundred years later in Grotius's work these same principles appear. The context of *De Jure Belli ac Pacis* was the historical experience of the cataclysmic century of conflicts fired by religious ideology during the period between the beginning of the Protestant Reformation and the end of the Thirty Years' War. Whereas Victoria looked mainly outside his own European culture to the conflicts created by interaction with the cultures of the Indians, Grotius looked inward to the conflicts that had divided Europe and created what were in effect two European cultures, one Protestant and the other Catholic. His response was the same as Victoria's: to attempt to bridge over such differences by employing natural law as a means of defining a common denominator for interactions among political communities on both sides of the divide, and to deny the right to use armed force except as a measure of self-preservation against the armed attack of another (Grotius 1949, 71–89, 269–82, and passim; cf. Johnson 1975, 209–31).

Self-preservation, which for Grotius was the fundamental natural right possessed by individuals, also becomes a right of political communities when these are formed by the banding together of people for the purpose of ensuring their own right to live and be left alone. Claims rooted in transcendent standards of belief, then, have nothing to do with the justification of the existence of civil society, and such claims correspondingly cannot justify the use of armed force between elements of civil society. What this meant in practice for Grotius was that he took the existence of separate nations for granted and laid out rules for their interrelations on the basis of their continued right to preserve themselves and do what is needful for the self-preservation of their inhabitants.

This theoretical conception coincided happily with the practical conclusion reached by the belligerents in the Thirty Years' War, which began as a religiously inspired conflict but ended as one over nonreligious claims. The Treaty of Westphalia, which formally concluded this lengthy dispute, established an internal order in Europe based on the acceptance of a plurality of political communities and made sovereignty, not right belief, the standard for interrelations among them. The modern state system may be said to begin here, though its roots are of course much earlier.

Grotius's ideas and the assumptions about the international order found in the Treaty of Westphalia were carried forward by the work of Samuel Pufendorf (particularly his *On the Law of Nature and Nations,* 1672, and *On the Duty of Man and Citizen According to Natural Law,* 1673). Like Grotius, Pufendorf defined his conception of society and the proper interrelations among nations on the basis of natural law, and he understood natural law, in turn, to be founded upon the right of self-preservation. By the time Pufendorf wrote, Hobbes had advanced the thesis that the natural condition of man was one of rights without duties, and Pufendorf responded by arguing to the contrary (with great influence on later thought) that all rights necessarily correlate with duties. The importance of this for the theory of international law, continuing to appear in jurisprudential discussion, is that it provides a foundation for understanding states as having not only rights one against the other, but also duties one toward the other. Pufendorf's statement of the natural-law conception of international law, incorporating the principles earlier identified and employed by Victoria and Grotius, was the vehicle through which this conception was transmitted to the era of the Enlightenment.

Reflecting back on this approach to understanding the relations among nations, several points stand out that are of importance for the issue of how to resolve conflicts between and among states. When the concept of just war coalesced in the Middle Ages, the right to wage war was gradually restricted (between the tenth and thirteenth centuries) to those political authorities who had no political superior (Johnson 1981, 150–65; Russell 1975, 55–212). In a culture within which every knight had the right to bear arms and might claim the right to use them at his discretion, this restriction of "right authority" to use armed force was a measure aimed at limiting armed conflict and ensuring that such force not be employed in the settling of disputes unless, in the judgment of the highest political authorities, it was justified and there was no other way to settle the conflict. Internal to a political community, the right to employ armed force became defined in terms of the police authority of the sovereign; between political communities whose sovereigns had no superior, it became the last resort for settling serious disputes that could not otherwise be settled, and thus a way of establishing peace between the parties in conflict. On the medieval conception the international order was not challenged by such trials by combat; to the contrary, that order would be challenged if the dispute were not resolved and peace restored.

These conceptions remain prominent in the work of the sixteenth- and seventeenth-century natural-law theorists of international relations. While Victoria defined limits to the justified use of armed force, he assumed that there would be times when, so far as any human could tell, there would be no way of resolving a serious dispute between sovereigns except by resort to arms. This concept, which I have elsewhere called the idea of "simultaneous ostensible justice" (Johnson 1975, 185–95), assumes the right of sovereigns to judge when they have a cause sufficiently grave to warrant the use of armed force. It also assumes a state of international affairs defined by a plurality of political communities whose sovereigns have no superiors. In such a context, is it possible for nations to live together without armed conflict?

The answer given by the naturalists, taken collectively and individually, is no. In attempting to remove the possibility of trying to justify war by appeal to religion, Grotius established a more formalized and less restrictive *jus ad bellum* than Victoria or his medieval predecessors would have accepted, in which the very existence of a state carried with it the right for its sovereign to judge whether or not to resort to armed force on behalf of the state's preservation, and in which the principal restriction on that right became the requirement that the sovereign publicly declare the reasons for any resort to force (Grotius 1949, bk. 3, chap. 3). This opened the way to the development of the idea of *compétence de guerre* in the international politics of the eighteenth and nineteenth centuries, according to which there were no external limits on a sovereign's right to judge whether to take up arms.

Rather than seeking to eliminate the use of armed force among sovereign states, which they believed impossible in any case and would have held to be contrary to the pursuit of order, justice, and peace, the natural-law theorists of international law concentrated on the problem of regulating and limiting the actual use of arms so as to protect innocent persons and restrain the overall destructiveness of war. That is, even as they deemphasized the inherited just war *jus ad bellum,* they put new stress on the requirements of the *jus in bello.*

While this direction of argument had the desired effect of removing the justification for war for religion, it had the less desirable result of providing little restraint on the readiness of sovereigns to go to war on the basis of material claims. The characteristic form of European warfare during the eighteenth century, the "sovereigns' wars," was accordingly one of frequent conflicts for often relatively minimal reasons. At the same time, though, these wars were also limited in terms of their political ends, their geographical extent, their targets, their impact on noncombatant society, and the resources put into them, reflecting the triumph of the idea that the conduct of war should proceed with restraint.

It is important to note the importance of this way of conceiving what is possible in restraining conflict among states for the development of positive international law on war. This law is principally a *jus in bello,* accepting the possibility of armed interstate conflicts and seeking to regulate their destructiveness by protecting certain classes of people as noncombatants and by setting limits on the means of war. (Indeed, the term "laws of war" technically refers *only* to those international legal instruments that address such issues. See Friedman 1972; Roberts and Guelff 1989; Schindler and Toman 1973.) As for the *jus ad bellum,* the requirement of sovereignty remains foremost, though the twentieth century has brought an effort to limit the incidence of war through agreements renouncing first resort to force in settlement of international disputes. More attention is given to both these aspects of international law below.

That the naturalistic theoretical system of international relations did not put brakes on the use of force by individual sovereign states was recognized as a failure by a competing line of theorists, the apologists for "perpetual peace." The term "perpetual peace" is that of Abbé de Saint-Pierre in his *Projet de traité pours rendre la paix perpétuelle en Europe,* published in 1713; the line of connecting works begins with Emeric Crucé's *Le Nouveau Cynée* in 1623 and includes Sully's *Le Grand Dessein de Henri IV* (1638), William Penn's *Essay toward the Present and Future Peace of Europe* (1693), Rousseau's unpublished essay, "Jugement sur la paix perpétuelle" (written in 1761), Kant's *Zum ewigen Frieden* (1795), Bentham's *Plan for a Universal and Perpetual Peace* (published in 1839, written a half-century before that), and William Ladd's *Essay on a Congress of Nations* (1840). These theorists attempted to resolve the problem of war among states by creating a higher framework of political order, above that of the state.

While many differences of detail distinguish the various approaches taken to this aim by the "perpetual peace" theorists, they collectively envisioned the desired higher order as a kind of parliament or congress within which the various states would be represented by a number of ambassadors related to the size and power of the individual states. The membership was conceived variously, with most of the theorists' attention focused on the need to dampen the frequency of intra-European warfare; thus what was proposed was at basis a "congress of Europe" (to borrow a later phrase), with some theorists also envisioning the membership of some non-European states. Held in common by most of the theorists in this tradition of thought was the idea that the states would give up some of their sovereignty, and particularly their right to wage war on their own account. On this conception member states would give up their military forces to the new higher entity, which would take on the function of protecting individual states against aggression, both from other members of the union and from states outside it (on this tradition of thought see further Johnson 1987, chaps. 4, 5).

Positive international law related to war and peace, then, has its roots in two rather different sources: the work of the naturalists, with their emphasis on the need for a strong *jus in bello* to restrict the destructiveness of war and make for less animosity that would hinder conclusion of peace, and with their reduction of the *jus ad bellum* to the idea of *compétence de guerre* and associated formalities; and the ideas of the "perpetual peace" theorists, with their effort to end war entirely by establishing a new and (at least for Europe) universal international order.

The two approaches differ in central respects. The thrust of the naturalist approach was compatible with the state system as it developed in the West following the Thirty Years' War; the thrust of the "perpetual peace" approach was to undercut and perhaps eventually to abolish the state system by replacing it with a higher and more inclusive form of political order. The naturalists' approach accepted war as a necessity for the settling of disputes among sovereigns (or, later, states) who had no superior; their goal was to moderate the severity of war and thereby to prevent the embitterment that might prolong conflicts and prevent their resolution. The "perpetual peace" theorists, by contrast, rejected war as a means of settling disputes, envisioned the parliamentary forum of nations as the vehicle for dispute resolution among nations, and accepted military forces for only two purposes: internally to the union, to police the peace among the members; externally, for security against other nations not a part of the common parliamentary system.

Despite the tensions and disagreements between them, both the naturalists' approach and that of the "perpetual peace" theorists are deeply embedded in contemporary positive international law: the former in the law of armed conflicts (including restraints on means of war and on the treatment of non-combatants in war); the latter in the United Nations regime, in restrictions against resort to armed force in the settlement of international disputes and in the provision of means for arbitration or judgment of such disputes by international bodies and neutral nations. I will look briefly at each in turn.

The Regulation of Violence as a Contribution to the Resolution of International Conflicts

Perhaps because it assumes the existence of war and focuses on moderating it rather than abolishing it, the international law of armed conflicts has not generally been regarded by theorists of international conflict resolution as a resource of any usefulness for them. This is a mistake. First, such recent influential theoretical interpretations as those of Myres McDougal and of Georg Schwarzenberger have focused on the humanitarian (McDougal and Feliciano 1961) or civilizing (Schwarzenberger 1967) purpose of this branch of international law, a purpose that is clearly consonant with the emphasis on protection of human rights and observance of law that is found elsewhere in the debate over what is wrong in international and intergroup armed conflicts and how best to end them. Indeed, there is an observable connection between the disregard of such rules for "good" fighting and the severity of impact on the whole social system in such recent and contemporary cases as the civil wars in Lebanon, Northern Ireland, Sri Lanka, Ethiopia, Sudan, Somalia, and the former Yugoslavia; the Iran-Iraq war; and the conflict between the State of Israel and the Palestine Liberation Organization. It is difficult to identify cause-and-effect relationships in such conflicts with any certainty (that is, whether the disregard of the rules for fighting makes for protracted conflict or whether the protracted bitterness of the conflict makes for disregard of the rules for fighting), but a common element in efforts to dampen such conflict and bring it toward resolution is the effort to get the parties to the conflict to exercise restraint in the means of violence they use and to observe the combatant-noncombatant distinction, protect the rights of prisoners, and so on. These are precisely the sorts of restraints laid out in the law of armed conflicts.

This leads to the second reason for paying attention to this branch of international law within the context of discussion of conflict resolution in the international sphere: the linkage between exercise of restraint in the conduct of hostilities and the likelihood of achieving a peaceful and lasting resolution to the conflict. The principles of noncombatant immunity and proportionality of means, which the law of armed conflicts embodies, implicitly define a context of belligerency in which not entire peoples but only particular elements of the belligerent societies are actively engaged in active hostilities with each other, and in which the dispute at the root of the conflict is not over ultimate values but of a character susceptible to human solution. The armed conflict is, after all, an attempt at a human solution; it is conceived as the last resort when no other means have worked, and in principle it could be replaced by other efficacious means, should they be found. Within this context of thought, the rules for armed conflicts attempt to keep the disputes in question under control of human reason. They are, in Clausewitz's (1949, 1:xxiii) words, "the continuation of state policy by different means," but the control imposed by the rules makes it easier to move back from armed conflict to a political solution to the dispute.

Historically, theoretical discussions have recognized this, linking the rules for conduct of hostilities closely to the rules for behavior at the end of a war: for example, how different categories of people within the vanquished state are to be treated, how far the victor may go in requiring the loser to pay the costs of the war, and so on. In a particularly insightful passage, John Locke used this linkage to strengthen the rules for armed conflict: destruction that has the effect of a long-term impairment of the economic productiveness of a nation is wrong, he argued, because of its impact on people after the war is over, when all are noncombatants (Locke 1924, Book 2, sec. 184; cf. 180–83).

Underneath the discussion, the reasoning involved is simple enough: the more bitter and unrestrained a conflict, the more hatred will mar the relations between the parties over the long term, and the more difficult it will be to reach any genuine state of peace between them. Thus the issue in applying the international law of armed conflicts is not simply to lay down a positive-law matrix for the conduct of hostilities but, more deeply, to achieve in each instance the conflicting parties' tacit acceptance of the idea that their conflict is not over ultimate, and hence nonnegotiable, values but susceptible to solutions that maintain such ultimate values while resolving the specific problems that led to the use of arms.

This said, however, there are three serious problematical issues in the international legal effort to regulate and restrain the processes of armed conflict: first, who is bound by the rules; second, how to ensure compliance with them; and third, their extent.

Who is bound by the rules of restraint in armed conflicts? International law is, by definition, between nations. The historical growth of the law of war reflects this: the rules for the conduct of hostilities that constitute this part of international law are the result of negotiations and agreements among nations and subsequent acceptance of the rules thus defined by other nations that were not party to the process that produced the rules. Nations that did not ratify the rules could claim not to be bound by them; even among nations that ratified them, sometimes significant reservations clouded their applicability. The case of the international convention banning gas warfare illustrates this problem. Iraq, for example, very likely employed chemical agents banned by the convention on gas warfare in its campaign of suppression against the Kurds, and possibly also in the war with Iran. Even among countries that accept the convention as forbidding the use of toxic substances in warfare, the United States and others hold that the ban does not apply to crowd-control substances such as tear gas. Against all such claims, there is a possible counterclaim that the convention is only the positive-law expression of the long-standing principles of customary international law that prohibit weapons that rely on poison and that are indiscriminate in their effects. Nonetheless, the strict letter of the positive law applies only to those nations that have formally ratified the applicable agreements, and even they may disagree on precisely what these agreements bind them to do.

An even more serious problem is caused by the fact that many belligerents in contemporary armed conflicts are not states, and that the rules of international law do not formally apply to such conflicts. A shift in terminology from "law of war" to "law of armed conflicts," undertaken in the 1970s and now for practical purposes universal, has been intended to imply that these rules should apply in such conflicts as well as in formally declared wars among states. Yet this approach is not universally accepted, and more importantly it has not had any great practical success. The conditions of many contemporary forms of armed conflict militate against the application of restraints aimed at disciplined armies serving under a responsible state authority. Further, the inspiration of much present-day armed conflict by religious, ethnic, or other passions tends to justify use of unrestrained force in the service of those passions and works against the idea that restraint in the use of force is the best way to protect high values. Even in war between states, the law of armed conflicts works to impose restraints and ameliorate suffering only because the belligerent parties recognize their common interest in such results. In nonstate conflicts that common interest and support is generally not recognized or admitted.

How is compliance with the rules to be ensured? The best answer to this question is that the parties to the agreements constituting the law are themselves to ensure compliance. While impartial third-party observers such as the International Red Cross or the Red Crescent may be involved, the belligerents themselves must permit such involvement, and they have the power to control, restrict, or terminate it, or to manipulate it for propaganda purposes. Further, the report of such observers implies no sanctions other than those of the war itself and, after the war, potential war-crimes trials by the victor. The threat of reciprocity provides the major intraconflict sanction; yet the exercise of reciprocity may be difficult to carry out for a belligerent that accepts the goals embodied in the laws of armed conflicts.

Civil wars, insurgency conflicts, and conflicts between religious or ethnic groups are notoriously "dirty." Compliance with such rules as protection of noncombatants from direct intentional harm is clouded by the tendency to define all of the "enemy" as combatants; prisoners may be treated as hostages, as criminals, as traitors, or simply as unworthy of any respect due to their membership in the opposition. Means prohibited in interstate conflicts may be employed on the excuse that the conflict in question is domestic. Lack of military discipline further contributes to the dirtiness of such conflicts. Attempts to impose sanctions through reciprocity may simply escalate the abuses, not end them. Finally, belligerents in such conflicts may judge that they simply have nothing to lose, and that all-out fighting is necessary if they themselves are not to be snuffed out.

The rules are limited as to their extent. While the principles of noncombatant immunity and proportionality of means lie behind the positive rules of the international law of armed conflicts, the black-letter law does not by far address all the implications of these principles. In the case of the principle of proportionality of means, it is doubtful that a law ever could fully capture the requirement of exercising proportional judgment in almost endlessly varied contexts. The case of the principle of noncombatant immunity is somewhat different: here the law is well specified, but the context of application is extremely broad and continually shifting. The Geneva conventions and attached protocols, the main expression of this principle, have historically sought protection of certain classes of persons within situations of combat, including prisoners of war, soldiers rendered hors de combat by wounds, medical personnel, chaplains, and civilians in the way of war. The context of these conventions has been set by the assumption that war would go on between nations and would have certain recognizable boundaries within which military forces would maneuver and fight each other. Combatants and noncombatants could be distinguished, and the effect of war on the latter could be minimized. Since 1940, however, the rules developed in this type of setting have had to be applied in a context that includes strategic air warfare; the destructive force of nuclear weapons and their utility for devastating population centers; the difficulty of preventing use of indiscriminate chemical and biological weapons (especially in internal conflicts); or the twentieth-century tendency, fanned by propaganda, ideology, religion, ethnic hatred, and even the needs of war mobilization in mass societies, to deny the traditional combatant-noncombatant distinction. This is all the more reason to think of these rules as not expressing the extent of all that is required for restraint of armed conflicts, but rather embodying a spirit of restraint and human control that has implications broader than the provisions of the positive law.

Restriction of the Right of Resort to Armed Force as a Contribution to the Resolution of International Conflicts

The idea that sovereigns possess the right to resort to force in settlement of disputes between them has been a feature of sovereignty throughout recorded history. Putting this concept into positive international legal form has, however, come to pass only in the twentieth century. Three major international agreements, the League of Nations Covenant, the Pact of Paris, and the United Nations Charter, define the effort to impose legal restrictions on the right of states to resort to armed force in disputes with other states. While the charter has superseded the earlier efforts, it is useful to look briefly at what they attempted as a way of setting the context for understanding this issue.

The League of Nations was a direct effort to embody the ideals of the "perpetual peace" tradition, but unlike the more robust conceptions of international order in that tradition, it did not constitute a "super-state" with any real powers over its members, and it possessed no military power at all. If any need for armed force arose, the only provision was for use of "forces of . . . Members of the League . . . cooperating to protect the Covenants of the League" (Article 16). The emphasis, however, was on settlement of disputes by arbitration, not resort to force. The relevant sections are Articles 10–17 of the covenant; these require a cooling-off period in case of disputes "likely to lead to a rupture," during which League members pledge not to resort to force but to seek an arbitrated settlement (Article 12); define the sorts of cases "suitable for submission to arbitration or judicial settlement" (Article 13); set up the Permanent Court of International Justice as the means for such settlement (Article 14); and establish sanctions against nations that do not abide by these provisions (Article 16).

The covenant of the League of Nations did not go so far as to render the resort to war illegitimate in the settlement of international disputes. The right of such resort remained to member states in the event of the failure of the measures summarized above. To take the further step of renouncing this right was the aim of the Pact of Paris or Kellogg-Briand Pact, concluded in 1928. This agreement bound its signatories to "condemn recourse to war for the solution of international controversies, and renounce it as an instrument of international policy in their relations with one another," as well as to seek solution of all disputes among themselves by peaceful means. It was optimistically to be kept open for signature so long as "necessary for adherence by all the other powers of the world." While sometimes called the "agreement to outlaw war," this pact did not in fact outlaw all war; it left undiminished the traditional right to resort to armed force in self-defense in case of attack by another nation. The League of Nations had also recognized this right, and the United Nations Charter made it explicit (see Falk and Mendlovitz 1966, 276–306).

In the operative international legal framework established by the United Nations Charter, Article 51 explicitly recognizes "the right of individual or collective self-defense if an armed attack occurs against a Member of the United Nations, until the Security Council has taken measures necessary to maintain international peace and security." While framed as a permission for self-defense, this passage has also been broadly interpreted as prohibiting all recourse to armed force *except* self-defense against "armed attack" for member states and regional groups of states. Coupled with the prohibition in Article 2 of "the threat or use of force against the territorial integrity or political independence of any state," this amounts to a prima facie delegitimizing of first resort to force and a legitimizing of second—defensive—use, often rendered as the distinction between "aggression" and "defense" (on the debate over this point see Falk and Mendlovitz 1966, 276–306; and Meyrowitz 1970). If universally followed, this understanding of the U.N. Charter (like the Pact of Paris before it) would mean the end to resort to armed force between or among nations, since without "aggressive" first use (prohibited), there would be no need for "defensive" second use (still legitimate).

Many factors have prevented this from eliminating all recourse to armed force, however. I will mention four major issues: reservation by nations of the right to use force in certain cases of national interest, international terrorism and covert activities, the question of preemptive use of force, and the increasing breadth of the concept of defense.

States have maintained significant reservations regarding the interpretation of the charter so as to protect what they regard as inalienable national rights. For example, the Soviet Union long maintained the right to support "national liberation" forces; the United States has held fast to its right to use military forces for reasons of national interest, including protection of American citizens in other countries; and various European countries have claimed the right to intervene in the affairs of their former colonies when necessary. In practice, the uses of force in this category have been directed to third world countries, and so the intent of the powers projecting force seems to have assumed a double standard of international behavior: that is, that they had rights toward the target nations that the latter did not have in return. Such a double standard is difficult to maintain, so the effect of this practice has been to undercut the general restraint on recourse to military action.

Some of the most prevalent and worrisome forms of contemporary armed conflict fall outside the arena of "armed attack" and "defense" between states. Insurgency conflicts and terrorist activity within states are by definition not included here. Further, insurgents and/or terrorist organizations may take refuge in one state and engage in armed actions across international borders against a second state. The second state may then project force back into the first state to punish the insurgents, force them back, or eliminate their military threat. This has been a familiar pattern in the conflict between Israel and the PLO forces in Southern Lebanon: though involving uses of armed force across an international border, this conflict is not formally one between states.

In a variation on this pattern, particular states may give outright support to terrorist organizations, providing them with safe havens, training bases, finances, and other forms of backing. The terrorist organizations, in turn, may act in the service of policy aims of the sponsor state. The resultant "state-sponsored terrorism," while violent, is covert as to its origin: it does not amount to an overt "armed attack" across national borders from the sponsor state against a target state. Indeed, the terrorist organization may base itself in a second state. The activities of groups trained and supported by Iran but based in Lebanon are cases in point.

How, in the framework of contemporary international law, is a target state to deal with such uses of force against it across international borders? Older customary international law had allowed for "reprisals" by force in cases of international wrongdoing. Recent international law has set limits on "reprisals," a concept that has gained a particular set of meanings associated with traditional forms of interaction between states, but has developed in its place a concept of "countermeasures" defining the right of self-defense by armed force against covert activity, including acts of violence sponsored by another state (see further Reisman and Baker 1992, chap. 5). Depending on the seriousness of the offense against which the countermeasures are directed, the latter may include acts of armed force: an example is the U.S. air raid against Libya in April, 1986, responding to Libyan complicity in the earlier terror bombing of the La Belle Discotheque in Berlin.

Other sorts of cases in which the right to employ countermeasures may be invoked include the use of subversion by one state against another, forms of coercion short of armed force, and various forms of proxy warfare (e.g., support for "movements of national revolution" or other revolutionary forces). Where measures and countermeasures employ force, the result has been to develop within contemporary international law and practice a concept of the limited use of armed force across international borders short of war between states. Regulation of the means of such conflict falls outside the positive law of armed conflict and thus depends on the self-restraint of the actors involved and the influence of international public opinion.

Can a use of force be defensive though preemptive? As noted above, alongside the concepts of "armed attack" and "defense" in Article 51 of the U.N. Charter there developed an association of "aggression" with first use of force across an international border and "defense" with second use of force in response. Arguably, however, the right of self-defense by means of force extends to preemption of an intended armed attack, even when the defensive action constitutes the first use of force across an international border. Accordingly, the effort to identify the first use of force as the legally prohibited use has proven impossible to maintain. The case that marked the turning point on this matter was the Israeli air strike against Egyptian and Syrian air forces at the beginning of the Six-Day War. In the subsequent debate the argument for legally prohibiting first use of force by one state against another, an argument based in the Pact of Paris and Article 2 of the U.N. Charter, lost ground to the concept of self-defense, protected by Article 51, as defined in customary international law to include genuine preemptive strikes against a military threat (see further Falk and Mendlovitz 1966, 276–306; and Meyrowitz 1970).

Finally, "defense" has turned out to be a most elastic term. The emphasis on defense alone in the positive international law as defined by the charter stands in contrast to the recognition of three just causes for a state's resort to arms in the overarching just war tradition: defense, punishment of evil, and retaking something wrongly taken. This latter list more clearly corresponds to the practice of nations. Accordingly, while positive international law has sought to do away with the latter two kinds of justification for resort to force, customary law as viewed through the practice of nations has reintroduced them under a broadened concept of defense.

Examples abound. Both Argentina and the United Kingdom tacitly appealed to the recovery of property wrongly taken as justification for their military actions in the Falklands/Malvinas conflict; yet their official self-justifications had to maintain the fiction that their actions were somehow those of national defense. Similarly, in the Gulf War one of the clear aims was to restore the territorial integrity of Kuwait; yet the formal justification focused on Iraq's "armed attack" against Kuwait, which was understood as continuous so long as Iraqi forces occupied Kuwaiti territory.

As for "the punishment of evil," the United States explicitly alluded to the punishment of wrongdoing in President Bush's enumeration of the justifications for the use of military forces in Panama and against Iraq; less clearly, it seems also to have been a justification behind the Grenada operation. Yet again, the larger formal context was that of defense. Finally, strategic nuclear deterrence is typically justified as "defense," though in fact it is nothing more than a threat to retaliate (punishment of evil) for a nuclear strike. With such elasticity in the concept of defense, it is clear that if defensive use of armed force is allowed, only the most blatant forms of aggressive use of such force is actually prohibited.

Again, however, there remains the matter of the context of expectation established by the treatment of use of armed force in the U.N. Charter. The old idea of a state having its own *compétence de guerre,* its own ability to decide whether a dispute justifies resort to arms, has been undercut by the provisions against resort to armed force written into international agreements from the League of Nations Covenant to the charter. Formal states of war between nations have been quite rare since the establishment of the United Nations, and this may in part be a result of the international legal effort to restrict recourse to war in the settlement of international disputes. The international regime of the cold war may also be cited, though, as a likely cause for this diminution in the number of formal wars between states. Armed conflicts have certainly continued to erupt, whether legally wars or not. In the present international legal context a state must go somewhat further in identifying and making known its justifying reasons for resort to arms than was the case in earlier periods, though whether this has meant a lessening in the resort to arms is not at all clear. A second effect of this context has been to encourage multilateral actions, signifying that the issues at stake are larger than any one state's own particular interests. One may suspect that this too has had a restraining effect on the actual resort to arms, though the thesis is impossible to test.

United Nations Uses of Force to the End of Peace

The peacekeeping provisions of the U.N. Charter set it sharply apart from earlier legal efforts to restrict resort to armed force in the settlement of international disputes. The value of U.N. peacekeeping forces, drawn from the national military forces of member nations not party to the conflict in question, has been great in establishing cease-fires, "breathing space," and "cooling-off periods" in any number of armed conflicts. In the context of the charter and related international law and institutions, the purpose of such forces is to assist the parties to a conflict in moving toward a settlement of their dispute by peaceful means. Thus the utility of these forces in any given case is affected by the willingness of the conflicting parties to move toward such a settlement and not pursue their own ends by continuing to use military force. The parties in conflict must first agree to a cease-fire and agree to have the U.N. forces on their soil. They must, moreover, continue in this resolve, since the peacekeeping forces by design are not heavily enough armed to allow them to dictate peace to the conflicting parties. That is, the United Nations forces do not *impose* a nonviolent solution to the conflict; they help to *enforce* such a solution in the event the disputing parties are willing to try it (see further Goulding 1993).

Going beyond traditional peacekeeping, Chapter 7 of the charter provides for the Security Council to authorize forceful measures by member states of the United Nations against "any threat to the peace, breach of the peace, or act of aggression" (Article 39). Such measures are to be a last resort, when it is determined that other means "would be inadequate or have proved to be inadequate" (Article 42); once the Security Council has determined to authorize force, however, "all Members" are called upon to take part as needed (Article 43).

In this regard the United Nations Charter builds on one of the conceptions of the "perpetual peace" tradition: the idea of collective use of force against renegades who threaten the common peace. Given the conditions of the cold war, however, the Korean War (a U.N.-authorized "police action") long stood as the only example of such Security Council action. In the post–cold war era, however, Security Council deadlock has proven less likely. Chapter 7 procedures were invoked during the Gulf Crisis, and the military action against Iraq was authorized by the Security Council under this chapter. Lower on the scale of military action, a determination that the crisis in Somalia constituted a threat to international peace justified the insertion of United Nations-authorized forces there for a range of purposes beginning with protection of humanitarian relief efforts and extending to an effort to impose civil order, more successful in some areas but notably unsuccessful in the capital city, Mogadishu.

The Somalia precedent is an interesting one that has led to much debate and discussion of the potential Chapter 7 reasoning holds for active United Nations military intervention in conflicts that have led to grave humanitarian need. A considerable consensus has formed around the concept that the United Nations has the right to authorize force to ensure delivery of humanitarian relief, an idea that opens the door to the possibility of more active military intervention under United Nations auspices in the future. Much more controversial, but nonetheless strongly supported in some quarters, are other projected uses of such force: for example, to protect human rights or to establish civil order, activities likely to involve fighting against the parties to the conflict (on the concept of humanitarian intervention, see further Roberts 1993).

International Law and the Resolution of Noninternational Conflicts

Many of the most virulent disputes of the contemporary period involve groups of people divided along various sorts of cultural lines: ethnicity, tribal membership, language, religion, ideology, and so on. Such conflicts may take place entirely within one state (e.g., Azerbaijan, Sri Lanka, Uganda or Northern Ireland) or may cross national boundaries but not directly involve a conflict of states (e.g., the Israeli-Palestinian conflict, the Hindu-Muslim conflict in South Asia), or may be mixed (e.g., the recent past conflicts in Central

America, the Angola-Namibia-South Africa conflict). Some such conflicts may actually be between states, but the issues may transcend those normally associated with international law (e.g., the Iran-Iraq war). Other conflicts may involve particular states as proxies (e.g., Soviet and Cuban support of the Sandinistas and United States support for the Contras in Nicaragua) or as "fraternal" participants without a declaration of war (e.g., Chinese "volunteers" in the Korean War, Cuban military personnel in Angola, military advisers in any number of conflicts).

By definition, many of these sorts of conflicts are not "international." Even when they are technically so, however, the causes of the disputes go well beyond the range of interests traditionally accepted as legitimate within positive international law—questions of territory, free passage, protection of neutral persons, and so on. The development of positive international law on human rights expands the latter list importantly, but much still remains to be determined as to the exact content of the rights to be protected, how far they are to be protected, and so on. Just as Victoria's flat declaration, "Difference of religion is not a cause for just war," did not prevent the virulent religious warfare of the following century, so the United Nations Declaration on Human Rights or the Helsinki Agreement should not be taken as ending (even for a time) the abuse in many areas of the globe of the rights identified in these documents—not to mention rights not mentioned there but claimed by some parties or rights in dispute in the various listings.

It has been recognized at least as long ago as Quincy Wright's *A Study of War* (Wright 1942) that conflicts across major cultural divisions are the ones least susceptible to moderation (see further Barkun 1968; Johnson 1981, chap. 3). Where values considered ultimate by each party are at stake, then the tendency is for the parties to justify measures that are also high on the scale of ultimacy. All the above-mentioned sorts of divisions along cultural lines have provided justification for conflict in the contemporary era, whether one thinks of Africa, South America, South and Southeast Asia, the Middle East, the southern rim of the Soviet Union, or Northern Ireland. Lacking political solutions that protect major values of the conflicting parties, such conflicts have every reason to be prolonged indefinitely, ending only with conquest or exhaustion of one or both sides.

There is, frankly, only limited scope for international law to serve directly as a moderator of conflict or a means for resolution of differences in such types of cases. International authorities lack jurisdiction, and the parties in dispute do not conceive their causes as susceptible to treatment in the international legal framework. They may even suspect or reject international law on the grounds that it expresses the values of Western culture, but not their own. This has become a significant problem with the growth of radical Muslim religio-political movements (for discussion see Mayer 1991). For such reasons, the field of conflict resolution applied to such disputes has developed largely alongside the framework provided by international law, not within it.

The positive potential of international law to affect such conflicts should not, however, be overlooked. The approaches embedded in international law are indeed historically tied to perceptions, values, and political structures from Western culture; yet they also enjoy a wide consensus in the international community, and the fact of that consensus argues that the underlying value structures and assumptions are a good deal more universal than would be the case if they were those of Western culture alone. Challenges to the legitimacy of international law on the basis that it is not "our law" turn out to fracture the consensus, not add to it, making everyone worse off. Efforts at conflict resolution may benefit from finding higher levels of consensual agreement between parties in dispute, and past acceptance of positions taken in international law may provide evidence of such commonality.

Further, in those cases that cross national boundaries, whether specific states are formally involved or not, the international legal framework may provide a more readily available matrix for dealing with the dispute than any other, which may need to be made up from scratch. It simply makes good sense to use whatever tools are already available for resolving disputes, and international law is already in the tool chest.

Thirdly, as argued above, the actual substance of black-letter law is perhaps less important than the nexus of customary law and principle that lies behind the positive law and that it expresses, though only in part. While international legal jurisdiction may not exist in substate conflicts, the presence of international consensus on the underlying principles and customs provides a further matrix for attempting to find a solution that preserves the values of the parties in conflict but ends their particular dispute.

Finally, it is important to observe that the role of international law relative to the resolution of interstate conflicts is rather different from the role of alternative dispute resolution methods vis-à-vis the legal system in the domestic sphere. In the latter, dispute-resolution approaches and procedures have developed as ways of avoiding the legal system and seeking a resolution that the legal system cannot, by its adversarial nature, provide. International law is quite different, though. In the first place, it is not "law" in the same sense as domestic law. As noted above, the positive law is only one element in the international legal framework. Moreover, the operation of international law, whether positive or other, is through consensus and agreement to be bound rather than by imposition of sanctions by superior authority. International law is thus inherently democratic in its operation and its effect, while domestic law is authoritarian. Historically, international law—even before there was much in the corpus of positive law—functioned as a framework for negotiated resolution of disputes among states, with particular statements of international legal requirements developing as concrete statements on particular points that could then be used as signs of the presence of consensus. Precedental cases have fed into the concept of international law in the same way.

All these observations about international law suggest that it has much more in common with the assumptions and processes of domestic dispute resolution than has been noticed thus far. This commonality is heightened by concentrating not on the analogy between international and domestic law, which is misleading at best, but on the functional patterns found in international law and in domestic dispute resolution.

Conclusion

Thomas Hobbes called the state of nature a "war of all against all." It has been one of the dogmas of political realism that nations are in a state of nature relative to one another, and that as a consequence, conflict is the rule rather than the exception. By contrast, idealists have often argued that peace is the ideal state toward which relations among nations trend, and international conflicts are by no means inevitable and will ultimately die out. International law has developed as a somewhat curious mixture of these two opposing points of view. On the one hand, the practice of states produces the customary international law of any given era, and much of positive international law has derived from past customary law. On the other hand, idealistic visions such as developed in the historic "perpetual peace" movement and among some of the supporters of the League of Nations, the Pact of Paris, and the United Nations have also influenced positive international law and the associated (but not identical) contemporary customary law. A similar mixture of realistic and idealistic influences also characterizes just war tradition, of which international law is one of the carriers in the modern era.

Because of its mixed heritage and intent, international law has two broad types of relationship to contemporary conflicts across state borders. On the one hand, it seeks to manage conflicts and turn them toward other means of resolution than by force: this is its realist side. On the other hand, it holds up broad goals, such as the absolute renunciation of resort to armed violence, that even though in the form of solemn international agreements simply have not produced the desired result; yet the goals remain, and the practice of states can be judged by them. This is the idealist side.

In both these respects international law depends on other institutions for its effect. The most fundamental of these is the institution of the state itself. Historically both the positive law and customary law have represented the practice of states and the agreement of states to abide by certain practices;

state interests and the readiness of states to abide by international agreements remain the core of international law's effect. In other words, it is largely self-policing. Even institutions such as the International Court of Justice and the United Nations, while they have some status of their own to enforce international law, ultimately depend on the willingness of states to abide by the established international rules or depend on the actions of other states to impose coercive measures, up to and including force, to bring about compliance.

As a result of its very character, then, international law has only a mixed record in regard to conflicts. Where it has been strongest, in such areas as the rules of war, a great deal of the activity of the International Court of Justice and United Nations peacekeeping efforts, this has been because of the interest of the parties involved to support the aim of the rules, abide by them, and assist in their enforcement. Yet by establishing common ends, rules, and procedures, and by bringing to bear the influence and assistance of other states, international law transcends each specific state's interests, taken alone. This is its value, and it is also where the realist and idealist aspects of its heritage tend toward convergence. In short, international law establishes a framework and a mechanism whereby particular actors (states and nonstate actors working across international borders) may rise above their own self-interest narrowly perceived to an understanding of that self-interest in larger terms as including international stability, justice, and peace. The result is not, as the most ardent supporters of international law would have it, a genuine "world order," but nonetheless a more orderly world than it would be in the absence of international law.

REFERENCES

Barkun, M. 1968. *Law without Sanctions: Order in Primitive Societies and the World Community.* New Haven, CT and London: Yale University Press.
Best, G. 1980. *Humanity in Warfare.* New York: Columbia University Press.
Black, C. E., and Richard A. Falk, eds. 1972. *The Future of the International Legal Order.* Vol. 4, *The Structure of the International Environment.* Princeton: Princeton University Press.
Clausewitz, C. von. 1949. *On War.* London: Routledge and Kegan Paul Ltd.
Falk, R. A., and Saul H. Mendlovitz. 1966. *The Strategy of World Order.* Vol. 2, *International Law.* New York: World Law Fund.
Friedman, L., ed. 1972. *The Law of War: A Documentary History.* 2 vols. New York: Random House.
Goulding, M. 1993. "The Evolution of United Nations Peacekeeping." *International Affairs* 63, no. 3 (July): 451–64.
Grotius, H. 1949. *The Law of War and Peace.* Roslyn, NY: Walter J. Black, Inc.

Johnson, J. T. 1975. *Ideology, Reason, and the Limitation of War.* Princeton, NJ and London: Princeton University Press.

———. 1981. *Just War Tradition and the Restraint of War.* Princeton, NJ and Guildford, Surrey: Princeton University Press.

———. 1987. *The Quest for Peace.* Princeton, NJ and Guildford, Surrey: Princeton University Press.

Locke, J. 1924. *Two Treatises of Civil Government.* London: J.M. Dent and Sons; New York: E.P. Dutton and Co.

McDougal, M., and F. P. Feliciano. 1961. *Law and Minimum World Public Order.* New Haven, CT and London: Yale University Press.

Mayer, A. E. 1991. "War and Peace in the Islamic Tradition and International Law." Chap. 8 in John Kelsay and James Turner Johnson, eds., *Just War and Jihad: War, Peace, and Statecraft in the Western and Islamic Traditions.* Westport, CT: Greenwood Press.

Meyrowitz, H. 1970. *Le Principe de l'égalité des belligérents devant le droit de la guerre.* Paris: A. Pedone.

Reisman, W. M., and J. E. Baker. 1992. *Regulating Covert Action.* New Haven, CT and London: Yale University Press.

Roberts, A. 1993. "Humanitarian War: Military Intervention and Human Rights." *International Affairs* 66, no. 3 (July): 429–50.

Roberts, A., and R. Guelff, eds. 1989. *Documents on the Laws of War.* 2d ed. Oxford: Clarendon Press.

Russell, F. H. 1975. *The Just War in the Middle Ages.* Cambridge: Cambridge University Press.

Schindler, D., and J. Toman, eds. 1973. *The Laws of Armed Conflicts.* Leiden: A.W. Sijthoff; Geneva: Henry Dunant Institute.

Schwarzenberger, G. 1967. *A Manual of International Law.* 5th ed. London: Stevens and Sons.

Scott, J. B. 1934. *The Spanish Origin of International Law.* 2 vols. Oxford: Clarendon Press; London: Humphrey Milford.

Victoria, F. de. 1917. *De Indis et De Jure Belli Relectiones.* Washington, DC: Carnegie Institution.

Wright, Q. 1942. *A Study of War.* 2 vols. Chicago: University of Chicago Press.

CHAPTER 9

The Power Cycle and Peaceful Change:
Assimilation, Equilibrium, and Conflict Resolution

Charles F. Doran

Why should a treatise on conflict resolution take seriously the possibility of applying such ideas at the world level among governments? More directly, why should advocates of conflict resolution read an essay that stems from essentially realist assumptions? More pointedly still, why should a practitioner of conflict resolution worry much about history, structural change, and notions of equilibrium, when they seem so removed from the arena of conflict resolution per se?

What I shall try to convince the reader of is twofold. First, a realist view of politics is far from incompatible with notions of conflict resolution. Properly conceived, political realism allows a holistic view of human behavior, encompassing ideals and ethical norms in the attempt to deal with power relations, and recognizing a variety of state goals and prudence as to the means employed.[1] Indeed, political realism offers *internal to itself* both a concept of justice and a quite compelling rationale for conflict-resolution ideas. Second, without a foundation in a just equilibrium between power and role for each of the leading states, the efforts to guarantee an international regime fostering cooperation and conflict resolution are likely to fail. These two arguments underpin this chapter and provide its justification.

Why Systemic Structure Shapes the Use and
Effectiveness of Conflict Resolution

In structural terms, the international system is entering a phase where the incentives to conflict resolution at the top are perhaps the greatest they have been since 1945. However, the structural constraints on conflict resolution must be kept in mind as well.

Conflict resolution is more necessary today because the structure of the international system is changing with more uncertain consequence than in recent decades. Structural change involves not merely movement up and down the power cycles of the respective states. More tellingly, structural change also involves sudden unexpected shifts in the trend of these power cycles—critical points of nonlinearity where surprise and shock are endemic to foreign policy conduct. Such a phase of uncertain structural change, occurring between the disappearance of one mature international system and the emergence of another, is systems transformation. Historically, the five instances of systems transformation have all ended in massive systemic warfare. Hence, conflict resolution is essential as a strategy to help manage the ensuing systems transformation.

Conflict resolution is perhaps also more possible today because of structural change. Because of internal economic difficulty and the response to that difficulty via *glasnost* and political reform, the former Soviet Union was responsive to the application of techniques of conflict resolution to world problems. In particular, the superpowers began changing the terms of their competition in the third world. Conflicts that a few years ago seemed ready to boil over onto the system now seem subject to resolution. In a few cases, disputes may even be effectively settled and definitively terminated by legal and diplomatic means. Conflict resolution today thus may enjoy a higher prospect of success, either under the auspices of the United Nations or in bilateral terms, because Russia and the United States are willing to use these techniques (Zartman 1991).

However, the very rapid structural change that makes conflict resolution more necessary also makes it more dangerously susceptible to failure. The structural changes constraining positive action during systems transformation are insidiously unexpected and counterintuitive, in contradiction with long-held foreign policy expectations within the system. These "shifting tides of history" are unexpected—and have historically led to massive warfare—because of conflicting messages within absolute and relative power change that contain a shocking surprise for statesmen: their long-held projections of future power and security are suddenly seen to be wrong. At base, the structural constraint on successful peaceful change is this abrupt yet monumental shift in *future expectations*—expectations regarding future power, future role, and the utility of force use.

Conflict resolution in world politics today must occur amid such intense structural uncertainty and tumult. Power cycle analysis seeks to enhance peaceful change by preparing states in advance for the difficult changes awaiting them during systems transformation. Incomplete understanding of relative power change supports dangerous fantasies regarding future power and role. Which expectations are mythical, and which are sustainable? When fully understood, the dynamics of structural change and the sources of structural friction in international relations suggest that systems transformation can be peaceful, secure, and just.

Peaceful change entails not the end of change, but a new beginning.

Ultimately, the capacity to manage international conflict in intervals of very rapid structural change is the capacity to establish a new form of equilibrium within the central system that could sustain world order. In practice and theory, quest for a more encompassing and enduring equilibrium is the logical consequence of efforts to overcome the shortcomings of the traditional balance-of-power concept. For while the balance of power may have deterred many wars, it was unable to preserve the peace during massive structural change. That the balance of power is insufficient as a guide to maintaining peace with security, however, does not mean that other schemes to achieve "universal peace," such as collective security, are necessarily superior.

Clues to resolving the dilemma of peaceful change—when to accommodate and when to oppose—are locked in history. Each transformation of the modern state system has been accompanied by hegemonic onslaught and massive warfare. Following each of these wars, statesmen have tried to create a new, restructured world order that would assimilate the defeated hegemonic states and provide a basis for security and peace. These great peace treaties— the aftermath of the hegemonic onslaughts of Hapsburg Spain (Peace of Westphalia, 1648), Louis XIV (Treaties of Utrecht, 1713), Napoleon (Congress of Vienna, 1815), Imperial Germany (Versailles, 1919), Nazi Germany (Yalta, 1945) and Imperial Japan (1945)—had to focus on static criteria for structures that would allow the new system to evolve and mature. To prevent collapse in world war, however, the new systems had to deal with the long-term relative power changes that inevitably would transform the new structure (Doran 1969, 1971, 1991).

The power cycle assessment of peaceful change grew out of the belief that analysis of these long-term changes "might provide a better understanding of the mechanism of systemic adjustment which must *precede* and *complement* any external alliances formed" (Doran 1969, 2). Reinforced by study of the diplomatic negotiations and concerns surrounding these peace treaties, power-cycle analysis proposes a more general and dynamic concept of equilibrium, which is explored in the second section. The third section of this chapter examines the effort to assimilate Germany and Japan at the end of World War II, and the implications for the resulting bipolar equilibrium. It then assesses how international political equilibrium may be managed as the system begins to collapse. The final two sections answer *machtpolitik*, showing how conflict resolution can be applied at the global level and assessing the limits and possibilities.

Dynamic Equilibrium and the State Power Cycle

Analogous to the balance of power is the chessboard. The number of pieces (actors) is specified, the rules are well understood, and a premium is placed on calculation, especially short-term calculation. The balance of power is an important part of the overall equilibrium of world politics, but it is only a part. Fundamentally, the balance of power is a static and partial conception of equilibrium. Analysts have sought to overcome this problem from a variety of perspectives and are converging to a dynamic conception of equilibrium that is truer to the reality of diplomatic behavior.

Toward a Dynamic Conception of International Political Equilibrium

Pluralism versus hegemony. The hegemonic leadership conception of world order is the most prevalent alternative to the balance of power in the recent literature. Finding support in the earlier writings of E. H. Carr (1939) or Ludwig Dehio (1962), a number of academic writers argue that each peaceful period of history is characterized by the "hegemony" of a single state—a Pax Britannica or a Pax Americana—that creates and maintains the system of rules and benefits (Modelski 1978; Organski and Kugler 1980; Gilpin 1981; Thompson 1992). Bertrand Russell's (1952, 106–7) vision of future peace invokes such a notion: "The preponderant Power can establish a single Authority over the whole world, and thus make future wars impossible." However, this depiction of international politics simply does not correspond to historical reality. In fact, it expresses conditions that emerged following the *failure* of peaceful change rather than successful peaceful change.

Worse, as Joseph Nye (1989) observes, the hegemonic thesis exaggerates the sense of present decline for principal states that are led to believe in some now-lost mythical past in which they alone established the rules of trade or of world order. It also inflates the hostility and the aspirations of potential rivals, who are encouraged to dream of singular predominance. In a word, these notions of hegemony distort.

At least since the Holy Roman Empire under Charlemagne, no individual state dominated any system. On the contrary, power has always been shared. Pluralism is the very gist of the modern state system. Single states could control regions or peripheries. Britain and later the United States employed navies for localized peacekeeping and to assure freedom of movement on the high seas. However, this is a far cry from military predominance in the central system where the essence of world order is determined.

Indeed, all of the major wars have been fought to preserve national autonomy and the decentralized character of the nation-state system. Aggressors, made abruptly aware of their shifted fate vis-à-vis power and role, have struck out against others, and have been beaten back by force. Hence the hegemonic theories assert just the opposite of reality, and of the Dehio thesis.[2] States coalesce in opposition to attempted hegemony, not in response to an effort to defend purported hegemony. Not always realized, hegemony and the idea of the balance of power, indeed of pluralism, are utterly at odds. In the conduct of diplomacy, it is well to remember this dynamic, and these limits of coercive power.

What is the balance of power? The balance of power is the process whereby states form a coalition in opposition to aggression.[3] When aggression is perceived to be imminent, states combine their resources to deter and, if deterrence fails, to defend against aggression. Balance is neither automatic nor totally strategic. Only the perceptive and politically nimble are able to concert a balance against an aggressor in time to safeguard peace and security. When the threat of aggression becomes overwhelmingly obvious, the balancing process does become virtually automatic (that is, for everyone, imperative), but by then it is often too late to prevent war.

Even if properly implemented, the balance of power alone is insufficient to prevent major war. It is necessary as an instrument to halt or counter aggression in the short term, but it does not cope effectively with the rise and decline of states. Designed to bolster the weaker and to oppose the power of the stronger state, balance-of-power logic is often the structural opposite of the strategy necessary to maintain long-term equilibrium in the system. It belies the need for systemic adjustment of role. Required is a more dynamic view of statecraft and a more complete concept of foreign policy behavior (Vasquez 1987; Smith 1987; Rosenau 1990). However, the dynamic of state rise and decline is neither simple nor kind, and it complicates order maintenance, especially during systems transformation.

The Dynamic of Power and Role. Making the notion of equilibrium more dynamic in the long-term temporal sense is a conception of the state "cycle of power and role." In the international system, the principal source of structural change is the slow alteration in the relative power of the component states. Differing absolute levels and growth rates among the leading states set in motion a single dynamic of relative power change at the systemic level (Doran 1969, 1971, 1991). The changing structure of the system is this single dynamic of relative power changes on the component power cycles.

What separates politics from economics is not just that the latter is preoccupied with wealth, the former with power. The conceptual difference is more fundamental. Power is a relative, comparative concept, and hence a level removed from the absolute output of interest in economics. A state's *absolute* power, and the rate of growth in its absolute power, are observable— for example, the current size of its GNP (or of its armaments base) and the yearly increments in GNP (or in its armaments). However, the state's international political behavior is conditioned by how its absolute power compares with the absolute power of other states in the system. The state's *relative* power on any indicator is the *ratio* of its absolute power compared to the absolute power of the other states in the system at that time. Statesmen must think in relative terms because a state's capability to create and sustain a foreign policy role is always relative to the other states in the system.

A most fundamental difference between absolute and relative power lies in the nature of their respective trajectories. State power follows a not-so-simple, and often counterintuitive, cycle of relative rise, maturation, and decline best described as a type of logistic growth and decay in a finite system.[4] Two principles underlie this dynamic. (1) A state's relative power (systemic share) will increase when its absolute growth rate is greater than that of the system (the systemic norm). Moreover, a single state growing faster than the systemic norm will initiate momentum of change on power cycles throughout the system. (2) Even when absolute growth rates continue unchanged, a state's relative power will accelerate for a time and then (at a point of inflection) begin a process of deceleration, due to the bounds of the system, which causes a logistic peaking and a turn into relative decline. Similarly, accelerating decline ultimately begins to decelerate to a minimum level prior to leveling out or beginning a new upturn.

Thus, on this state power cycle, there are four "critical points" of sudden, massive, and unanticipated change where the projection of future role and security is very abruptly proven wrong. These critical points—the upper and lower turning points, and inflection points on the rising and declining trajectories—are the result of different levels and rates of absolute growth within the system, and competition for the finite systemic shares (the bounds of the system). More important, the critical points of sudden shift in the prior trend of *relative* power can occur even when absolute trends do not change throughout the system. Each critical point corresponds to the intuitive notion of the "shifting tides of history"—and explains the sense of surprise so often expressed at their occurrence.

The critical point is as troubling as it is unexpected because a disjuncture occurs in the state's long-standing view of security and place in the system. Historically, such an inversion in the trend of prior foreign policy expectations has not been easy for government or society—or for other states in the system. The critical points in a state's foreign policy have been the times where major war has been of the highest probability.

Note that the power cycle is a "cycle of power and role." Future power and role projections are embedded in the cycle, providing the basis for an encompassing notion of power-role equilibrium for the state. While realists have long acknowledged the importance of state interest and foreign policy role, it is necessary to conceive of how role changes as power changes on the state cycle to address issues of legitimacy and justice in power relations. The relation between power and role, and these concerns about justice, become imperative at the critical points where foreign policy adjustment, so precarious for systems stability, is so difficult to achieve.

Critical points and the structural causes of major war. Three basic processes underlie the impact of the power cycle dynamic on the occurrence of major war. First, passage through critical points is itself destabilizing, for the future power and role expectations of the state are suddenly and unexpectedly constrained by the bounds of the system. The tides of history abruptly seem to shift against the state, proving its future security projections dangerously misguided.

Second, power-role gaps long in the making are squeezed to the surface of foreign policy consciousness at these points, and appear formidable indeed as the state tries to cope with the shifting tide. Power-role gaps aggravate the uncertainty and tension that already exist at critical points. Since power and role are necessarily systemic, strains between power and role for the state ricochet throughout the system, demanding adjustment.

Third, the process of the inversion of force expectations worsens conflict behavior of states in a critical interval. Normal force expectations become inverted as the uncertainties and shocks to foreign policy sensibility cause both deterrer and aggressor to now regard force use, previously thought of as "unthinkable," as "thinkable." This transmutation of mentality is roughly analogous to the inversion of demand and supply expectations that occurs in so-called inverted markets, such as during the stock market collapse of 1929 and the oil price run-up of 1973 and 1979.

What happens in the critical interval to cause this inversion of force expectations? The decision atmosphere hardens. The inelasticity of "role ascription" and "power achievement" increases sharply as various sources of anxiety come together to intensify the sense of threat throughout the system. Attitude and action rigidify. The sense of uncertainty becomes monumental and exaggerates foreign policy response. All this is magnified and multiplied as to effect in a period when a number of leading states are confronting the uncertainties and tensions of shifting tides on their own power cycles.

A more general notion of equilibrium must confront two essential aspects of international political behavior: (1) long-term structural change on the state power cycles, most notably the shifting tides that occur so abruptly at critical points in the state's foreign policy experience; (2) the concept of state interest, or state foreign policy role. Collapse of the balance of power and peace twice in this century could have been avoided.

Failure of static, partial conceptions of balance. When a state faces superior power accompanied by suspected hostile intent, it always prescribes external alliance aggregation or coalition formation. This is both the strength of the balance of power prescription and the crux of its greatest weakness.

Power-cycle analysis exposes its flaws. While defenses must always be maintained against aggression, in the long term, rising power cannot be artificially halted, and declining power cannot be artificially bolstered. However, the balance of power attempted and promoted precisely these objectives.

External aggregation of power was used both to halt the advance of an ascendant state and to shore up the fortunes of a declining state (Carr 1939). No distinction was made between legitimate and illegitimate interests of the rising and declining states. While this formula to preserve stability worked most of the time, it was a recipe for cataclysmic misjudgment when the system was in rapid transformation. The consequence was intense structural strain within the central system—a systemswide crisis. War became the vehicle to forcibly "adjust" the hierarchy along lines that put power and interests once again into harmony. Designed to deter aggression and to provide peace and security, the balance of power wrongly conceived ended up precipitating war against the crumbling system it was supposed to protect.

World War I and the attempt to constrain rising power. Faced by the rapid ascendancy of German power in the late nineteenth century, the other members of the European system banded together to try to offset the German advances in relative power. So rapid was the rise of German power, and hence the relative decline of Britain, Austria-Hungary, and France, that the fears of the latter blinded them to the need for (and justice in) a transfer of role and status. While the allies denied intent, the effect was to "encircle" Germany according to the traditional conception of the balance of power so as to constrain this country "so powerful and yet so restless" (Trevelyan 1922, 443). In 1914, suddenly confronting the reality that it had peaked even as it remained so role-disequilibrated, Germany contested these constraints, using as a pretext defense of Austro-Hungarian interests in the Balkans. German challenge to the constraints of the balance of power precipitated a war that became major because of the degree of disharmony that had accumulated among the great powers in terms of power and role.

A more dynamic understanding of the structural situation, taking into account both foreign policy role and power, resolves this classic "dilemma of peaceful change." The structural constraints that caused the war, and that are the key to conflict resolution, are clear. (1) Britain, France, and Austria-Hungary were in severe decline in terms of relative power, but they did not wish to admit this decline nor to make adjustments for it in terms of interests in Europe or within the colonial empires. (2) German power was in ascendancy, yet none of the other governments was prepared to acknowledge this ascendancy, nor to transfer status or role to Germany in consequence of its greater power. Bent upon a larger international political role, Germany became a very dissatisfied actor, but it was willing to "wait" for greater status and role, so long as it could anticipate future relative power growth. (3) Russia

was beginning a slow ascent on its power cycle due to accelerated industriali-
zation, but it was also preoccupied with serious internal developments. (4)
The United States was isolationist according to the precepts of the Monroe
Doctrine, and it could not act as a moderator in the dispute between Germany
and its European neighbors.

In the late nineteenth century, instead of allowing role to shift toward
ascendant Germany, the rigidity of the balance-of-power system prevented its
occurrence. Then accelerated growth for Britain, Austria-Hungary, and France
led to improvements in their rate of decline (the second inflection point) and
the illusion that adjustment was not necessary. Germany's rise bumped
against the upper limit to its relative growth and, by 1914, was suddenly
pulled onto a declining trajectory by Russia's rapid rate of growth. The tides
of history had shifted monumentally. The system was experiencing the throes
of a critical, severely disequilibrated transformation. When this confluence
of critical changes exposed and tested the contradictions in the system, war
became by default the only apparent instrument available to offset the severe
structural strains (Doran 1989, 1991).

World War II and the attempt to appease declining power. In 1939,
neither equilibrium nor justice flowed from the allies' attempt to learn from
their past mistakes and to correct the deficiencies of the balance of power
(May 1973; Jervis 1976). Having been too harsh on Germany after World
War I, and too indifferent to German demands for a larger systemic role prior
to it, the allies sought to compensate Hitler, to temporize, and even to appease.
Attributed (correctly) to the British Labor leadership, this was also the policy
of virtually all the allies, from Stalin to FDR, and from the American wheat
farmer and the French industrialist to the Canadian Prime Minister MacKen-
zie King. Everyone sought to correct the wrongs done to Germany prior to
World War I by yielding position and role to Hitler.

By 1936, however, Germany was already in aggravated decline in relative latent capability, notwithstanding its great absolute strength and its passage through the second inflection point of lessened rate of decline. Germany
could make no further claims on the system for a larger role or greater status.
Moreover, Hitler's territorial demands were inherently aggressive and had to
be confronted on these grounds alone. The correct strategic response to Hitler,
evident from a larger concept of equilibrium, was a firm policy of balance and
opposition. Appeasement was exactly the wrong policy to follow. Again, an
incomplete and too static understanding of the balance of power led governments to make mistakes that at the time Churchill quite rightly concluded
were avoidable. It was a tragic misunderstanding of the dynamics of international political equilibrium.

General international political equilibrium. World War II showed that
states ignore the balance of power at their peril and that illegitimate interests

must never be appeased. World War I showed that states also ignore power-role equilibrium at their peril and that rising power cannot be halted. A minimum public morality requires both policies of balance and policies of accommodation regarding nonvital issues of foreign policy role and status, properly timed to changes on the state power cycles.

A genuine international political equilibrium is sensitive to the dynamics of structural change and facilitates the shift of interests from the declining to the ascendant state. As the rising state assumes more systemic responsibilities, it also has the obligation to respect the legitimate rights of states in decline. However, there is a tendency for interests to lag behind rising power because the system is reluctant to yield role to the ascendant actor. Likewise, there is a tendency for interests to lag behind declining power, creating overextension for the actor in decline, because the predominant state finds the transfer of role to others difficult.

A true international political equilibrium does not tolerate the effort to bolster declining power or to constrain rising power artificially through external alliance barrier. Equilibrium emerges through the internal harmony between interests and power within each of the major states, and therefore the external harmony among the foreign policies of all of the leading states. In the absence of centralized authority, such an equilibrium is difficult to affect, and once achieved, difficult to maintain (Keohane 1985). These difficulties in no way deny the logic of international political equilibrium itself. They only point to the complexity of managing equilibrium, especially in a period when the structure of the system itself is changing radically.

Moreover, international political equilibrium is not a recipe for passivism or for indifference to the security needs of the state. Aggression must always be halted. Sufficiently threatened in the short term, governments will always tend to unite in opposition according to the most basic precept of the balance of power. "Collective defense" is not sufficient to prevent major war and may even contribute to its magnitude and severity. If war is to be prevented or avoided, with security intact, then the long-term dynamics of power and role must be thoroughly understood and respected, and the dynamics of equilibrium initiated well in advance of the outbreak of hostilities. Security and peace can be achieved even during the tumultuous intervals of systems transformation, but the balancing process must overcome the tendencies toward static response and partial conceptions of adjustment.

The Mansbach-Vasquez Model and Power Cycle Analysis

A very helpful correspondence can be drawn between the Mansbach-Vasquez (1981, chap. 6) model of spiral conflict escalation and the process of the inversion of force expectations in power-cycle theory. "In a conflict spiral, disagreement (issue position) leads to the use of negative acts (conflict behavior), which in turn produces hostility (attitude). The presence of hostility encourages more disagreement ..." (Vasquez, chap. 7, herein). Inversion of force expectations during a critical interval on the power cycle corresponds to a "negative affect calculus" that generates an intractable conflict via such a spiral of issue position, conflict behavior, and attitude.

To explore the correspondence, let us collapse the three dimensions of the conflict-spiral mapping of conflict-cooperation into the two dimensions of power achievement and role ascription viewed at different times (positions) on the state power cycle. Future foreign policy expectation— expectation regarding future power, future role, and force utility in the short term—is the key variable in the power-cycle model. During normal (noncritical) periods on the power cycle, future expectations are "rewarded" by a continuation of the prior trend. The sudden inversion in the trend of power and role expectations that occurs at a critical point is the "trigger" that starts the process of inverted expectations regarding force utility.

More specifically, at a critical point, an issue position emerges when long-standing expectations regarding future status and security are suddenly proven wrong. The existence of a sizable and/or growing gap between achieved power and ascribed role increases the likelihood of disagreement regarding this issue. The dynamic concept of *increasing inelasticity* in power-cycle theory encompasses aspects of both attitude and conflict behavior. It reflects the increasing salience of the issue and hence increasing *rigidity* regarding the issue position, the *hardening of the atmosphere* vis-à-vis perceived threats to that issue position, and ultimately the very *inversion of expectations* whereby massive force use is viewed as acceptable. The conflict spiral is thus causally similar to the mechanism operating within a critical interval in the power-cycle conception of major war.

In the Mansbach-Vasquez model, conflict resolution occurs when the conflict spiral is reversed or interrupted by a positive policy intervention. The issue at stake becomes less salient, cooperative behavior is enhanced, and/or the general attitude surrounding the situation is improved. In the power-cycle model, conflict resolution must achieve one or more things: (1) increased elasticity, that is, increased receptivity to structural change, (2) minimization of the gap between power and role, and/or (3) a return to normal force expectations. In practice, all these components of conflict resolution are interrelated, as the Mansbach-Vasquez model so nicely demonstrates.

Order Maintenance at the Birth and Death of International Systems

Assimilation of Defeated Expansionist States as Conflict Resolution

Historically, a new international system has been ushered in at the end of each great expansionist attempt to dominate the international system by force. At the monumental peace treaties that signified the end of the one international political era and the emergence of a new era, the architects of the nascent system had to plan for a new equilibrium of power and role. The resulting peace treaties constituted the structural anchors for the new system. The goal was to create a new and better system that would not end in such a massive world war. A primary preoccupation of the drafters of these treaties was thus prevention of revanche by the most recent militarist state.

Not without reason, the architects of new structures at Yalta in February of 1945 worried about revanche. On two prior historical occasions, the defeated military hegemon rose against to try to dominate the international system by force: Napoleon followed Louis XIV; Hitler continued in the path of Wilhelmian Germany. At Yalta, and at Potsdam (July, 1945), Roosevelt, Stalin, and Churchill shaped the contours of the new system around a strategy to prevent Germany and Imperial Japan from ever again threatening the pluralism of international politics.

Assimilation of defeated hegemonic states is not without problems. A danger exists that a former hegemonic state will again attempt military expansionism, the condition of *underassimilation*. There is also a danger that the defeated hegemon will be so weakened by the war and the terms of the peace, *overassimilation*, that it will not be able to perform its function in a new reconstituted equilibrium to offset other potentially expansionist powers from attempting forceful domination.

Two general processes are operative in assimilative statecraft, the *media of consonance* and the *media of constraint*. The media of consonance are "those political, military, social, and economic forces which tend to *induce* the hegemon to resume a normal political relationship with other states during the order-maintenance phase" (Doran 1971, 195). Media of constraint are "those factors and forces operating between and among the hegemon and the other actors to *force* the hegemon to comply with the norms of the international system." The essence of assimilative strategy is to match consonance and constraint so effectively that the defeated hegemonic state is neither overassimilated nor underassimilated. Self-interest of the victors will often lead them to abuse assimilation to their own short-term advantage and to the long-term harm of structural equilibrium. That is why a number of systems have gotten off to a very bad start, notably, that following World War I and the Peace of Versailles, as already demonstrated, as well as the first two assimilative attempts (1648 and 1713) (Doran 1971).

The Peace of Westphalia (1648), after a half-century of warfare that followed the Spanish Hapsburg peak in relative power circa 1580,[5] was not a propitious application of the notions of balance and of equilibrium. Nor did it prevent the outbreak of European-wide war again. The problem was over-assimilation by breakup of the defeated hegemonic state, the Hapsburg Complex, thus permitting the too-rapid rise of France on the world scene. However, the problem was also the tardy transfer of prestige and interests from the Hapsburgs to Sweden and Holland, who enjoyed a meteoric rise, and to France, consolidating its power under Richelieu. To a government that is supremely concerned about status, such as that of the Sun King, matters of protocol, place, and precedence were almost more real than substantive power. By ignoring the early seventeenth-century disparity between excess Hapsburg interest and declining Hapsburg power, the system was only encouraging an assertive Louis XIV to attempt to take by force what French ascendancy had earned but had not heretofore obtained through more benign means.

The chaos of the Thirty Years' War had done little to bring about timely equilibration of power and interest. Focused efforts to maintain a balance of power that would constrain France did little to halt the accretion of French power since that power growth was indigenous, was incremental, and could not be stopped by external means. The balance of power could attempt to prevent territorial aggression by France, as for the most part it did, though not without considerable bloodshed. However, equilibration of interest and power internal to the Hapsburg Complex and internal to France, that is, a shift of interest from the Spanish-Austrian focus to that of France, was at least as essential as power balancing to the stability and peace of Europe. Lamentably, power balancing was mistaken for a thoroughgoing reexamination of power-interest equilibria before and after Westphalia.

Whereas the Peace of Westphalia failed to equilibrate Hapsburg interests with its declining power base, the Treaties of Utrecht (1713) failed to constrain the potential for French expansionism. Several reasons explain the neglect of the balance of power at Utrecht. First, Louis XIV had died, leaving French finances and military capability in disarray after so many years of fighting. With something of a vacuum apparent in French government, French latent capability was perhaps underestimated. Decline in actualized power symbolized by the demise of the Sun King obscured the reality that French power was still the preeminent factor in eighteenth-century diplomacy and had to be balanced. Rising more slowly toward its peak, however, it did not require a transfer of interests and prestige to ensure equilibrium. On the contrary, other governments, principally Britain and Prussia under Frederick II, were in ascendance and were demanding a larger place for themselves within the international political hierarchy. However, Utrecht did little to accommodate the new players or to contain the old.

Second, because of the death of the Emperor Joseph, thus threatening once again unification of the entire Hapsburg Complex under Charles VI, and because of the removal of Marlborough from command of the Grand Alliance, a series of parallel but bilateral negotiations with France (1711–13) emerged at the end of the War of Spanish Succession. This splintering of diplomatic effort reflected the division of the allies on the battlefield, and led to separate deals that were far more generous to France than was necessary or desirable, and far less indicative of the reality that France's relative power in the system was decelerating toward its upper limit. More than this, no clear sense of the need to establish firm bulwarks to possible future French expansionism emerged from these negotiations.

It is true that for a decade thereafter, Europe enjoyed greater peace than it had during any decade in the past two centuries. However, this peace arguably resulted from the exhaustion of the war economies and the astuteness of the diplomacies of Walpole and Fleury, rather than from the structure of the system as shaped at Utrecht. Even Catherine in the first years on the Russian throne saved money and avoided war rather than face a reopening of bellicosity on the grand scale of the prior century. The pirouettes of the mid-eighteenth century did little to make up for the weaknesses of the Utrecht effort to assimilate France, however, and nothing to generate a lasting balance of power that would place the threat of French revanche at its fulcrum.

In contrast, the Congress of Vienna (1815) was far more effective at establishing a lasting peace. This peace arrangement could not, to be sure, outlast the structural underpinnings that were its origin. When structure changed substantially, a new set of equilibria and a new balance of power would become essential. However, the Congress of Vienna did establish a structural basis for world order that would remain serviceable for decades.

At the heart of the Vienna solution to world order was awareness that French power, although in decline, was still dangerous and had to be balanced. However, the emergent balance of power was neither a creature of continentalism nor of maritime interest. It was neither the sole product of Metternich's genius nor of Castlereagh's acumen. Flexible and sensitive to the possibility that any of the five actors could upset the peace, the balance was also the product of overlapping alliances, the so-called *Quadruple* and *Holy Alliances*. This resiliency combined with flexibility kept all of the major governments on guard against a renewal of hostilities that would threaten core interests and therefore possess a high likelihood of escalation to world war.

Also at the heart of the Vienna approach was a successful equilibration of power and interest. The Congress of Vienna left no government seriously discontent or frustrated because of a disparity between its interest and power. Britain, the dominant power, found solace and preoccupation in a far-flung colonial empire, as well as a reservoir of resources outside the central system. Not until later in the century would Prussia attempt to consolidate its territory, and then not in a fashion that would lead to a risk of major war on the scale, for example, of the American Civil War. Thus, all of the major actors were comparatively satisfied with their role and status within the system. There were few surprises well into the century concerning future position on each nation's power curve. Linear projections of future position seemed adequate. Power and role for the most part remained in alignment.

The Congress of Vienna thus reinforced the existing structural relations among governments and the existing balance of power. So long as the power cycles of the leading states did not seriously distort this comparative balance and equilibrium, the system as a whole remained stable and peaceful. At the very least, the Vienna settlement did not get in the way of equilibrium and balance. The diplomatic record suggests that these policies may have been intended, so it probably actually contributed to their proper functioning.[6]

If statesmen at Vienna were indeed sensitive to the need for a broader concept of equilibrium, addressing concerns of role and status, it is all the more ironic that the long nineteenth-century peace was shattered by a refusal to yield increased role and status to Germany during its meteoric rise later in the century. So preoccupied was Britain with the possibility of renewed French expansionism that it had failed to consider the implications for equilibrium of the rise of a new dominant continental power. When that reality occurred, all of Europe demonstrated how incomplete and insufficient was that broader notion of equilibrium that had served the peace so long.

Assimilation of defeated militarist powers is a preoccupation at the birth of an international system because the prior system died in massive warfare. For assimilation to meet its full success within a mature international system, however, the larger concept of general international political equilibrium must become an element of order-maintenance in the new system. As that system itself begins to fade, and history moves into a phase of systems transformation, the management of equilibrium becomes even more important, though more difficult. By carefully nursing the process of international political equilibrium, statesmen may be able to help the old system to die and the new system to be born without the occurrence of massive world war.

Assimilation at Yalta: Creating the New World Order

How does the post–World War II assimilative process at Yalta fare by the previous standards of statecraft?

The structural anchors must be examined. It is often said that the foundations of bipolarity were laid on the battlefield where Patton's tanks and the Red Army met. While this observation may in part be true, the provisions at Yalta already prefigured the outcome. Yalta led to two results.

First, it determined that Germany would be divided and its society transformed politically into the image of the respective victors. Never before in the history of the modern state system had the media of constraint been so apparently coercive. To appease the Soviet Union, Poland and Czechoslovakia were reinforced with territory taken from East Prussia and the German Sudetenland, respectively. Despite words about free elections in the agreement, Soviet occupation of Eastern Europe and the establishment of Communist regimes there were foreordained. For Japan, too, unconditional surrender was to be its fate. While use of the atomic bomb, the symbol of total coerciveness, had not yet been decided (indeed the terms of the Yalta agreement in Far East Asia were strongly tilted toward getting a Russian declaration of war against Japan), the intent of total submission was everywhere evident. Although Germany was divided and Japan was occupied by the United States, their constitutions provided that neither would have a military place in the system.

Second, the Soviet Union, the principal target of the German war machine (with six million military dead, twenty times that for the United States), became the largest beneficiary of the peace. Not only was an Eastern European buffer created with Stalin's stamp, but the territorial transfers along the Soviet western border, illegally obtained in the 1941 barter with Hitler, were made official at Yalta. To obtain Soviet military support for a last attack on Japan, the democracies gave Stalin a free hand in Manchuria at the cost of China, the southern half of Sakhalin Island lost in the 1904–5 Russo-Japanese War, and the Kurile Islands. Yalta substantially strengthened the Soviet Union in international political and territorial terms. Thereby, ideological difference with the West was frozen into the structure of the system.

A plausible deduction from such a peace, which neither of the former hegemons attended, was that overassimilation was the inevitable result. Such a conclusion is premature. With the benevolence and perhaps naïveté of the predominant economic power, the United States, the media of consonance were to play an equally important part. Almost as a quid pro quo for the adoption of democratic institutions and the disproportionate benefits and weight obtained by the Soviet Union at Yalta, the United States proceeded to help rebuild the economies of both of the defeated hegemonic states with an industrial base much more modern than its own. In fact, as a further offset to the ever-growing military prowess of the Soviet Union, the United States spread its nuclear umbrella over both the Federal Republic of Germany and Japan, thus absolving them from much of the costs of defending themselves.

The post–1945 assimilative effort thus was the product of intensive application of the media of constraint—keeping troops on the territories of the defeated military hegemons under the guise of their own defense for almost a half-century—and the media of consonance—rebuilding technical and economic strength (the so-called *Wirtschaftswunder*) unparalleled in the twentieth century. Never before had both of these media been applied so zealously and yet so evenly. The result was a balanced and completely controlled form of assimilation that postponed many tough structural choices until much later in the century, when a combination of relative military decline for the superpowers and a diminution of Soviet ideological fervor would once again raise the question of the nature of systems transformation. From the narrow perspective of peace and comparative stability in the context of bipolarity, the assimilative effort at Yalta was a remarkable success, remarkable in part because of the deep offsetting operation of its two media.

Unfinished business. Yalta necessarily reflected to some extent the configuration of power at the end of the World War II. The bipolar configuration of power, and the resulting geo-strategic conflict trouble spots, were to some extent a product of the decision making at Yalta and Potsdam. When combined with the intense ideological polarization of the cold war on the one hand, and the collapse of the great colonial empires on the other, the unfinished business during the assimilative effort would become the source of the worst wars of the latter twentieth century. However, these wars were still "limited" and did not reenact the first half of the century. They did not constitute a qualified failure of the assimilative process, however imperfect that process was by the absolute standards of unsullied peace.

Unfinished business came in the form of the divided societies. The assimilative process for the most part dealt with Germany by dividing it. Likewise, in the aftermath of the Japanese withdrawal from Manchuria, the Soviet Union was allowed to control Korea above the 38th parallel, thus dividing it. Eventually, a division between North and South Vietnam, in the wake of French defeat in Indochina, would claim many lives on both sides and some 300 billion dollars of U.S. resources before ending in capitulation to the Communist government in Hanoi.

Divided societies as an assimilative solution became the focal points for international political tension after 1945. In 1948–49, Berlin was the locus of crisis during the airlift. Again in the 1950s, tensions emanating from societal divorce led to the East German construction of the Wall, which, more than any other action, symbolized the cold war and global division. The Korean War and the Vietnamese War were also products of attempted assimilative compromise. Societal cohesion proved damaging to world order when arbitrarily tampered with on behalf of larger global visions. Ethnic and linguistic solidarity, like the atom in physics, released enormous explosive energy when split. In the future, assimilation cannot rely on this method of international policy coordination.

Structural anchors and the avoidance of revanche. Some 45 years after the assimilative effort at Yalta, analysts are taking stock of the quality of the solution worked out regarding Germany and Japan. As the Federal Republic incorporates the German Democratic Republic in the midst of some European anxiety over German reunification, this aspect of the design seems to receive the most attention. Does German reunification signify a failure of the assimilative design? Does reunification create a threat to the stability of the global system? Our answer to each of these questions is a firm no.

Assimilation can only guide a young system into maturity. It cannot guarantee peace into perpetuity. It can give both a former hegemon and the system time to adjust, to adapt to a new international political equilibrium, and to allow new norms to become routinized. Moreover, the unfinished business of the Yalta design involved coping with the divided societies of which Germany was one. Eventual German reunification was essential to the welfare of the international system. The only matters were when, by what means, and upon whose terms.

Adaptation may be easier for the United States than for states on the German border. However, the global system has grown up around Germany and has reduced its potential for harm. Continent-sized states now exercise global leadership. Germany has neither the population nor the economy to challenge this leadership again, even if it chose to do so, which it does not. A reunified Germany will not threaten the peace; a splintered and unhappy pair of Germanies might. For Germany, the assimilative "bottom line," in a bipolar system itself beginning to experience transformation, is that it will assume the posture of a normal, saturated territorial state.

For Japan the bottom line may look quite different than for Germany. Power-cycle analysis reveals that Japan is in the ascendancy both economically and politically. While Japan, too, experienced the joint impact of the media of constraint and consonance, the latter were far more predominant than in the German case, even though two atomic bombs were dropped on Japan, killing more than two hundred thousand people (estimates were that over a million would have died in a conventional attack), and even though foreign troops continued to reside inside the borders of this densely populated nation nearly five decades after World War II. Thanks to accelerated economic growth that became the hub of world manufacturing industry, Japan by 1970 had returned to the same trajectory of growth it had been on prior to the war (Doran and Parsons 1980; Doran 1991). The media of consonance operated not only to fund Japanese recovery but to provide rich markets in the United States through the Korean War and on into the next decades of liberalized world trade. Japan has twice the population size of Germany, a much larger and more dynamic economy less burdened by military expenditures, and growing financial leadership.

Despite a constitution that prohibits certain kinds of militarization, a strong Socialist Party allegedly critical of rearmament, and important pacifist groups in the population, Japan has a powerful defense force and the capacity to become a military power possessing the most sophisticated armaments high technology can produce. Thus Japan is in a very important position on its power cycle, growing very rapidly, albeit at a diminished rate.

From the assimilationist perspective, perhaps the most important fact about Japan is that it has participated in one hegemonic attempt on the system, not two as was the case for both France and Germany. Moreover, Japan has not reached the upper turning point on its power curve, an event that, when it occurs, may tax the Japanese political capacity to accept a declining role in the international system.

Can Japan avoid the pattern of revanche of other ascendant military-expansionist powers of the past? Every indication to date is that Japan is quite prepared to accept whatever role the system bestows upon it, and that the expansionism of the past is not a role that Japanese society would tolerate or that the government of Japan would promote, much less carry out. However, might a new generation of Japanese feel differently if suddenly confronted with unexpected relative decline and a perception of severe role deprivation? For Japan to adjust fully and completely to the strains that await it on the upward path of its power growth, and when that growth peaks, much understanding and flexibility will be necessary on the part of other players in the system with whom Japan must interact, and from whom much will be required.

In sum, after fifty years of success, the process of assimilation will meet its greatest challenge. For assimilation to reach fruition, as the international system begins to enter transformation for the second time in the twentieth century, the fuller and more dynamic conception of international political equilibrium will become a theoretical and practical necessity.

Will the Impending Systems Transformation Be Peaceful?

The bipolar international system is dying; a new system has yet to be born. General equilibrium takes on its greatest meaning in terms of the structural specifics of the particular systems transformation. In the late twentieth century, this dynamic involves essentially five actors: the two superpowers, Japan, China, and if constituted into a single actor with a single foreign and defense policy, a united Western Europe. The current preoccupation is understandably with the former Soviet Union, still a nuclear giant, as it struggles to remake itself. However, we must focus our analysis here on the final stage of assimilating Germany and Japan into the system.

In terms of the long-term success or failure of assimilation at Yalta, the principal question during the impending systems transformation involves the future not of Germany, though this is important in European regional terms, but of Japan. Japan will avoid the mistakes of prior military hegemons that have undergone two expansionist attempts if international equilibrium is maintained throughout the transformation interval. What conditions must apply if this happy circumstance is to come to pass?

For equilibrium to be successful, Japan must assume a role that is commensurate with its power. The danger today is that Japan and the United States are deluding themselves. They continue to pretend that the United States can assume all order-maintenance responsibilities while Japan continues to be the principal foreign-exchange earner in the system. As long as international credit and the sale of domestic American assets to Japanese firms will permit this behavior, such a disharmonious set of relations can perhaps continue. At the same time, some Japanese citizens and opinion makers continue to assert that Japan is or should be uninterested in a larger world role. As the debate over voting rights in the IMF revealed, this mentality defies political and psychological reality. It amounts to a suppression of feelings that eventually may surface in resurgent nationalism.

The greater danger is that Japan's peak may occur as suddenly and expectedly as did Germany's, and that the failure to increase its world role during its period of rapid rise will be viewed as lost opportunity, or even as a denial by the United States and other states of its "rightful" place in the system. Better a long, slow adjustment of interests to power.

Such adjustment will require from the United States and Russia great understanding and perhaps coordinated strategies. Japan not only must legitimately seek a larger place in international financial and monetary circles. It must take a lead in liberalized international free trade talks since Japan more than any other big state stands to benefit from such a trade order. In addition, Japan will have to assume responsibility for its own defense. Nuclear capability is a bitter issue for Japan, but insofar as burden sharing cannot properly be worked out with the United States, Japan will become a nuclear power with some of the most advanced technological capability in the system. Territorial matters such as were acknowledged by the United States in Okinawa must be acknowledged by Russia with respect to the Kurile Islands.

In short, for assimilation ultimately to succeed, the principles of general equilibrium must be observed with regard to Japan. Role and power must be brought into harmony throughout the system. The United States and Russia will gradually have to transfer some role functions to Japan. Japan must learn to exercise these responsibilities of far broader leadership with some of the prudence it has displayed politically since 1945. Likewise, the other leading states in the system, including China and Western Europe, must grow accustomed to a Japan that adopts a more assertive political role than has been experienced recently.

China, an important entrant into the central system, continues to vacillate widely in both its domestic and its foreign policies. Still in the first phase of ascendancy on its power cycle, China will one day face passage through a first inflection point. However, given the variance among the points tracing its slow ascendancy, this event may perhaps be less troubling for China than for other states of the past having both more consistent policies and greater overall momentum in their rise in power. China will increasingly impact on the foreign policies of other governments, especially those within the Asian region. Systems transformation will not be complete until China finds a stable place within the general international political equilibrium.

Perhaps four to six decades or more will be necessary, judged by historical standards, for bipolarity to merge into some new form of mature multipolarity (Rosecrance 1963). Each international system is stable, based on its own norms and equilibrium (Russett 1985). Fully assimilated into the new system, Japan can be a very responsible player, supportive of that equilibrium. The trick will be to manage systems transformation smoothly in the intervening years of high international political uncertainty.

From Conflict to Conflict Resolution at the Level of the Global System: Answering *Machtpolitik*

To understand power is to understand its limits (bounds on relative growth), its issues (systemic role legitimacy and adjustments), its surprises (discontinuous expectations), and hence the shocks and uncertainties and sense of injustice conducive to violence.

Is war the creator of all things, as Heraclitus proclaimed? Is major war the Machiavellian instrument to coerce a necessary restructuring of world relationships? According to Liska (1968, 59), "the evolution of a European or any other international system is the story of conflicts which create the system and then later on lead to its destruction." Thompson (1988, xii) states that "global war emerged as a systemic mechanism for resolving policy-leadership disputes in the late 15th century. Since then the mechanism continued to evolve." Gilpin (1981), Organski and Kugler (1980), Modelski (1978), and Kennedy (1988), among others, argue that major war appears to be the vehicle whereby a new hierarchy of states is born. Reluctant governments will not yield privileged power positions except by force.

A number of points require clarification for the analysis to proceed. First, many structural conflicts between states have been resolved through the use of force. These were "contests of power" in the strictest meaning of the phrase. Therefore, history does reveal such examples of confrontation, not just at the top of the system, in support of the view of war as vehicle of structural change. However, most of these structural conflicts were fought over border disagreements (Vasquez 1993) or a range of other territory-related issues (Holsti 1991).

Second, when speaking of the relationship between war and systems structure, the assumption is that *major* war is the motor of change; not minor uses of force, but force at the highest levels. This use of force is not limited or limiting, albeit perhaps accompanied by the speculation that war will be over quickly, but this speculation is commonly associated with all endeavors of force use. It facilitates cooperation internally in support of the mission. However, the assumed brevity of the war to the contrary, the amount of force necessary to restructure world order at the top of the system has always been regarded as maximum force.

Third, insofar as major war today means the possibility not only of nuclear war, but nuclear war of unlimited dimension between two states with second-strike nuclear capability, using force at the highest levels is no small matter. According to classical deterrence theory, a government must be willing to defend its territory and that of its allies without flinching. But would a state defend the existing structure of world order, that it and others had created, with the unflinching determination to confront nuclear second-strike capability? Or, conversely, would potential challengers be willing to risk an all-out nuclear response from the defender of the existing order to the extent of triggering nuclear war against an opponent possessing second-strike nuclear capability? This puts the major war-as-the-vehicle-of-structural-change thesis in quite a different light.

Fourth, historical reality, for example vis-à-vis the origins of World War I, is far more complicated than the thesis envisions. World War I did not cause the relative decline of German power, any more than it toppled British dominance within the international system. These structural changes were long in the making. British power was long in relative decline. German power had peaked a decade prior to the war. Russia, the United States, and Japan were rising on the outskirts of the system. It was these dynamics that brought about the relative decline of both Britain and Germany, notwithstanding all the paired rivalries within the central system.

Thus the notion that war was necessary to restructure world power in 1914 belies historical fact. Restructuring was already going on in terms of power relationships. Role was admittedly more dilatory, and the war accelerated role change—but *not in the direction the parties intended.* Role shifted after World War II to the Soviet Union and the United States rather than to either the initial belligerents or the defenders of the old order. Major war neither precipitated the important changes in power nor was a reliable purveyor of role.

There is a threefold flaw in assertions that the war caused one contender (Germany) to decline, allowing another contender (Russia) to rise. (1) The central system was not composed of just two contenders: The full dynamic among all the leading states is essential to an understanding of relative power change. (2) Structural change was long in the making before major war actually occurred: Decline for Germany was intrinsic to economies and to relative power relationships. (3) The issue was *systemic adjustment of role*—an issue that assumed existential significance when Germany had to confront decline in relative power. War was an aberration not essential to systems change. Rather, it was an effect of failure to accommodate Germany's rise with role adjustments before it was too late. Only by comprehending the limits and surprises of power change can one hope to address questions of legitimacy and justice underlying the dilemma of peaceful change.

Contained within the dilemma of peaceful change are two strategic problems. First is the problem for the older declining state. The temptation is to resist yielding role for fear of the newly rising state. The fear is that the rising state will want to demand *more* in the future, possibly when it becomes a hegemon dominating all. Thus the logic for the declining state becomes, why yield now, when it will be expected to yield even more in the future? This is the invitation to preemptive attack, to strike now so as to avoid an ever-worsening situation in the future (Gilpin 1981; Levy 1987).

Second is the problem for the newly rising state. Why should the rising state assume role now instead of later when it can do so more easily and on its own terms when it has more power? This is the temptation of deferred gratification. It is also, partially, the mentality of the "free rider." The free-rider mentality is to let others do what they must and then to come in under their umbrella since that coverage is collective and cannot be denied.

In the former case, the contradiction is glaring. On the one hand, there is never a "right moment" for preemptive attack since the state is involved in a very long interval of relative decline. On the other, even more problematical, why should the declining state assume that another state is poised to attack if there is no historical evidence for this contention. Very likely, there will also be no current intelligence to conform such a notion. However, during periods of high uncertainty and regarding high-stakes matters, the paranoia of the subject is likely to distort the actual intention of the object. Aggressive fear will replace the normal prudence of statecraft.

In the latter case, the blemish is equally obvious. If the rising state waits to assume responsibility until later, it creates a power-role gap in the system, or what diplomatic historians have traditionally described as a "political vacuum." This places burdens on other governments incapable of funding the costs of a more extensive foreign policy. More seriously perhaps, by postponing responsibility, the state also postpones its own gratification associated with increased status and diplomatic visibility. The predicament for the state is that it will eventually peak. When that happens it will discover that it has forgone opportunity—foreign policy opportunity for leadership and visibility that is never likely to return. The shock to government and elites upon abruptly discovering this reality, having postponed gratification, is likely to be all the more destabilizing.

In short, the twin problems of the dilemma of peaceful change—the declining state's fear about future security and temptation to preemptive attack, and the equally serious propensity of some rising states to postpone responsibility until too late—are problems that confront all international systems in all periods of history. To resolve the dilemma of peaceful change that emerges out of political realism and neorealism, one must recognize the limits within the essence of power itself. The bounds of the system, that is, competition from even the smallest state in the hierarchy, force the rising state to peak in relative power and, ultimately, to enter decline on its power cycle. Rising states, then, will not defer role gratification on the mistaken assumption that they will be able to make it up in the future. Declining states will not deny increased role to the rising state out of fear that it will overwhelm and dominate the system.

Thrasymacus was rightly criticized by Socrates for believing that, internal to the state, justice meant that the strong should rule. However, ironically, external to the state, the injustice that has precipitated the most massive wars is even more egregious than that of Thrasymacus. The *decreasingly powerful* want to claim all of the perquisites, status, and influence that they had enjoyed when they were indeed at the top of their power cycle. The *increasingly powerful,* either because they foolishly postponed assuming responsibility until too late or because the system refused to adjust for them to allow them a timely assumption of rightly earned status and influence, find that they have been denied an appropriate role.

Thus Thrasymacus has been gone one better: The no-longer strong, who can no longer rule effectively, think they should continue to rule. That is the essence of the problem. The increasingly weak attempt to rule at the cost of the increasingly strong. This is a recipe for structural catastrophe. It is a recipe that not even conflict-resolution techniques alone can overcome.

A structural resolution to the problem of peaceful change must precede more tactical measures of conflict resolution per se. When the structural foundation is made propitious for the application of conflict-resolution effort, then the truest benefits of the conflict-resolution enterprise can become available to world politics, but only in the context of such general international political equilibrium.

Limits and Possibilities of Conflict Resolution at the Global Level

This chapter has made three arguments. First, for conflict resolution to proceed at the international level, a foundation is essential, namely, a structural equilibrium between power and role for the leading states in the system. Power-cycle analysis suggests how that equilibrium is to come about and how it is to be sustained. Such an equilibrium faces its toughest test during systems transformation. Gaps between power and role must be eliminated before states pass through critical points of abrupt change in foreign policy expectation. The transformation to new power trends need not be aggravated by a crisis of role adjustment.

Second, the assimilation of defeated expansionist states is conflict resolution of the broadest sort. This occurs after the major wars when the great international peace treaties are signed forging the terms of a whole new era of statecraft. Some progress and learning are evident here. Embedding structural and institutional arrangements have made management of future international relations marginally more certain. Underassimilation of Germany and Japan had to be avoided to prevent revanche by one or both as they rebuilt their positions on their respective power cycle. Likewise, overassimilation had to be avoided or the Soviet Union might have become too great a threat to the stability of the system. The concurrent development of the United Nations was an auxiliary mechanism for the collective management of stability at lower levels of intensity. Assimilation in 1945 established a framework of conflict resolution that lasted for over half a century.

Third, political realism need not embrace the pessimistic assumption that major war is the arbiter of future systemic relations. That major war was associated with each prior interval of systems transformation is indisputable, but even a perfect correlation across time is not determinative of the future. Past correlational results are subject to new circumstances, understandings, and ideas. States can prevent the severe disequilibrium of power and role that exacerbated the strains and tensions of prior systems transformations. Both increase in the destructiveness of weaponry and learning from past failure make major war less likely to be the architect of future international systems. However, just as conflict resolution becomes more feasible in this era, it also becomes more necessary, given even a small probability that states may lose their security through force use or threatened force use at the highest levels.

Why then is conflict resolution not a more commonly used strategy at the global level? In the international context, the limits as well as potential of conflict resolution are somewhat daunting. Regarding mediation, the "strongest relationship" seems to hold for the "level of conflict" (Wall and Lynn 1993, 174). The higher the conflict level, the more the "likelihood of successful mediation" decreases. This is a thought-provoking finding, since some of the greatest successes of conflict resolution internationally, such as the Camp David Accords, have been through mediation. It is perhaps for this reason that Raimo Vayrynen and associates argue that instead of resolving international conflict, conflict must be transformed by redefining modes of operation, issues, and even the actors themselves (Vayrynen 1993).

According to Ernst Haas (1990), international organizations are managing conflict through "adaptation" or "learning." Alexander George (1991, 3–4) observes that Moscow and Washington have "gradually learned to better understand and respect each other's vital interests, to regulate and somewhat restrain their global rivalry, and to deal with specific conflicts of interest in ways that do not plunge them into new war-threatening crises." Having reviewed a number of international crises, Glenn Snyder and Paul Diesing (1977) conclude that the crisis will end in "capitulation" if one party has clearly established its "dominance of resolve" during the confrontation, in "compromise" if it has not. Perhaps governments are slowly learning, under the compelling pressure of circumstance at the highest force levels, to shift more cases into the latter category.

In terms of the Mansbach and Vasquez paradigm, learning to make conflict resolution work will require policy intervention to reduce the salience of an *issue* for the disputants, to enhance cooperative *behavior,* or to improve the general *attitude* surrounding negotiations. The conflict spiral proceeds through issues, to behavior, to attitude, but presumably could be altered favorably through intervention at any of these loci. Similarly, conflict resolution regarding the most serious instances of security loss and war ought to address the situation prior to a critical interval on a nation's power cycle. Such policy intervention can occur by learning to minimize gaps between power and role (issue manipulation), to return the intense behavior caused by inverted force expectations to a more normal condition (behavior modification), or to increase "elasticity," that is, relax the general attitude surrounding diplomatic talks (attitude change). In their model and power-cycle theory, there are alternative vehicles and times of entry to wind down the conflict spiral or to navigate a critical point on the power cycle. Another common lesson is that late entry makes conflict resolution terribly difficult. Early impact on elasticity or attitude change is indispensable. Avoiding international conflict is better, other things being equal in security terms, than attempting belatedly to manage it.

In short, there is nothing in the realist or neorealist outlooks that is inherently antithetical to conflict resolution. In fact, assessment of the limits, issues, surprises, and shocks associated with changes in relative power suggests a propitious structural framework for conflict resolution—and a concept of justice to guide conflict resolution at the international level. Practitioners and theorists of the art of conflict resolution should recognize, however, that the nature of war in a decentralized international system, where the means of destruction are so available and so final, makes conflict management and resolution more complex and difficult than in other arenas.

NOTES

1. Hence, political realism must not be confused with *machtpolitik*—the drive for power, by any means, for power's sake, made famous most recently by Hitler. Nor is it the polar opposite of idealism or liberalism. Properly conceived, realism can meet Vasquez's (1983, 1987) criteria for a more comprehensive view of political behavior than "power politics." Neorealism recognizes as well (as I interpret it) the paramount necessity of matching power with role. Critics should distinguish these variants of realism and forgo caricature. Analysts should establish the assumptions and probe in depth the ethics and prudence required for holistic realist-cum-idealist behavior.

2. Thompson (1992, 128) recognizes Dehio as "an exemplar of the balance-of-power tradition," but uses his distinction between continental and maritime powers to support the thesis of long-cycle hegemonic leadership by a maritime state. The latter, Thompson adds, explains the absence of continental hegemony in the middle of the seventeenth and eighteenth centuries (1992, 147). In my view, Dehio sees the maritime state as one type of fringe power rising on the outskirts of a system, which helps pull the aspirant for continental hegemony into relative decline, and thus plays a balance of power role. See Doran (1971) and the third section of this chapter.

3. Hume (1752) disputes Butterfield's (1966) assertion that the Greeks did not know the balance of power, faulting Roman translations. Waltz (1979) adds that pursuit of a balance-of-power strategy need not be conscious to be effective—Athenians may have practiced such a strategy without theorizing about it.

4. See Doran (1971, 191–94) and Doran (1991, chap. 3), noting in particular the very helpful figures.

5. Doran (1971). *The Harper Atlas of World History* (1986) gives a precise date for the Spanish peak, 1580. Most historical accounts provide a broader interval, and emphasize how long-standing economic and financial policies undermined Spain's power base from within, accelerating its relative demise as much smaller states began to consolidate power. Only eight years after this peak, in 1588, Spain struck out against the British fleet, and the fateful "Protestant wind" defeated its Armada. The massive changes in structure eventually strained the system at its core, witnessed by the web of tensions in the Thirty Years' War.

6. Historian Paul Schroeder (1986) documents this conscious effort to obtain a broader equilibrium that would balance interests with power. He also stresses how

smaller European states in the post-Vienna period acted as a buffer for the absorption of conflict. I put a bit more weight on structural factors, notably the Tsar's willingness to accept a France intact, and the British effort to build "pillars" around France without strengthening either Austria or Russia unduly. Schroeder (1992) seeks a structural basis in terms of hegemonic stability theory, but Enno Kraehe (1992) and Wolf Gruner (1992) show that the appropriate term is "cooperative great power hegemony," what in older parlance are called "spheres of influence." Austria, Prussia, and France were individually too powerful for either Britain or Russia to dominate the peace even if sufficient cooperation between Castlereagh and Alexander I, to the exclusion of these smaller states, had been possible. Robert Jervis (1992) attempts to account for the strategic logic of the parties through the Prisoner's Dilemma analogy. The analogy does convey the willingness of the principals to accept second-best outcomes that in turn created a first-best solution for the system as a whole.

REFERENCES

Butterfield, H. 1966. "Essay on the Balance of Power." In H. Butterfield and M. Wight, eds., *Diplomatic Investigations*. London: Allen and Unwin.

Carr, E. H. 1939. *The Twenty Years' Crisis, 1919–1939: An Introduction to the Study of International Relations*. London: Macmillan.

Dehio, L. 1962. *The Precarious Balance: Four Centuries of the European Power Struggle*. New York: Alfred A. Knopf, Inc.

Doran, C. F. 1969. "The Politics of Assimilation: A Comparative Study of the Integration of Defeated Hegemonic States into the International System." Ph.D. Diss., The Johns Hopkins University, Baltimore.

————. 1971. *The Politics of Assimilation: Hegemony and Its Aftermath*. Baltimore: The Johns Hopkins University Press.

————. 1989. "Systemic Disequilibrium, Foreign Policy Role, and the Power Cycle: Challenges for Research Design." *Journal of Conflict Resolution* 33, no. 3 (September): 371–401.

————. 1991. *Systems in Crisis: New Imperatives of High Politics at Century's End*. Cambridge: Cambridge University Press.

Doran, C. F., and W. Parsons. 1980. "War and the Cycle of Relative Power." *American Political Science Review* 74, no. 4 (December): 947–65.

Druckman, D. 1973. *Human Factors in International Negotiations*. Beverly Hills, CA: Sage Publications.

George. A. L., ed. 1991. *Avoiding War: Problems of Crisis Management*. Boulder, CO: Westview Press.

Gilpin, R. 1981. *War and Change in World Politics*. New York: Cambridge University Press.

Gruner, W. D. 1992. "Was There a Reformed Balance of Power System or Cooperative Great Power Hegemony?" *The American Historical Review* 97, no. 3: 725–32.

Haas, E. B. 1990. *When Knowledge Is Power: Three Models of Change in International Organization*. Berkeley, CA: University of California Press.

Haas, R. N. 1990. *Conflicts Unending: The United States and Regional Disputes.* New Haven, CT: Yale University Press.

Holsti, K. J. 1991. *Peace and War: Armed Conflicts and International Order 1648– 1989.* Cambridge: Cambridge University Press.

Hume, D. 1752. "Of the Balance of Power." Reprint, in J. A. Vasquez, ed., *Classics of International Relations,* 2d ed., 273–76. Englewood Cliffs, NJ: Prentice Hall.

Hyland, W. G. 1990. "America's New Course." *Foreign Affairs* 69, no. 2: 1–12.

Jervis, R. 1976. *Perception and Misperception in International Politics.* Princeton, NJ: Princeton University Press.

———. 1992. "A Political Science Perspective on the Balance of Power and the Concert." *The American Historical Review* 97, no. 3: 716–24.

Katz, M. N. 1991. "Superpower Conflict Resolution: Lessons for the Future." *The Annals* (special volume edited by I. William Zartman), 518(Nov.): 177–87.

Kennedy, P. 1988. *The Rise and Fall of Great Powers: Economic Change and Military Conflict from 1500 to 2000.* New York: Random House.

Keohane, R. O. 1985. *After Hegemony: Cooperation and Discord in the World Political Economy.* Princeton, NJ: Princeton University Press.

Kolodziej, E. A. 1991. "U.S.-Soviet Cooperation: The Role of Third States." *The Annals* 518(Nov.): 118–31.

Kraehe, E. E. 1992. "A Bipolar Balance of Power." *The American Historical Review* 97, no. 3: 707–15.

Kremenyuk, V. A. 1991. "Rules of Conduct in the Settlement of Regional Conflict." *The Annals* 518(Nov.): 143–52.

Levy, J. S. 1983. *War and the Modern Great Power System, 1495–1975.* Lexington, KY: University of Kentucky Press.

———. 1987. "Declining Power and the Preventive Motivation for War." *World Politics* 40:82–107.

Liska, G. 1968. *War and Order: Reflections on Vietnam and History.* Baltimore: The Johns Hopkins University Press.

Long, F. A., and G. W. Rathjens, eds. 1976. *Arms, Defense Policy, and Arms Control.* New York: W. W. Norton & Co., Inc.

Mansbach, R. W., and J. A. Vasquez. 1981. *In Search of Theory: A New Paradigm for Global Politics.* New York: Columbia University Press.

May, E. R. 1973. *Lessons of the Past: The Use and Misuse of History in American Foreign Policy.* New York: Oxford University Press.

Midlarsky, M. I. 1988. *The Onset of World War.* Boston: Unwin Hyman.

Modelski, G. 1978. "The Long Cycle of Global Politics and the Nation-State." *Comparative Studies in Society and History* 20, no. 2 (April): 214–35.

Nye, J. S., Jr., ed. 1984. *The Making of America's Soviet Policy.* New Haven, CT: Yale University Press.

———. 1990. *Bound To Lead: The Changing Nature of American Power.* New York: Basic Books.

Organski, A. F. K., and J. Kugler. 1980. *The War Ledger.* Chicago: University of Chicago Press.

Rosecrance, R. N. 1963. *Action and Reaction in World Politics.* Boston: Little, Brown.

Rosenau, J. N. 1990. *Turbulence in World Politics: A Theory of Change and Continuity.* Princeton: Princeton University Press.

Russell, B. 1952. *The Impact of Science on Society.* London: Unwin Hyman.

Russett, B. 1985. "The Mysterious Case of Vanishing Hegemony." *International Organization* 39:207–31.

Schroeder, P. W. 1986. "The 19th-Century International System: Changes in the Structure." *World Politics* 39:1–26.

———. 1992. "Did the Vienna Settlement Rest on a Balance of Power?" *American Historical Review* 97, no. 3(June): 683–706.

Smith, S. 1987. "The Development of International Relations as a Social Science." *Millennium* 16:189–206.

Smoke, R. 1977. *War: Controlling Escalation.* Cambridge, MA: Harvard University Press.

Snyder, G. H., and P. Diesing. 1977. *Conflict among Nations: Bargaining, Decision-Making, and System Structure in International Crises.* Princeton, NJ: Princeton University Press.

Stein, J. G., ed. 1990. *Getting to the Table: The Processes of International Prenegotiation.* Baltimore: Johns Hopkins University Press.

Thompson, W. R. 1988. *On Global War: Historical-Structural Approaches to World Politics.* Columbia, SC: University of South Carolina Press.

———. 1992. "War and Systemic Capability Reconcentration." *Journal of Conflict Resolution* 32, no. 2 (June): 335–66.

Thornton, T. P. 1991. "Regional Organizations in Conflict Management." *The Annals* 518(Nov.): 132–42.

Trevelyan, G. M. 1922. *British History in the Nineteenth Century and After (1782–1919).* London: Longmans, Green and Co., Ltd.

Vasquez, J. A. 1983. *The Power of Power Politics: A Critique.* New Brunswick, N.J.: Rutgers University Press.

———. 1986. "Capability, Types of War, Peace." *Western Political Science Quarterly* 38:313–27.

———. 1987. "The Steps to War: Toward a Scientific Explanation of Correlates of War Findings." *World Politics* 40 (October): 108–45.

———. 1993. *The War Puzzle.* Cambridge: Cambridge University Press.

Vayrynen, R., ed. 1993. *New Directions in Conflict Theory: Conflict Resolution and Conflict Transformation.* Newbury Park: Sage Publications.

Wall, J. A., and A. Lynn. 1993. "Mediation: A Current Review." *Journal of Conflict Resolution* 37, no. 1 (March): 160–94.

Waltz, K. N. 1979. *Theory of International Politics.* Reading, MA: Addison-Wesley.

Winham, G. R. 1976. *Negotiation as a Management Process.* Halifax, Nova Scotia: Center for Foreign Policy Studies, Dalhousie University.

Zartman, I. W., ed. 1991. *Resolving Regional Conflicts: International Perspectives.* Special volume of *The Annals of the American Academy of Political and Social Sciences* 518(Nov.): 8–187.

Zartman, I. W., and M. R. Berman. 1982. *The Practical Negotiator.* New Haven, CT: Yale University Press.

Part 4
Conclusion

CHAPTER 10

The Learning of Peace: Lessons from a
Multidisciplinary Inquiry

John A. Vasquez

Peace, like war, is something that is learned, and both are deeply affected by
the ideas people have about peace and war. Mead (1940, 402) tells us that
warfare is a social invention like writing, marriage, or trial by jury. It is a
practice that groups develop to handle certain situations; a group learns from
its folklore that when confronted with certain situations (having characteristics X, Y, Z), war is the appropriate response (Vasquez 1993, chap. 1).

Groups learn not only for what reasons it is legitimate to go to war, but
also how to conduct war. War should not be confused with "ubiquitous
violence" (Bull 1977, 185). War is an institution with an order to it. It has a
purpose and is fought on a certain basis, often following well-known rules
and norms that vary through history. The presence of war therefore does not
mean that all is a Hobbesian anarchy; rather the strength of order in global
society is reflected in how it makes war. A political order, whether it be at the
global, domestic, or local level, involves an understanding of when and for
what reasons violent institutions (like war, coups d'état, or child beating) may
be initiated and who can engage in these practices (Vasquez 1993, chap. 1).

Peace is also something that is learned. People and groups learn to get
along with others and develop a variety of ways to settle disputes and resolve
deep underlying conflicts without the use of collective violence. We can and
do make peace all the time at the interpersonal, domestic, and interstate levels
(Boulding 1987). Peace does not just happen, however; it is subject to structural influences and the conscious actions taken by groups. Peace is the
outcome of a set of practices that permit the resolution of disagreements and
the establishment of relations that embody a minimal level of respect and
tolerance. The analysis in this chapter is based on the assumption that how
peace is made is not fixed and unchanging. People make peace in a variety
of ways and some ways are more effective than others.

An understanding of peace and war must keep in mind how the two are
related and in what ways peace is maintained by providing functional equivalents to war and other violent practices. Within the modern global system,

211

war has been an institution by which binding political decisions can be made. To the extent that there are other ways of making authoritative decisions, war will be less frequent. Only rarely in established states does war (either in the form of civil war or social revolution) become a way of resolving a political issue. Most political issues are resolved nonviolently by the political processes of the established government.

If we view war as a social invention, then we must also see government, and politics itself, as a social invention. Everyday politics (like party politics or diplomacy) is distinguishable from war in that it is an interdependent system of decision making, whereas war is a unilateral attempt to escape that interdependence. Government is useful because it not only institutionalizes interdependencies, but provides ways of breaking stalemates to which very equal interdependencies are prone. War is not simply an act of violence, but a way of conducting politics. Like government, it is also a way of breaking stalemates, but unlike government it provides a unilateral solution for the resolution of issues, and this has been the main reason why actors have found it so attractive, despite its costs. War, government, and politics, then, must be seen as different ways of resolving issues and making collective decisions. In that sense, they are functional equivalents (see Vasquez 1994).

Not all conflict, however, takes the form of a political issue that needs to be resolved. Within domestic society at both the local and national levels, there are many conflicts that do not so much require the passage of new laws for their settlement as they do the application or interpretation of existing law. For these kinds of disputes, the criminal courts and legal system provide a set of practices for maintaining the peace. The presence of such an institution not only prohibits the use of violent practices (e.g., gang warfare, vendettas, or vigilantism) for settling disputes, but presents the parties with rules, principles, and procedures for ending their differences. Likewise, civil suits provide a way for individuals and corporations to settle claims in a routinized manner rather than taking the issue into their own hands by using violence (e.g., first fights or duels) or economic coercion (breaking contracts, boycotts). These, as well as a variety of other domestic practices, provide an alternative to violence by setting up channels for authoritatively settling disagreements.

The ways in which disputes are settled are not fixed, however. One of the reasons for the growth of alternative dispute resolution (ADR) techniques and the spread of conflict-resolution ideas in the domestic arena is the realization that litigation may not be the best or most efficient way to settle disputes or resolve deep-seated conflict. U.S. society has become terribly litigious and such action may have long-term negative effects on individual relationships and the community as a whole. Increasingly within the United States there is a recognition that the way in which individuals, couples, neighbors, classes (labor-management), and races make peace with one another can be changed and improved. Internationally, with the end of the cold war, there is a recognition that power politics behavior is not the most efficient or the most appropriate way to resolve conflicts.

In this analysis, the previous chapters will be reviewed with an eye to how we might learn to make peace better and what specific lessons might be worth exploring in more detail. Different disciplines have provided varying insights that can be useful in broadening knowledge even where the approaches are not always complementary. More significantly, the variety of practices and experiences of using conflict-resolution techniques in different settings from the family and corporate context to the neighborhood, legal, and interstate context provide a wealth of experience that needs to be systematically analyzed for its possible lessons. The next section reviews conflict-resolution practices to see which techniques seem to work in which contexts and how conflict resolution at the interpersonal and domestic level might inform conflict resolution at the interstate level. It also examines to what extent differences in structure at the interpersonal, domestic, and global levels make certain applications of theory and practice across levels problematic. The chapter concludes with a summary of what techniques seem most applicable across fields and contexts and what areas of conflict-resolution theory and practice would benefit from further exploration across disciplines and levels of analysis.

Learning from Conflict-Resolution Practice

Most of the chapters in this book have addressed the question of how solutions to problems in one area might be relevant to other areas, with particular focus on the global arena. If we are to learn how to improve conflict resolution, broadly defined, it is important to investigate what conflict-resolution strategies and specific techniques work and what might be applicable across contexts. This involves reviewing existing practices to see how similar problems are treated in different contexts and what solutions and techniques might be adapted from one area to the other and which might not. Kolb and Babbitt explore in detail some of the problems faced in mediation, which is one form of conflict resolution, and outline how these problems might also arise in international mediation. Ronald Fisher provides a similar discussion of third-party consultation and problem solving, with more of a focus on how such techniques might be applied at the global level. Kriesberg and Pruitt in their respective chapters attempt to identify what theoretical constructs, assumptions, and practices are most applicable across levels of analysis. Burton challenges the presupposition that the distinction between domestic and international politics is meaningful for understanding conflict and its resolution. Baruch Bush looks at the effect of structure on the way disputes are settled and conflicts resolved within the United States, while Johnson examines the effect of international law and Doran the role of power in the way conflict resolution operates in the global political system.

What have these efforts revealed? The most basic conclusion is that mediators and third parties involved in problem solving face common obstacles they must overcome if a resolution is to be found. Regardless of the context, common obstacles and problems that appear within intense conflict have similar effects. This suggests that common solutions or strategies might be applicable and a number of analysts offer very similar advice.

It is practically common knowledge among conflict-resolution theorists that mediators and third parties must establish trust between themselves and those they are trying to aid. Disputants must have a certain level of trust in the mediator or consultant if they are going to take suggestions seriously. Tactics for establishing trust have been the focus of much research (see Kressel and Pruitt 1989).

One of the most important tasks of mediators is to facilitate discussion, but how a mediator structures what and when things are communicated will have an important impact (Kolb and Babbitt, in this volume). Open communication between the parties can often do as much harm as good. This is especially the case when communication raises hostility levels or focuses on repeating stories of past injustices rather than focusing on shared interests or on seeing if there is common ground and a possible solution that might be the basis for a way out of the conflict and the subject of serious negotiation. Mediators and third-party consultants can help the parties to keep on track, to avoid the harmful, and to see things in a different light.

Kolb and Babbitt (in this volume) provide specific advice (based on empirical research) on what tactics a mediator might employ to deal with these and related problems. This advice is clearly relevant to mediators working at the interpersonal, intergroup, and interstate levels even though the specific nature and content of the problem may vary. Fisher also provides specific advice for third-party consultants based on an identification of the stage of the conflict. He also reviews the empirical research of Bercovitch (1986) and Frei (1976) to see what factors are associated with success and which with failure.

Pruitt (in this volume) reviews some of the psychological barriers that often prevent disputants from breaking away from a conflict and that a mediator must deal with if progress is going to be made. These include the tendency of both parties toward selective perception, biased information search, biased attribution, and engaging in behavior producing a self-fulfilling prophecy.

Kriesberg (in this volume) shows that even if conflicts are at different levels, the outside party may face similar problems depending on the stage of the conflict. Conflict resolution can involve preventing conflict, limiting escalation once conflict emerges, getting adversaries to the table, problem-solving negotiation, and/or reaching high-quality agreements. Since each of these activities poses similar goals, they are often amendable to a set of common strategies the outside party can adapt to the specific circumstance.

Clearly, these analyses suggest that the behavior and skill of the mediator and third-party consultant are a variable in whether a conflict is resolved or a dispute settled, and empirical research confirms this (see the discussions in Kolb and Babbitt, and in Fisher). However, the previous chapters also suggest that other factors are important as well. These include: (1) the nature of the relationship between the disputants, (2) the type of issues over which they are contending, (3) the nature of the proposals that are being offered by each side to resolve the conflict or settle the dispute, and (4) whether the structure of the system (including institutions and beliefs) in which the conflict occurs offers channels for the pacific resolution of conflicts.

Many analysts see the underlying relationship between parties as critical for explaining the dynamics of conflict and for assessing the prospects for conflict resolution (see Fisher, in this volume; Pruitt, in this volume). As both Pruitt and Vasquez have pointed out, hostile relationships are characterized by festering issues and spirals of escalation. When relationships are negative and hostile, it is hard to reach the agreements that would be reached if relationships were more neutral. Knowing how differences in position and behavior toward one another affect psychological hostility and friendship is important if attempts to reverse a conflict dynamic are to succeed. Various factors that might bring about such reversals, such as unilateral conciliatory initiatives or hurting stalemates (Pruitt, in this volume; Kriesberg, in this volume; Zartman 1989) have been the subject of investigation.

What the parties have done and do toward each other are the most important factors in shaping a relationship. Thus, prior interactions are often the best guide for understanding and predicting current interactions. Nevertheless, outside parties can change a relationship by trying to change behavior and moderate attitudes that might give immediate efforts to reach an agreement or begin a negotiation more of a chance of success. Short-term strategies like trying to get the parties to see things from the other side's perspective, to empathize with the other party, and to avoid public posturing while simultaneously trying to create a positive psychological and physical environment can play an important role in successful talks (Pruitt, in this volume). In more intractable disputes, long-term strategies intended to change the basic relationship by changing the attitudes of important individuals or the structure in which the groups operate may be necessary. Such strategies include things like increasing activities that are incompatible with violence, for example increased trade or economic interdependence (Pruitt, in this volume), cultural exchanges (Mitrany 1943), or reaching agreement on issues that are less important but where fewer differences are present (Vasquez, in this volume; Dean and Vasquez 1976).

Outside parties can also play an important role by pointing out the costs of continuing the conflict and finding alternative ways for the parties to meet their basic needs and interests. Whether such efforts will succeed will depend on other factors shaping the relationship between the disputants. These include whether the relationship between the disputants is long-term and can be expected to continue and whether the relationship involves important interdependences. In such a situation it behooves each to settle the dispute in a way that will help the relationship. Likewise, the extent to which class, race, or economic differences between the parties are fueling the conflict of interests is an important dimension. Finally, the extent to which the parties are relatively equal in power and status, or whether one side is trying to maintain dominance and the other is trying to break free are important factors shaping the dynamics of the conflict and its possible solution. Such socioeconomic and structural factors are important sources aggravating conflict. At the same time, however, attempts to directly address these conditions can help to ameliorate the situation.

The relationship between the parties is an important element in determining the dynamics of conflict and the prospects for conflict resolution, but it must be kept in mind that the original hostility in the relationship and the likelihood that a mediator will be able to reduce that hostility will depend in part on the nature of the issue under contention. Issues that link a number of stakes into a single overarching issue are extremely difficult to negotiate and resolve and usually must be de-coupled before any progress can be made (Vasquez, in this volume).

Similarly, issues that are infused with symbolic and transcendent qualities are less likely to be compromised. Thus, issues that are discussed in terms of interests can often be settled by compromise, whereas those discussed in terms of rights or involving matters of principle are less prone to splitting the difference or to any negotiation at all. Kolb and Babbitt (in this volume) find that issues of pay are easier to negotiate than issues involving the prerogatives of labor and management. Bercovitch (1986) finds that disputes over tangible interests are more likely to be successfully mediated than disputes involving ideological differences. Likewise, Vasquez (1983) finds that intangible issues are more conflict-prone than tangible issues. Whether one views the disagreement in terms of interests, rights, needs, values, or costs and benefits will have an effect on the dynamics of conflict. Since this is the case, political systems that have a tendency to frame issues in one way rather than another are more likely to give rise to intractable conflicts.

The reason some issues become harder to resolve than others, as Vasquez (in this volume) points out, is that the nature of the issue and how it is defined shapes the kinds of proposals the parties are likely to offer or consider. Issues that are seen in zero-sum terms are going to give rise to proposals that basically say, "I win and you lose." Obviously such proposals are not likely to be accepted and must be imposed. Conflict resolution is most likely to be successful with issues that are susceptible to a win-win solution (Pruitt and Rubin 1986). Since only some issues are clearly defined this way, often successful conflict resolution involves making the parties redefine their true issues and needs so that a win-win solution is possible.

The kinds of disputes in question and how parties define the issue then can be of critical importance. When a relationship becomes so hostile that the issue becomes the other, rather than some visible stake, then hurting the other, regardless of costs, may become the main point (Vasquez, in this volume). Mediators can do little in such a situation except to point out that the parties are moving in that direction and the costs may not be worth it. If, as often happens (see Pruitt and Rubin 1986), the parties become entrapped in an escalating conflict where the costs of staying in are outweighing any future likely benefit, then mediation, although difficult, has a clear role to play.

A society as a whole, however, can mitigate the effects of such intractable disputes by channeling them into a settlement process that reduces negative social effects. For example, civil suits may be preferable to murder or vendetta. In the international realm, coercive diplomacy or limited wars may be preferable to total wars. Peace therefore need not depend on eliminating even the most conflict-prone issues, so long as channels exist for settling or resolving these in a nonviolent manner. One of the things that distinguishes relatively peaceful societies from violent ones is the presence of such channels. Nevertheless, even the most stable domestic polities can be disrupted by the emergence of an issue that involves conflicting ways of life that touch upon moral questions. Such issues are often seen as involving questions of life and death, and both sides are more likely to fight than accept a negative outcome from a previously accepted settlement procedure. Indeed, the issue can become so salient that all other practices and agreements are interpreted in light of the issue. Slavery was such an issue in the United States, which, despite numerous compromises, eventually resulted in a fight to the finish. This seems to especially be the case if such issues are linked with the control of territory, as they often are in sectional disputes that escalate to secession attempts or in interstate wars between neighbors (Vasquez, in this volume; see also Vasquez 1993, chap. 4).

These examples should make it clear that the structure of the system is an important factor influencing the prospect for successful conflict resolution. Peaceful systems have two characteristics. First, the ability to keep certain life-and-death issues off the political agenda and second, the presence of channels that are accepted by contenders for nonviolently resolving conflicts or imposing settlements (i.e., determining winners and losers). Conflict is a social event and how it is dealt with will vary by culture (see Kolb and Babbitt, in this volume). Tradition and custom play a large role in determining how a conflict is pursued and resolved. In this light, it should be made clear that modern techniques of conflict resolution provide a social construction of reality. To the extent that they become accepted and embedded within the culture and institutions of a society, as ADR has within the United States (see Bush, in this volume), they form yet another channel by which disputes can be settled and conflict resolved. Violence often occurs when contenders see no other way of solving the problem confronting them. Research findings support this generalization at both the interpersonal (see Pruitt, in this volume) and interstate levels (Barringer 1972). One of the reasons why international relations may be prone to war or certain unstable states may be prone to civil war or coups d'état is that there are no legitimate channels for resolving issues (see Vasquez 1993, chap. 7).

Even when formal institutions do not exist or their use is not required, the mere presence of laws and norms can have an ameliorating effect. Johnson (in this volume) notes that international law provides voluntary channels that have resolved a variety of disputes even though they have not eliminated war. Several researchers have suggested that one of the factors that distinguishes peaceful periods of international relations from very violent ones is a consensus on certain rules of the game. Peter Wallensteen (1984) provides evidence to show that when major states work out a set of rules to guide their relations, no wars among major states are fought, military confrontations are drastically reduced, and even wars and confrontations between minor and major states are somewhat attenuated. Conversely, when major states are unable to create rules of the game and fall back on "unilateral actions," then wars break out and confrontations are much more frequent. Further evidence along these lines is provided by Kegley and Raymond (1990), who find that in periods when norms, particularly alliance norms, are seen as binding, the incidences of war and confrontations are reduced. Likewise, Väyrynen (1983) finds that wars go down when the system of "political management" restrains unilateral actions.

Certainly, the establishment of certain rules of the game between the United States and the Soviet Union went a long way in controlling conflict during the cold war so that the risk of escalation to nuclear war was minimized (see Kremenyuk 1994). Eventually, concern about nuclear war was instrumental in bringing about a change in the relationship that made détente possible and an end to the cold war crises feasible. Tacit rules about limited war, treaties and norms regulating the nuclear arms race, explicit discussions of confidence-building measures that would reduce tension, and attempts at crisis management and then crisis prevention (George 1983) all played a critical role in preventing the cold war from becoming a nuclear war and eventually ending nuclear crises as well as the cold war itself.

In the post–cold war era, mutual security among the major states (United States, Russia, China, Britain, France, Japan, and Germany) involves extending rules to cope with a host of domestic and regional disputes that confront the world. The establishment of a new world order can be facilitated through the extension of a number of conflict-resolution techniques and strategies to areas where they have heretofore not been applied because of cold war rivalry. Regional and ethnic disputes, rather than disputes among the superpowers, are now the major threats to world peace. If the major states can continue to work together as they have been since the Persian Gulf War, they can establish rules for resolving some of these conflicts, imposing settlements, and/or controlling the spread of violence if it breaks out. The adoption of conflict-resolution ideas at the global level will help them spread to domestic areas, such as intrastate and intercommunal conflicts in Eastern Europe and ethnic and nationalist conflict within the former Soviet Union, where they have not heretofore been needed because the dominance of the powerful prevented these disputes from getting out of hand.

As Kriesberg (in this volume) points out, the way in which we think about conflict and the ideas we have about conflict resolution affect the chances we have of settling disputes or resolving conflict. Techniques and strategies of conflict resolution are not fixed. They can flourish or atrophy depending on the structural factors present. New techniques and norms can be invented and adopted. Moreover, modern Western conflict resolution is not the only source of ideas. There are older traditions in non-Western societies that emphasize reconciliation rather than bargaining that can be drawn upon. In areas where disputes and conflict have an ethnic dimension to them, such traditions may provide the basis for finding some common ground even where there are religious and ethnic differences. Conceptions of reconciliation prevalent in many societies are essential if peace settlements are to be lasting and truly *resolve* conflict. Western approaches to conflict resolution have much to learn from these traditions.

Likewise, although this book has focused on mediation, third-party consultation, and problem solving, other forms of dispute settlement and conflict resolution such as arbitration, good offices, negotiation, fact-finding, and peacekeeping have a long history in diplomacy and domestic politics. Undoubtedly, new practices to fit new times, like the development of Track Two diplomacy (McDonald and Bendahmane 1987) during the détente era, can be expected to occur. If ideas about conflict resolution are to play an important part in creating a new world order, it is essential that the Western social science version of them not be seen as the only or best method of conflict resolution. To take that approach would make conflict resolution simply the latest in a series of attempts to impose Western rationalistic hegemony on the rest of the world. Rather, a new world order must be built collectively, by developing a common language and set of ideas about what constitutes good settlements and resolutions. As the work on problem solving shows (see Kelman 1982), some of the best solutions may come from the parties themselves and not third parties; the same is true for the creation of a new world order.

The ending of global rivalries makes traditional and new conflict-resolution techniques more relevant to the world than at any time since the breakdown of the one hundred years of "peace" in 1914. Power politics and coercion need not be the only or main instruments available to states for achieving order and resolving issues. The adoption of conflict-resolution techniques, however, should not imply that power will not play an important or key role. The history of ADR within the United States shows that (see Bush, in this volume). Nor should it imply that justice will prevail. Major states working in concert may impose settlements that may better protect their interests than those of regional or minor states (see Betts 1993, 282). Mediation with muscle (Stein 1985; Touval and Zartman 1985; see also Rubin 1980) may take the form of providing inducements or it may be based on threats and coercion. The use of conflict resolution in global politics will not be a panacea. It cannot assure justice, but it can help reduce the incidence of war and violence, and may aid in the creation of order in a world where stability is becoming more problematic.

The analyses in this book have shown that a dialogue between domestic conflict-resolution and global conflict-resolution theorists and practitioners can be mutually beneficial. Common problems exist, and even where solutions in the one area are not directly applicable to the other, they often provide important insights. One of the major conceptual obstacles to pursuing such a dialogue has been the realist belief that the structures of domestic and international politics are so fundamentally different that domestic notions of government and conflict resolution could never work at the interstate level. In order to take conflict resolution seriously, the validity of this claim has to be examined, and part 3 of the book gave it extensive treatment.

There can be no question that the structure of the system is important. Nevertheless, as Vasquez (in this volume) demonstrates, global anarchy has not been as pervasive as realists (e.g., Waltz 1979) assert. Just because a system may not have a government does not mean that it is a Hobbesian state of nature that some realists, but not all, assume. As Bull (1977) and Johnson (in this volume) show, the contemporary international system is much more akin to a global society, in that it has evolved certain rules and customs that have patterned behavior, including the way force and war may be used. This does not mean that differences in structure are unimportant, only that it cannot be assumed that the global structure is always anarchic and the domestic structure always ordered. The extent to which any system is ordered is an empirical question that must be determined on the basis of each case. Many domestic systems in protracted conflict, like Lebanon or Northern Ireland, lack the order of contemporary global society and much more closely approach the Hobbesian image of anarchy, as Vasquez (in this volume) points out.

To see the modern global system as "anarchic" is to hide the historical fact that an arbitrary system of organization (i.e., nation-states and a capitalist world economy) evolved at a particular period of history and has been guided by clear principles that make this system much more of a society than a state of nature. Anarchy as a state of nature probably never was an eternal verity of world politics. Hence, there is no inherent reason why some of the techniques of conflict resolution that have been applied at the domestic level would not be relevant to problems occurring at the global level. Indeed, most of the analysts in this book who have sought to make connections between the two realms have found it rather easy to do so.

Thus, for Burton (in this volume) the distinction between domestic and international is not meaningful. For Burton, what is important is knowing the difference between "disputes" and "conflict." "Disputes" involve disagreements over interests that are negotiable and can often be settled through the application of well-known techniques, while "conflict" involves disagreements over issues reflecting fundamental needs that cannot be compromised but must be "resolved" through creating a solution that would satisfy the needs of all parties. Likewise, Vasquez (in this volume) elaborates a general framework for explaining the dynamics of conflict, regardless of whether it appears at the domestic or global level. How and whether conflict is resolved, of course, will depend on the nature of the political system in operation, and Burton outlines ideas about how the practice of conflict "provention" can build better political systems.

The chapters by Bush, Johnson, and Doran discuss how system structure can offer both incentives and barriers to conflict resolution. Bush's review (in this volume) of the growth of the ADR movement shows how private actions can change a structure and in turn how the structure can be an incentive to the use of dispute-settlement procedures. Obviously, court-ordered mediation or arbitration goes a long way in mandating certain ways of dealing with issues and has the effect of institutionalizing conflict-resolution techniques. However, as mediation becomes more widespread, questions of training, certification, and even licensing are raised, thereby giving the government some say over the nature and content of these techniques.

Nevertheless, it is significant that ADR has developed and has been applied to new areas, like environmental mediation and to consumer arbitration outside the legal structure and sometimes, as with divorce mediation, in opposition to powerful elements within the legal structure. This demonstrates that new ways of making peace and new channels for resolving issues can be constructed and applied without a prior change in the structure of a system. This is an important lesson for world politics, because it shows that conflict-resolution techniques can be adopted on a voluntary basis without there being any implication that a world government or some other utopian design is being created or is necessary for global conflict resolution to work.

One of the advantages of the nonhierarchical structure of the global political system is that there is no need to gain approval for the use of conflict-resolution techniques. Parties interested in using them can just go ahead. There need be no deadlock of government that prevents action from taking place. Conversely, there is sufficient order within the current global political system that there exists fertile soil in which conflict resolution can grow.

Johnson (in this volume) makes it clear that international law, although it is not law in the way domestic U.S. law is law, has created a structure that helps bring order to global relations. He points out that international law, by regularizing and regulating relations among states, helps to avoid many disputes and peacefully resolve others. It does this by establishing through custom and consensus a structure of expectations, rights, and duties. This is most evident in the area of commercial international law, where every ship crash need not provoke an international incident.

An even more important function of international law, as Johnson emphasizes, is the regulation of conflict, including violent conflict, once it breaks out. International law attempts to contain conflict so as not to damage the overall relationship between states, and it likewise tries to limit the negative effects of such conflict, particularly war, on the global system as a whole. As such, international law can be seen as more similar to ADR than it is to the domestic legal system. Therefore some of its lessons are relevant to those engaged in conflict resolution in domestic societies that are very fractured and look more like a society of sovereign states than a society with a single hierarchical government. Johnson shows how the conceptual problems facing classical international law theorists are not that different from those facing analysts of domestic wars.

Johnson makes it clear that traditional international law has created a foundation for peaceful society. This is especially the case when there is a broad consensus among major states about the rules of the game, and it is in the general interest of the major states to have conflicts resolved peacefully, a condition that appears to be emerging in the post–cold war era. He also shows that despite initial objections to international law by some third world states as being biased to the West and Eurocentric in its intellectual sources, third world states have since the sixties accepted large areas of international law as their own, making it much more of a global consensus than it was prior to 1945. Johnson's analysis (in this volume) reminds us that the world is not fixed and given; it need not always be a permanent struggle for power, but is subject to the creation of regimes that vary over history and cultures.

Doran's analysis (in this volume) looks explicitly at the power foundations of any political order. For him, as for Bush (in this volume), the structure of the political system will reflect the biases and interests of those who created the system, and the creators are inevitably the most powerful groups in the system. For Doran, some structures are more conducive to peace and hence to conflict resolution than others. Doran's analysis is based on a theory that predicts the periods in a system's history that are most likely to produce severe conflict and war. Whether the conflict will end in war or be resolved peacefully depends, according to Doran, on whether major states that are rising in power can be assimilated into the system. This in turn depends on whether the political structure of the system has channels that allow the demands of rising states to be accommodated.

To think about peace and about conflict resolution, it is necessary to think in systemic terms. Peace involves not simply the construction of the emergency room procedures of mediation, peacekeeping, and crisis management, but also crisis prevention and war avoidance. This involves the creation of a peace system—an international society of rules and norms that will permit states to articulate demands and allow them to take actions that will permit them to bring about change. Such actions might involve negotiation, mediation, or limited use of coercion. The exact nature of the system is something that must be worked out in practice. In the post–cold war era it is now possible for the major states to set out the parameters and basic rules for a new system of world order and to apply that system to a host of regional and ethnic conflicts that are now threatening world peace. In such a system, the availability of conflict-resolution practices for use by disputants or major states acting as third-party intervenors will be an important resource for all parties. This was dramatically revealed by Jimmy Carter's deal with Haiti's military leaders which was able to avoid war.

Doran's analysis suggests that long-term shifts in economic capability and their eventual impact on military capability are providing new opportunities and dangers at the systemic level. If the current system is to remain peaceful, it must assimilate a rising Germany and Japan as well as a declining Russia and United States. It must also deal with a potentially much more powerful China. So far the way the U.N. Security Council has been used by all concerned has struck an optimistic note. The ending of the cold war rivalry clearly has brought about an opportunity for creating a new world order, and that opportunity has been seized by all the major states to bring about a kind of concert of power, as Vasquez notes in chapter 7. The current structure of the international system, rather than forming a barrier to the use of conflict-resolution techniques, provides the greatest opportunity since 1815 for creating a new political structure that would allow these techniques to flourish and be supported by a concert of major states. At the same time, the end of Soviet dominance in Eastern Europe and the inability of the United States to serve as the sole guardian of a hegemonic order (to the extent it was ever able to fulfill such a role) have created areas of instability that demand the application of conflict-resolution and dispute-settlement techniques, if crises and war are to be avoided and mitigated.

Bush's review (in this volume) provides an illustration of what a political system that has extensive and varied conflict-resolution procedures might look like. It would involve parties voluntarily using specific channels and procedures because it was in their mutual interest. It would also involve some parties being required to use those channels because the system as a whole found that to be in its interest or the most efficient way of handling and containing certain disputes. In domestic society, the courts are the institution that requires mediation or arbitration. In global society, a concert of major states might perform this function on a more informal basis. As major states draw closer together, the use of mediation through muscle can be expected to be more frequent and to extend to new areas.

In any case, for global and regional conflict resolution to work, it will need more of an organizational base and more diplomats and scholars will have to have some familiarity with its procedures. The development of a transnational group of theorists, researchers, and practitioners who are experts on conflict resolution would make private and international organizations dedicated to conflict resolution more able to assist groups or states to deal with global conflict (internal ethnic conflict or interstate conflict). One of the main lessons of this inquiry is that the current structure of the global system is shifting in a direction that makes conflict-resolution ideas and practices more relevant than in any time in recent memory. The concluding section briefly examines this and other lessons that have been learned.

Conclusions

Several important lessons have been learned from this inquiry. The first is that peace is something that is learned and that it is possible to improve the ways in which peace is maintained. The use of conflict-resolution and dispute-settlement techniques often produce better outcomes and/or are more efficient than existing ways of deciding conflicts—namely litigation at the domestic level and war or coercion at the global level. In addition, with increased knowledge, conflict-resolution and dispute-settlement techniques can be improved and applied to new areas. This is particularly the case in areas of the world where these techniques have not been applied, such as in Eastern Europe.

Second, existing practices of conflict resolution at different levels of analysis, for example interpersonal, intergroup, and interstate, have much to learn from each other and can benefit from further discussion. The problems faced in some areas, such as intergroup disputes, are often not that different from problems in other areas, such as interstate conflicts. At times, even conflict-resolution practices focusing on interpersonal disputes can provide insights for dealing with group conflicts. This is in large part due to the fact that the dynamics of conflict and conflict escalation frequently evince a similar pattern of behavior.

Third, in order for there to be real progress in conflict resolution and dispute settlement there needs to be a concerted multidisciplinary effort to develop a unified theory of conflict and conflict resolution. In particular, the disciplines of international relations, political science, law, and history need to be made more aware of the relevant theory and research in social psychology and sociology; attempts to integrate these theories and findings into the perspectives of these disciplines should be encouraged. Ultimately, systematic multidisciplinary research on the dynamics of conflict, cooperation, and conflict resolution across levels of analysis will be the best way to spread ideas. Why conflict emerges; why it escalates and becomes intractable; and why and how it can be mitigated, resolved, or settled are questions relevant to interpersonal, intergroup, and interstate conflict. Answering them will be the best way to advance knowledge, improve practice, and move toward a unified theory.

Fourth, one of the keys to resolving conflict and settling disputes is to understand the relationship between the disputants, the nature of the issue dividing them, and how the kinds of proposals they are offering are aggravating the relationship between them. One of the factors that makes for successful conflict resolution is the ability of outside parties to change the relationship, redefine the issue, and come up with proposals that are not zero-sum. The science of conflict resolution can identify the key variables that need to be manipulated. The art of conflict resolution lies in successfully manipulating them.

Fifth, structure can be an incentive or a barrier to the pacific resolution of conflict. Structure itself, however, is not fixed. New practices, like collective bargaining and environmental mediation, can have profound effects on the dynamics and impact of conflict on the social system. The distinction between domestic and international politics is often more obfuscating than illuminating. Global society is not the Hobbesian state of anarchy it is often portrayed to be. Conversely, some domestic societies approach that kind of anarchy. The emergence of a post–cold war era provides an opportunity to build a new world order that will incorporate conflict-resolution ideas and techniques.

Sixth, there are several areas where both domestic and global conflict resolution might benefit from a further exploration. These include: (1) The use of mediation and problem solving—what factors promote success and what factors are associated with failure; who can do it, and what are the best times to try to mediate or engage in third-party problem solving; which strategy (mediation, problem solving, good offices, etc.) should be used when? (2) Negotiation theory and practice—how can parties be brought to the table; how can negotiation be productive; what is the relationship between formal negotiation and extra negotiation techniques, like Track Two diplomacy and problem solving; how can outcomes (settlements, resolutions, or agreements) be structured so as to create a lasting peace? (3) The structural characteristics of peace systems—what separates political systems that are relatively peaceful and stable from those that are prone to periodic violence; how are systems that have experienced widespread violence or the use of violent practices (like vendettas or labor strife) transformed into more peaceful systems; what factors have made some international peace systems, like Westphalia and the Concert of Europe, work while others have failed? (4) A systematic review of existing and recent cases attempting to resolve interstate conflicts or settle disputes—what were the common problems; were they handled differently and if so why; what seem to be the reasons for success or failure; and are these cases relevant to other cases where conflict resolution was not tried?

While dialogue and multidisciplinary research is important, the ultimate test is to tackle specific problems in the field. Unfortunately, the withdrawal of the Soviet Union from Eastern Europe, as well as ethnic and nationalist conflict within the former Soviet Union, have provided a number of potential cases, all of which have important international implications. In some of these areas, for example the Balkans, there is little tradition of conflict resolution. These cases provide a challenge to those studying and practicing conflict resolution. How they are handled, particularly in reaching peace settlements, will provide important precedents for the new global order. Much will be learned about conflict resolution from these cases; we can only hope that multidisciplinary efforts like the one in this volume have generated enough insights to ameliorate and limit the inevitable suffering these conflicts will generate in the last years of one of the most violent centuries of world history.

REFERENCES

Barringer, R. 1972. *War: Patterns of Conflict.* Cambridge, Mass.: MIT Press.

Bercovitch, J. 1986. "International Mediation: A Study of the Incidence, Strategies and Conditions of Successful Outcomes." *Cooperation and Conflict* 21:155–86.

Betts, R. K. 1993. "Systems of Peace as Causes of War? Collective Security, Arms Control, and the New Europe." In J. Snyder and R. Jervis, eds., *Coping with Complexity in the International System,* 265–301. Boulder, Colo.: Westview.

Boulding, E. 1987. "Learning Peace." In R. Vayrynen, ed., *The Quest for Peace,* 317–29. Beverly Hills, Calif.: Sage.

Bull, H. 1977. *The Anarchical Society.* New York: Columbia University Press.

Dean, D. P., Jr., and J. A. Vasquez. 1976. "From Power Politics to Issue Politics: Bipolarity and Multipolarity in Light of a New Paradigm." *Western Political Quarterly* 29 (March): 7–28.

Frei, D. 1976. "Conditions Affecting the Effectiveness of International Mediation." *Papers of the Peace Science Society (International)* 26: 67–84.

George, A. L. 1983. *Managing U.S.-Soviet Rivalry: Problems of Crisis Prevention.* Boulder, Colo.: Westview Press.

Kegley, C. W., Jr., and Gregory A. Raymond. 1990. *When Trust Breaks Down: Alliance Norms and World Politics.* Columbia, S.C.: University of South Carolina Press.

Kelman, H. C. 1982. "Creating Conditions for Israeli-Palestinian Negotiations." *Journal of Conflict Resolution* 26: 39–75.

Kremenyuk, V. A. 1994. "The Cold War as Cooperation." In M. Midlarsky, J. Vasquez, and P. Gladkov, eds., *From Rivalry to Cooperation: Russian and American Perspectives on the Post–Cold War Era,* 3–25. New York: HarperCollins.

Kressel, K., and D. G. Pruitt, eds. 1989. *Mediation Research.* San Francisco: Jossey Bass.

McDonald, J. W., and D. B. Bendahmane, eds. 1987. *Conflict Resolution: Track Two Diplomacy.* Washington, D.C.: Foreign Service Institute.

Mansbach, R. W., and J. A. Vasquez. 1981. *In Search of Theory: A New Paradigm for Global Politics.* New York: Columbia University Press.

Mead, M. 1940. "Warfare is Only an Invention—Not a Biological Necessity," *Asia,* 40, no. 8: 402–5.

Mitrany, D. 1943. *A Working Peace System.* London: Royal Institute of International Affairs.

Pruitt, D. G., and J. Z. Rubin. 1986. *Social Conflict: Escalation, Stalemate, and Settlement.* New York: Random House.

Rubin, J. Z. 1980. *Dynamics of Third Party Intervention: Kissinger in the Middle East.* New York: Praeger.

Stein, J. G. 1985. "Structures, Strategies, and Tactics of Mediation: Kissinger and Carter in the Middle East." *Negotiation Journal* 1: 331–47.

Touval, S., and I. W. Zartman, eds. 1985. *International Mediation: Theory and Practice.* Boulder, Colo.: Westview.

Vasquez, J. A. 1983. "The Tangibility of Issues and Global Conflict: A Test of Rosenau's Issue Area Typology." *Journal of Peace Research,* 20 (no. 2): 179–92.

———. 1993. *The War Puzzle.* Cambridge: Cambridge University Press.

———. 1994. "Building Peace in the Post–Cold War Era." In M. Midlarsky, J. Vasquez, and P. Gladkov, eds., *From Rivalry to Cooperation: Russian and American Perspectives on the Post–Cold War Era,* 208–18. New York: HarperCollins.

Väyrynen, R. 1983. "Economic Cycles, Power Transitions, Political Management and Wars Between Major Powers." *International Studies Quarterly* 27 (December): 389–418.

Wallensteen, P. 1984. "Universalism vs. Particularism: On the Limits of Major Power Order." *Journal of Peace Research* 21 (no. 3): 243–57.

Waltz, K. N. 1979. *Theory of International Politics.* Reading, Mass.: Addison-Wesley.

Zartman, I. W. 1989. *Ripe for Resolution: Conflict and Intervention in Africa.* Updated ed. New York: Oxford University Press.

Contributors

Eileen F. Babbitt is deputy director of the Program on International Conflict Analysis and Resolution at the Center for International Affairs at Harvard University. She is also an associate at the Program on Negotiation of the Harvard Law School, where she teaches a seminar in mediation theory and practice. Her current research interests include preventive diplomacy and roles for third parties in protracted intergroup disputes. She received her Master's in public policy from the Kennedy School of Government, Harvard University, and completed her Ph.D. at M.I.T.

John W. Burton, B.A., Ph.D., D.Sc. began his career in the Australian public service, becoming permanent head of the Australian Foreign Office in 1947 and high commissioner for Ceylon in 1951. After his retirement from government service, he taught and did research on conflict resolution at a number of universities and centers, including the University of London, Centre for the Analysis of Conflict in Canterbury, University of Kent, University of Maryland, and George Mason University. He has participated in numerous problem-solving workshops, including efforts to resolve conflicts in Ceylon, Cyprus, Northern Ireland, the Falklands-Malvinas Islands, and Lebanon. He has published a number of very influential books, including *Systems, States Diplomacy and Rules* (1968); *Conflict and Communication* (1969); *World Society* (1972), *Deviance, Terrorism and War* (1972); *Dear Survivors* (1982), *Global Conflict* (1984), and most recently the four-volume *Conflict Series* (1990).

Robert A. Baruch Bush is the Rains Distinguished Professor of Alternative Dispute Resolution Law at Hofstra University School of Law. At Hofstra he directs a mediation clinic and has conducted research on ethical dilemmas in mediation, funded in part by the National Institute for Dispute Resolution. He has written extensively on mediation and alternative dispute resolution, including articles in *Wisconsin Law Review, Florida Law Review, Journal of Contemporary Legal Issues, Denver Law Review, Journal of Legal Education, Ohio State Journal on Dispute Resolution, Missouri Dispute Resolution Journal,* and *Negotiation Journal.* Several of these have won awards from the

Center for Public Resources, including the monograph, *The Dilemmas of Mediation Practice* (1992). He has recently coauthored (with Joseph P. Folger) *The Promise of Mediation: Responding to Conflict Through Empowerment and Recognition* (1994).

Charles F. Doran is Andrew W. Mellon Professor of International Relations at The Paul H. Nitze School of Advanced International Studies, The Johns Hopkins University. He is author of numerous books and articles including *The Politics of Assimilation* (1971), *Myth, Oil, and Politics* (1979), *The Forgotten Partnership: U.S./Canada Relations Today* (1984) and studies on the Power Cycle in *American Political Science Review, Journal of Conflict Resolution,* and *International Studies Quarterly.* His most recent book is *Systems in Crisis: New Imperatives of High Politics at Century's End* (1991).

Ronald J. Fisher is professor of psychology at the University of Saskatchewan. During 1989–91 he was formerly a fellow at the Canadian Institute for International Peace and Security. His main interests are in social psychology and conflict resolution. He has published in numerous journals, including *Journal of Conflict Resolution, Professional Psychology, International Journal, Negotiation Journal,* and *Journal of Peace Research.* His most recent book is *The Social Psychology of Intergroup and International Conflict Resolution.*

Sanford Jaffe is director of the Center for Negotiation and Conflict Resolution at Rutgers University and teaches at the School of Law and the Bloustein School of Planning and Public Policy at Rutgers. As officer in charge of the Government and Law Program at the Ford Foundation, he directed its program in legal education and dispute resolution for a number of years. A graduate of Harvard Law School, he is the author of a number of publications in the fields of dispute resolution, public interest law, and legal education, including articles in *New Jersey Law Journal, Connecticut Law Tribune, Legal Times,* and *ABA Journal,* among others. He has mediated a number of cases involving large-scale public policy issues as well as disputes involving a few parties at high management levels in several large institutions.

James Turner Johnson is university director of international programs, professor of religion, and associate of the graduate department of political science at Rutgers University. His research and teaching have focused principally on the historical development and application of moral traditions related to war, peace, and the practice of statecraft. His books include *Ideology, Reason, and the Limitation of War, Just War Tradition and the Restraint of War, Can Modern War Be Just?, The Quest for Peace,* and (coedited with John Kelsay)

Cross, Crescent, and Sword: The Justification and Limitation of War in Western and Islamic Traditions, and *Just War and Jihad: Historical and Theoretical Perspectives on War and Peace in Western and Islamic Traditions.*

Deborah M. Kolb is professor of management at the Simmons College Graduate School of Management, director of the Simmons Institute for Leadership and Change, and a senior fellow at the Program on Negotiation at Harvard Law School. She is author of *The Mediators* and has edited *Hidden Conflict in Organizations* and *Making Talk Work: Profiles of Mediators.* Professor Kolb is currently carrying out field research on gender issues in negotiation, dispute resolution, and diversity, and on work/family practices in corporations. Her B.A. is from Vassar College, her M.B.A. from the University of Colorado, and her Ph.D. from M.I.T.'s Sloan School of Management.

Louis Kriesberg is professor of sociology, Maxwell Professor of Social Conflict Studies, and former director of the Program on the Analysis and Resolution of Conflicts at the Maxwell School of Syracuse University. He received his Ph.D. in 1953 from the University of Chicago. His writings include: *International Conflict Resolution: The U.S.-USSR and Middle East Cases* (1992), *Social Conflicts* (1973, 1982), *Social Inequality* (1979), and *Mothers in Poverty* (1970). He edited *Social Processes in International Relations* (1968) and edits the annual series *Research in Social Movements, Conflict and Change;* he coedited *Intractable Conflicts and Their Transformation* (1989) and *Timing the De-escalation of International Conflicts* (1991). He is a former president of the Society for the Study of Social Problems.

Dean G. Pruitt is Distinguished Professor at the State University of New York at Buffalo. He received his Ph.D. in psychology from Yale University in 1957 and did postdoctoral work in psychology at the University of Michigan and in international relations at Northwestern University. He specializes in the psychology of social conflict and does laboratory and field research on negotiation and mediation. He is author or coauthor of *Theory and Research on the Causes of War; Negotiation Behavior; Social Conflict: Escalation, Stalemate and Settlement; Mediation Research;* and *Negotiation in Social Conflict.*

Linda Stamato is deputy director of the Center for Negotiation and Conflict Resolution at Rutgers University and teaches at the School of Law and the Bloustein School of Planning and Public Policy at Rutgers. She is the author of a number of articles on mediation and negotiation, including articles in *Mediation Quarterly, Negotiation Journal, The Arbitration Forum, The Judges Journal,* and *National Civic Review.* She has mediated a number of disputes both in the public policy area and in high-level management. A graduate of Rutgers University, she has served as a consultant to the Ford and Rockefeller Foundations and as chairman of the Board of Governors of Rutgers University.

John A. Vasquez is professor of political science at Vanderbilt University. His major areas of specialization are international relations theory and peace research. He has published numerous books and articles, including *The Power of Power Politics, In Search of Theory: A New Paradigm for Global Politics* (with Richard Mansbach), *Classics of International Relations, The Scientific Study of Peace and War: A Text-reader* (with Marie Henehan), *From Rivalry to Cooperation: Russian and American Perspectives on the Post–Cold War Era* (with M. Midlarsky and P. Gladkov), and most recently *The War Puzzle,* which constructs a new scientific explanation of the causes of war and the conditions of peace.

Index